FRANK FRAZETTA

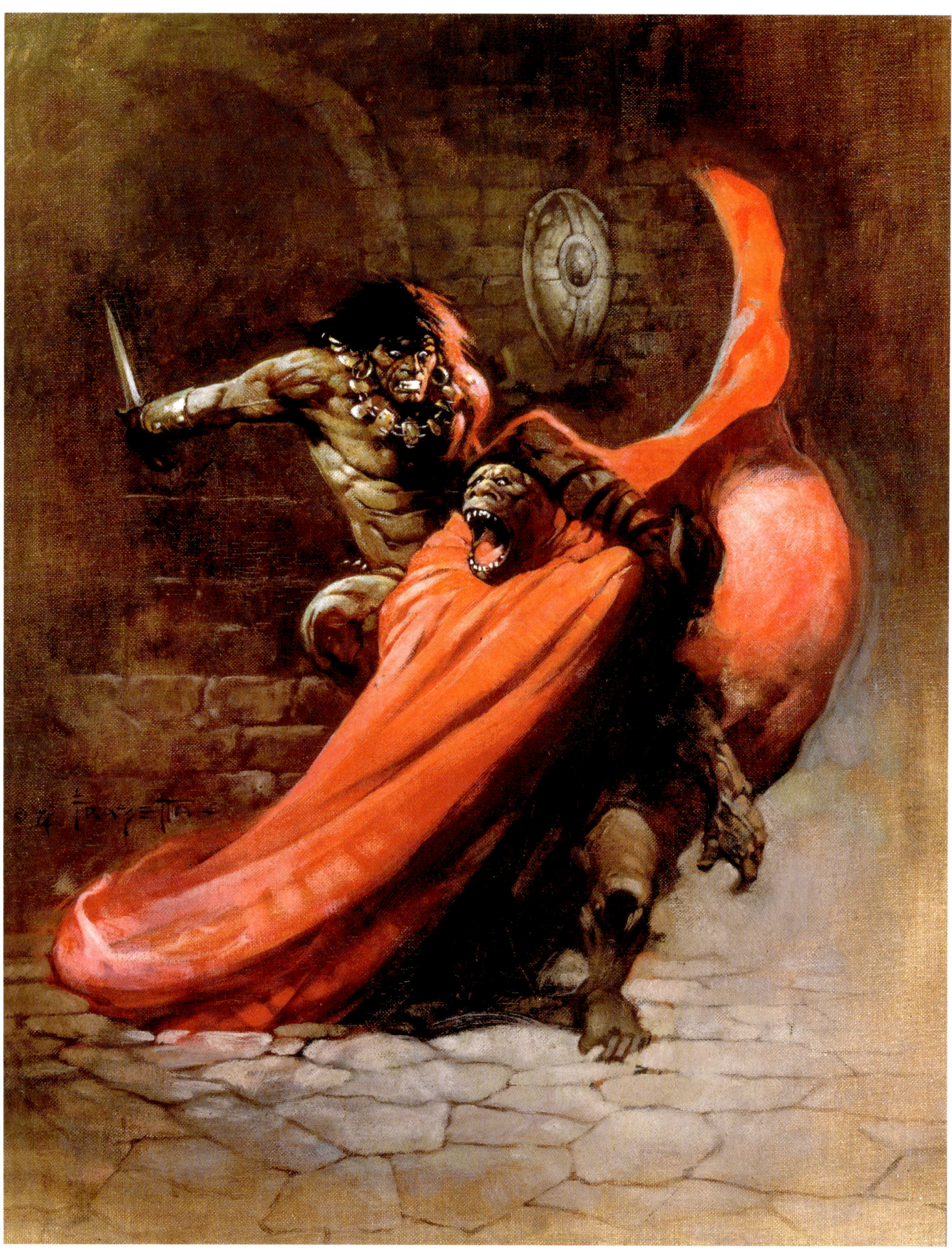

Dian Hanson (Ed.)
Dan Nadel / Zak Smith

Frank Frazetta

1928–2010

Godfather of Fantasy Art

TASCHEN

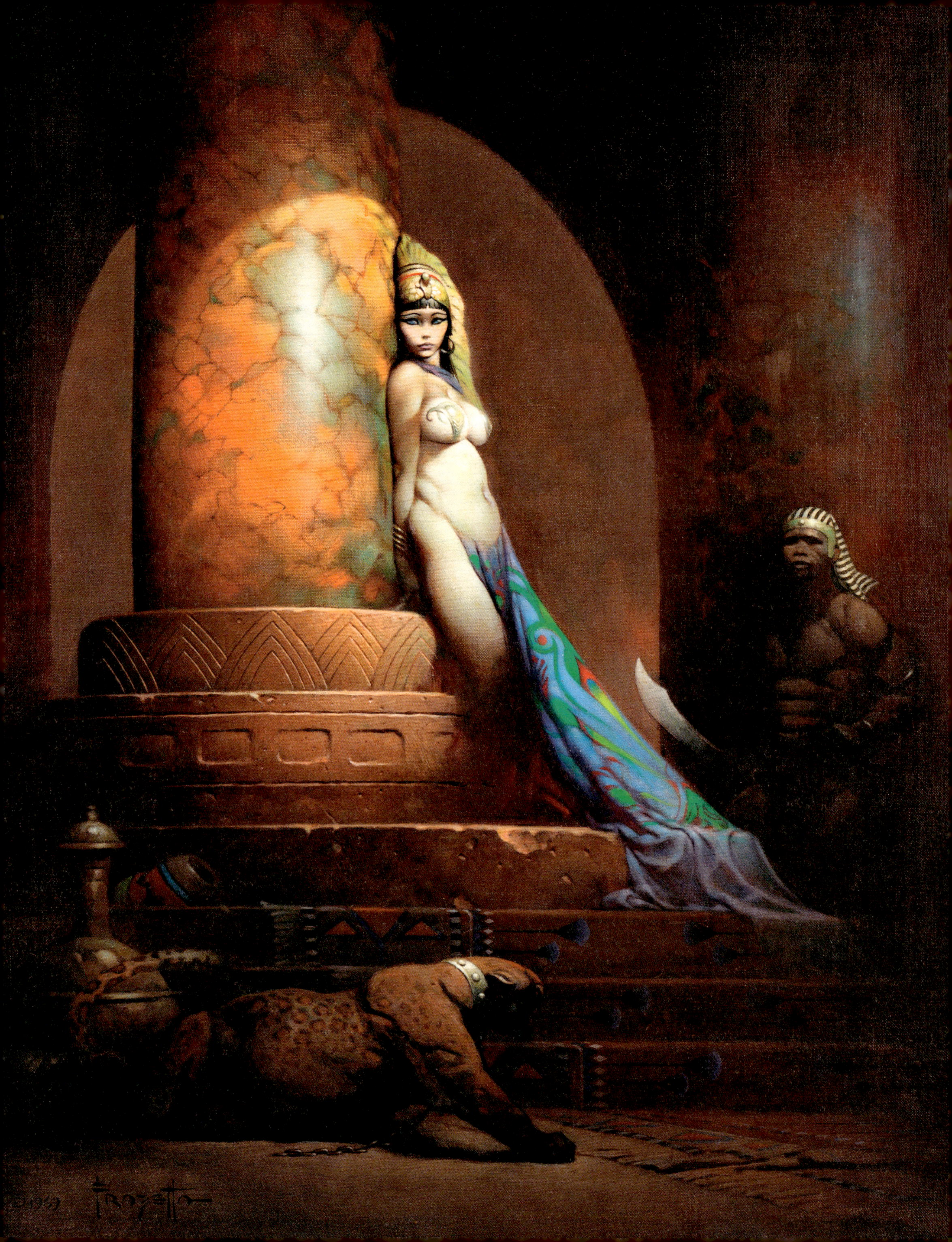

Contents

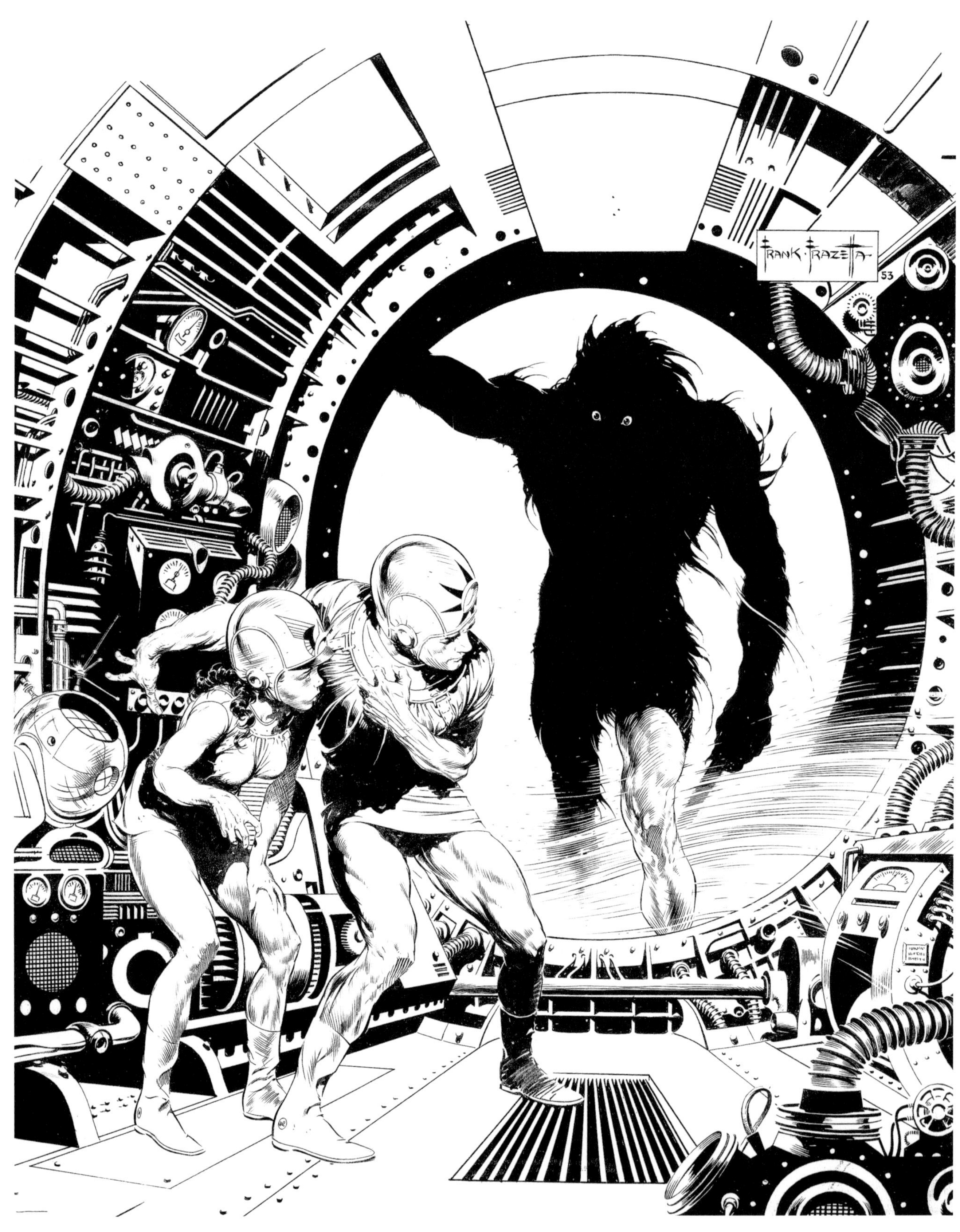

FRANK FRAZETTA
53

Frank Frazetta:
Hold and Release

Back in 1969, a few comic book and fantasy fans put together a magazine called *Promethean*. Psychedelic master Rick Griffin contributed a cover drawing, printed black on silver, of engorged eyeballs in mortal battle with a demonic Mickey Mouse stand-in. Above the carnage, instead of a logo, is the word "Frazetta" in Griffin's near-unreadable Baroque lysergic script. The image is a perfect transmutation of the Frank Frazetta project: a centralized image of otherworldly brutality composed in fluid darks and lights and rendered with precisely vigorous brushstrokes.

And yet Frazetta was a politically conservative paragon of the kind of all-American virility that was hostile to the counterculture. Where the two factions of white guys met—Northern California communes and Hells Angels' clubhouses, let's say—was in their love of imagined verdant realities where a man could have his woman and defend his land. Frazetta was on the same misty mountaintop as Led Zeppelin and King Crimson, liberated and exploratory, but still firmly rooted in traditional art, politics, and sex. That last part: all those nude or nearly-so bodies, bottoms out, in impossible danger or triumph, is as fundamental to the artist as the action in which they feature. It is the not-uncomplicated crossing of tradition and liberation that makes Frazetta's work so intriguing.

A Brooklyn-born hustler and brawler, Frazetta was not like his hero Hal Foster, a soft-spoken Canadian whose early-1930s *Tarzan* newspaper strip he called his "Encyclopedia Britannica." In 1937, Foster began the decades-long comic strip story of Prince Valiant, a noble, upright, and righteous adventurer whose medieval world Foster rendered with stunning accuracy and vigorous life. Frazetta took Foster's upstanding example, first urbanized it, and then blew it out into a landscape of forbidding darkness. If Foster was noble, then Frazetta was gloriously vulgar. But, like, say, Led Zeppelin, Frazetta was transcendently so. He didn't imagine narrative scenes so much as emotional and psychological spaces not so dissimilar from the psychedelic mind space in which no rules apply. Drawings like his 1954 *Weird-Science Fantasy* cover or his 1967 painting for *Conan the Conqueror* are pictures of unbearably intense, nearly animated moments. His figures do it all in those instants—they're lit purely for design purposes, bent, pulled, crossed precisely as he needs them, like the way a kid might abuse an action figure to get the pose he

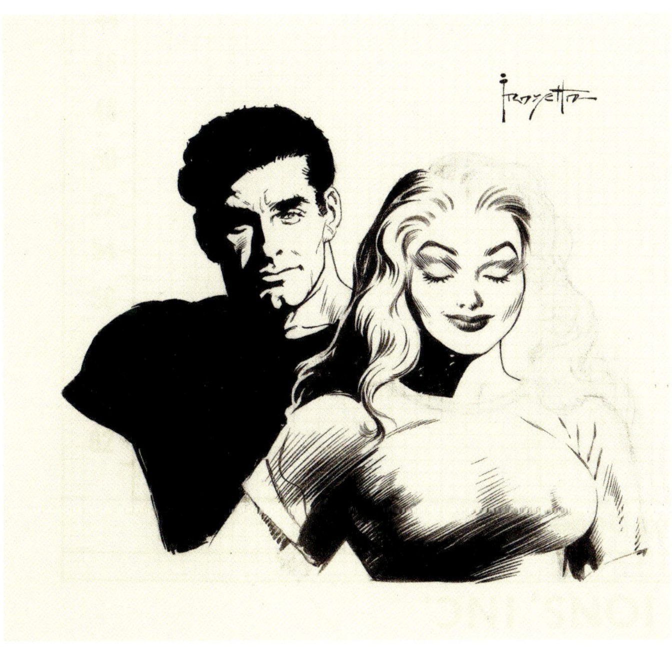

"Came the Dawn" was assigned for EC's *Shock Illustrated* No. 4 but never published. The doomed duo: a rugged outdoorsman resembling the artist in idealized form, and the buoyantly breasted blonde who seeks shelter in his cabin, finding love, and death. Ink over graphite on paper, 1954, 22.8 x 22.8 cm (9 x 9 inches). *Courtesy of Heritage Auctions.*

Buck Rogers in the original cover art for *Famous Funnies* No. 213. Frazetta had already mastered his art form at age 25, after 10 years of daily drawing. Ink over graphite on paper, 1953, 71.1 x 63.5 cm (28 x 25 inches). *Courtesy of Heritage Auctions.*

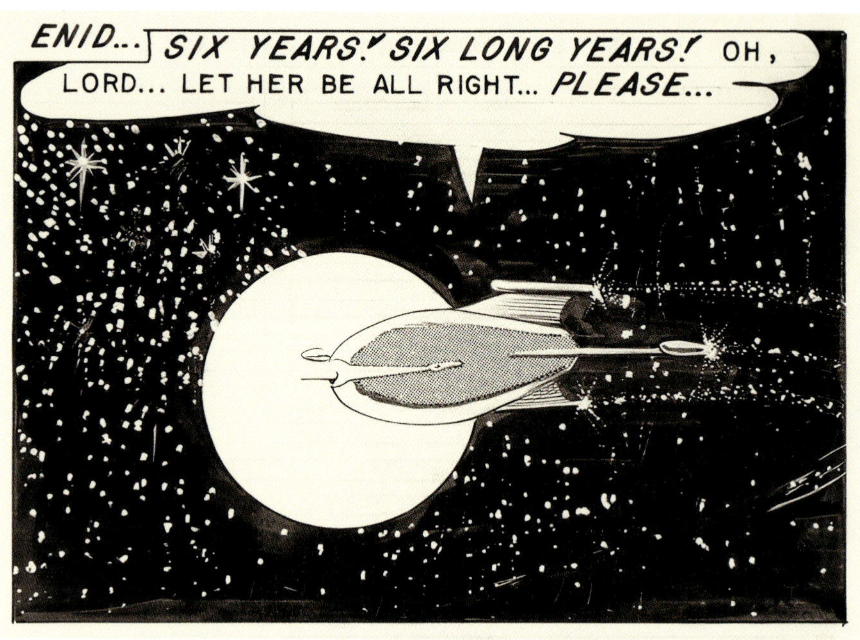

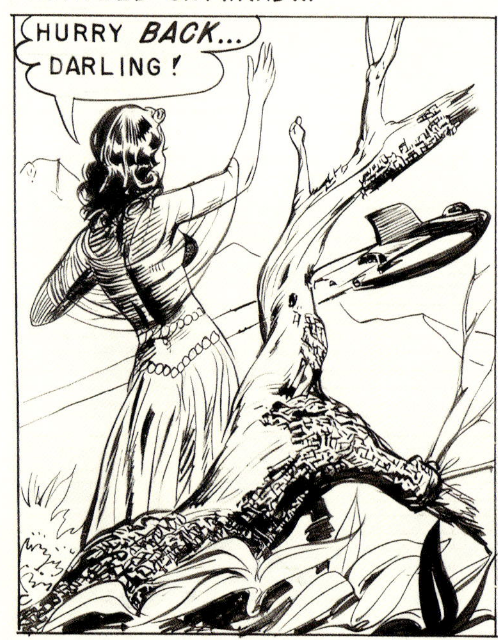

needs. This feel is enhanced by the eerie fact that Frazetta put his face on so many of his characters: conqueror, racist, sheriff, lothario. His face, his physical and mental states, are both text and subtext in his work.

Frazetta came by his coiled intensity honestly. He was born in 1928 and raised in a Catholic Sicilian family in a squat working-class home in Italian and Jewish Sheepshead Bay, Brooklyn. Surrounded by a supportive and female-dominated family, he was a physical prodigy in drawing and athletics. Edgar Rice Burroughs was some of the first (and per the artist, only) reading Frazetta ever did. He remembered finding a stack of six or seven *Tarzan* books at age four—among them *Tarzan of the Apes*, *Return of Tarzan*, *The Beasts of Tarzan*—left in his cellar by an uncle who lived downstairs. Fascinated by the J. Allen St. John illustrations, he eventually read them all.

While attending grade school, young Frazetta began taking classes with Michele Falanga, an Italian neoclassical painter who was the sole proprietor of a single-floor all-ages school called the Brooklyn Academy of Fine Arts just on the edge of Brooklyn Heights. Falanga taught drawing and painting rooted in the 19th-century Roman neoclassical movement, emphasizing painting from life and humble subject matter. It was with Falanga that Frazetta learned brush control for subtle gradients, washes, and thin, taut lines. According to Frazetta, Falanga believed the boy was a prodigy, and planned to send him to Rome to further his education, but died just short of Frazetta's 14th birthday, without having secured the travel plans. Frazetta never did make it to Italy, nor anywhere outside of the United States. For a couple years after, Frazetta and his classmates continued on their own, but it became "more like a club. I did life drawings and still lifes … we could go out in the field and paint some old church or whatever."

Alongside classical drawing, Frazetta was absorbing the curves and spaces of Disney cartoons, including his favorite *Fantasia* (the "Night on Bald Mountain" sequence designed by Baroque Surrealist Albert Hurter and art nouveau fantasist Kay Nielsen was an easily recognizable influence), E. C. Segar's *Popeye*, with its incredible energy and violence, and Milton Caniff's *Terry and the Pirates*. In his boyhood drawings Frazetta was pulling and pushing Caniff's slim patrician figures into stout forms and exaggerated poses. He was making people as he saw them in his neighborhood: dark-eyed, full-figured men and women. Like a lot of other artistic children of immigrants in New York, Frazetta was drawn to comic books, then still a young industry populated mostly by artists who fell on either side of the draft: teenagers and middle-aged men. At 16 a family friend introduced him to the illustrator John Giunta, who was working for packager Bernard Bailey assembling comic books to sell to publishers. Giunta inked Frazetta's pencils on the teenager's character "Snowman." Bailey placed it in *Tally-Ho* No. 1, December 1944, and at age 16 Frazetta was a published cartoonist.

Frazetta did a few more jobs for Giunta, but shortly after, in what would become a pattern, he said, "I dropped out of it because I felt they were not paying me what I deserved." From 1945 to 1953 the young cartoonist bounced around studios, drawing funny animal comics and a Li'l Abner knockoff called Looie Lazybones. He found fans in the future comic book horror master Graham Ingels, an alcoholic savant who kept Frazetta in jobs at Better Publications, and Ralph Mayo, who replaced Ingels at Standard Publications. Mayo thought the kid promising, but in need of some structure, so he loaned Frazetta the standard anatomy books by George Bridgman and Victor Perard,

Golden Girl was produced as Frank's first limited edition print by independent publisher Russ Cochran in 1978. As with many other early works, it bears the date of copyright, not the date of creation. Watercolor on paper, circa 1950, 28.5 x 33.6 cm (11.25 x 13.25 inches).

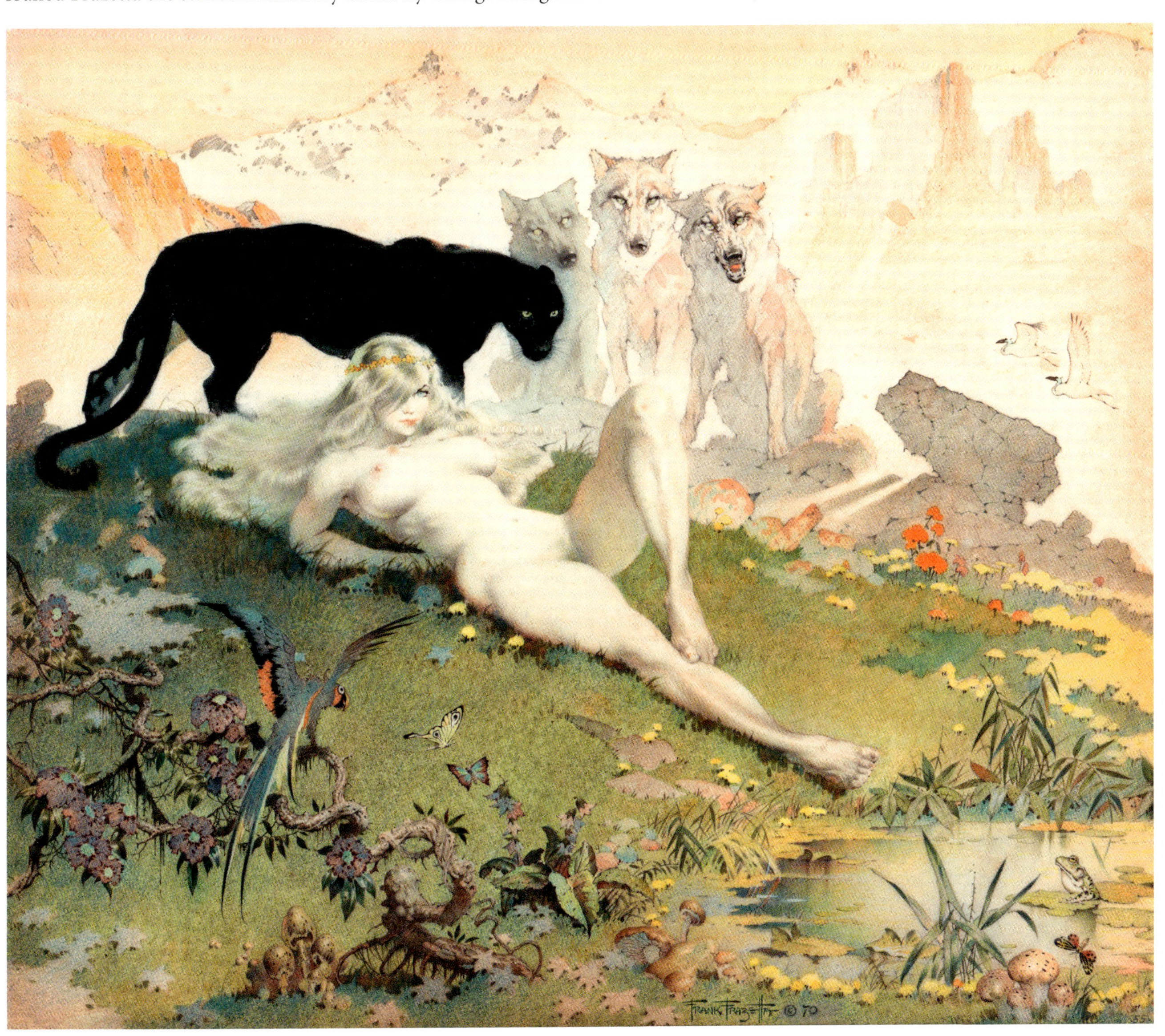

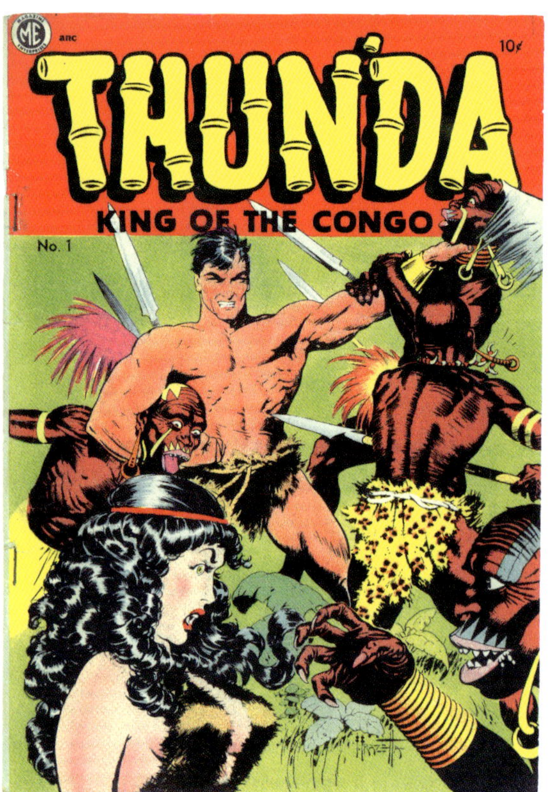

Thun'da, from 1952, is the only comic book drawn entirely by Frazetta. Though just 24 at the time he was already an established artist.

The title page for *Thun'da, King of the Congo* No. 1, done by Frazetta for Magazine Enterprises in 1952. Legend has it that Frazetta hoped to take over the *Tarzan of the Apes* newspaper comic strip once drawn by his childhood hero Hal Foster. Ink over graphite on board, with title and text corrections stripped in. 45 x 33 cm (18.5 x 13 inches). *Courtesy of Heritage Auctions.*

which Frazetta remembers bringing back the next day, claiming to have learned anatomy. This is the first of numerous "overnight" stories Frazetta told or encouraged—paintings, cover drawings, comic strips completed in marathon sessions. True or not, they attest to the competitive athlete and obsessive craftsman in Frazetta. He got some popularity behind him and gradually fell in with a bunch of like-minded young cartoonist/illustrators, many of whom, like Ingels, would go on to work for the most literate and visually advanced comic book publisher of the time: EC Comics. Al Williamson, Roy Krenkel, Angelo Torres, Nick Meglin, and Frazetta, dubbed "The Fleagles" after an early 20th-century gang of bank robbers, palled around Brooklyn (Frazetta, Torres would later remember, would never come into Manhattan—the boys came to him), modeled for and worked on each other's stories, and generally came up together in the 1950s and '60s.

From 1949 through 1953 he flourished as a cartoonist, producing comic book stories for Magazine Enterprises, National (now DC), and EC, including *Shining Knight*, *The Ghost Rider*, and *The Durango Kid*. In 1952, he drew his own comic book for Magazine Enterprises called *Thun'da*, which he hoped might get him a shot at the Tarzan comic strip. *Thun'da* is a beautifully drawn jungle adventure story with plenty of panels swiped from Foster, and it did indeed make Frazetta's name in comics. It is also, like the original Tarzan story itself, mired in the racist politics of colonialism. The larger white savior/black devil dynamic is baked into so much of 20th-century sci-fi and fantasy that it's hard to grapple with its ubiquity. Filmmakers like Jordan Peele are only now beginning to get inside of it and explicate it. Racially charged imagery is a constant in Frazetta's work: the white man (or sometimes woman) is forever battling back a dark-skinned adversary, if not an "African" then a "Martian" or "mongoloid." This isn't to condemn the artist, but just to state the obvious. Frazetta's first great love was forbidden to see him because, as a Sicilian-American, he was considered ethnically inferior and lower class. So, it's possible that the beasts were sometimes the artist himself. It bears more examination, as do so many of our fantasy constructs.

Working hard, for a guy who always claimed laziness, following *Thun'da*, Frazetta perfected his pen-and-ink drawings. First up was a year-long stint on a race car comic strip called *Johnny Comet* (known as *Ace McCoy* halfway through its run), which offered a chance to draw fast cars and beautiful women at impossible angles. During and after this run he produced eight Buck Rogers covers for *Famous Funnies* from 1953 to 1955 that shaped the look of drawn fantasy art for decades. Each drawing, like his best paintings, resembles a sudden inhalation and long-held breath: a giant alights on a spaceship overwhelmed by Mars; a monster blows through a hull, only its eyes visible in the chaos; an octopus viciously ensnares a woman as Buck Rogers glides to her rescue; and in a drawing first rejected by *Famous Funnies* and ultimately published as EC's *Weird Science-Fantasy* No. 29, a gnarled lone white man beats back dark brutes, bodies viciously splayed in every direction. These covers are drawn with not just evident relish, but the thing that is more difficult to pull off: real presence as both original drawings and printed objects. They radiate tension. Frazetta's compositions of impossibly contorted bodies set the tone but his linework creates an atmosphere—knotted muscles, billowing smoke, and cascades of hair. Every component of these images flows so that there are no resting points for a viewer's eye—the effect is vertiginous.

In this period, hovering around the edges of EC Comics, he drew his finest comic book story, "Squeeze Play" (published in *Shock SuspenStories* No. 13, 1954), which follows a criminal physically modeled on the artist himself, who kills a woman atop Coney Island's Cyclone and is then lured by a group of women into the ocean, where he drowns. The tale offers up a clear view into Frazetta's subconscious image of himself—hustler,

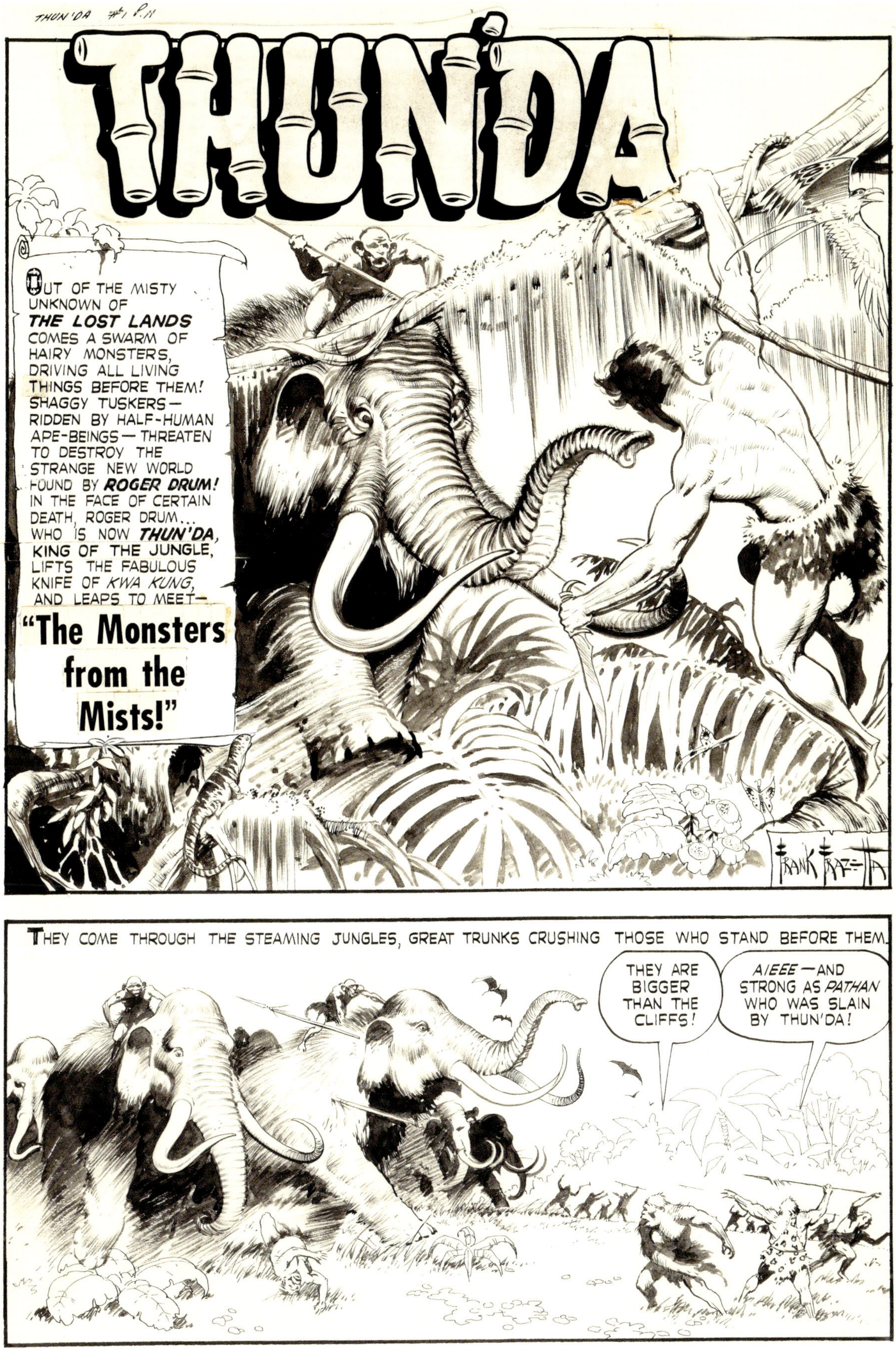

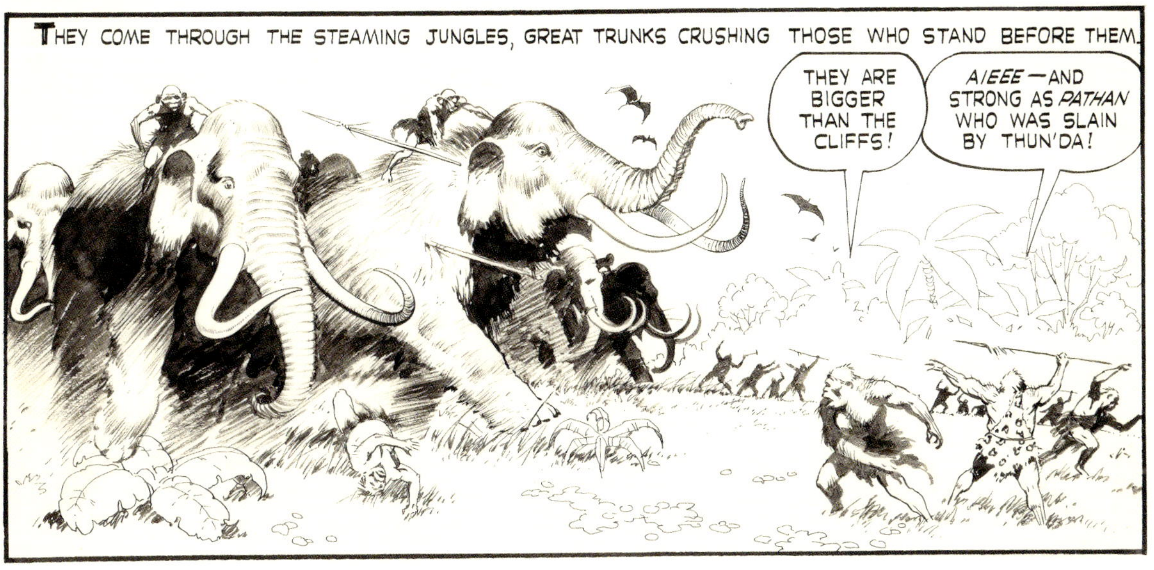

THUN'DA

OUT OF THE MISTY UNKNOWN OF THE LOST LANDS COMES A SWARM OF HAIRY MONSTERS, DRIVING ALL LIVING THINGS BEFORE THEM! SHAGGY TUSKERS— RIDDEN BY HALF-HUMAN APE-BEINGS— THREATEN TO DESTROY THE STRANGE NEW WORLD FOUND BY ROGER DRUM! IN THE FACE OF CERTAIN DEATH, ROGER DRUM... WHO IS NOW THUN'DA, KING OF THE JUNGLE, LIFTS THE FABULOUS KNIFE OF KWA KUNG, AND LEAPS TO MEET—

"The Monsters from the Mists!"

FRANK FRAZETTA

THEY COME THROUGH THE STEAMING JUNGLES, GREAT TRUNKS CRUSHING THOSE WHO STAND BEFORE THEM.

THEY ARE BIGGER THAN THE CLIFFS!

AIEEE—AND STRONG AS PATHAN WHO WAS SLAIN BY THUN'DA!

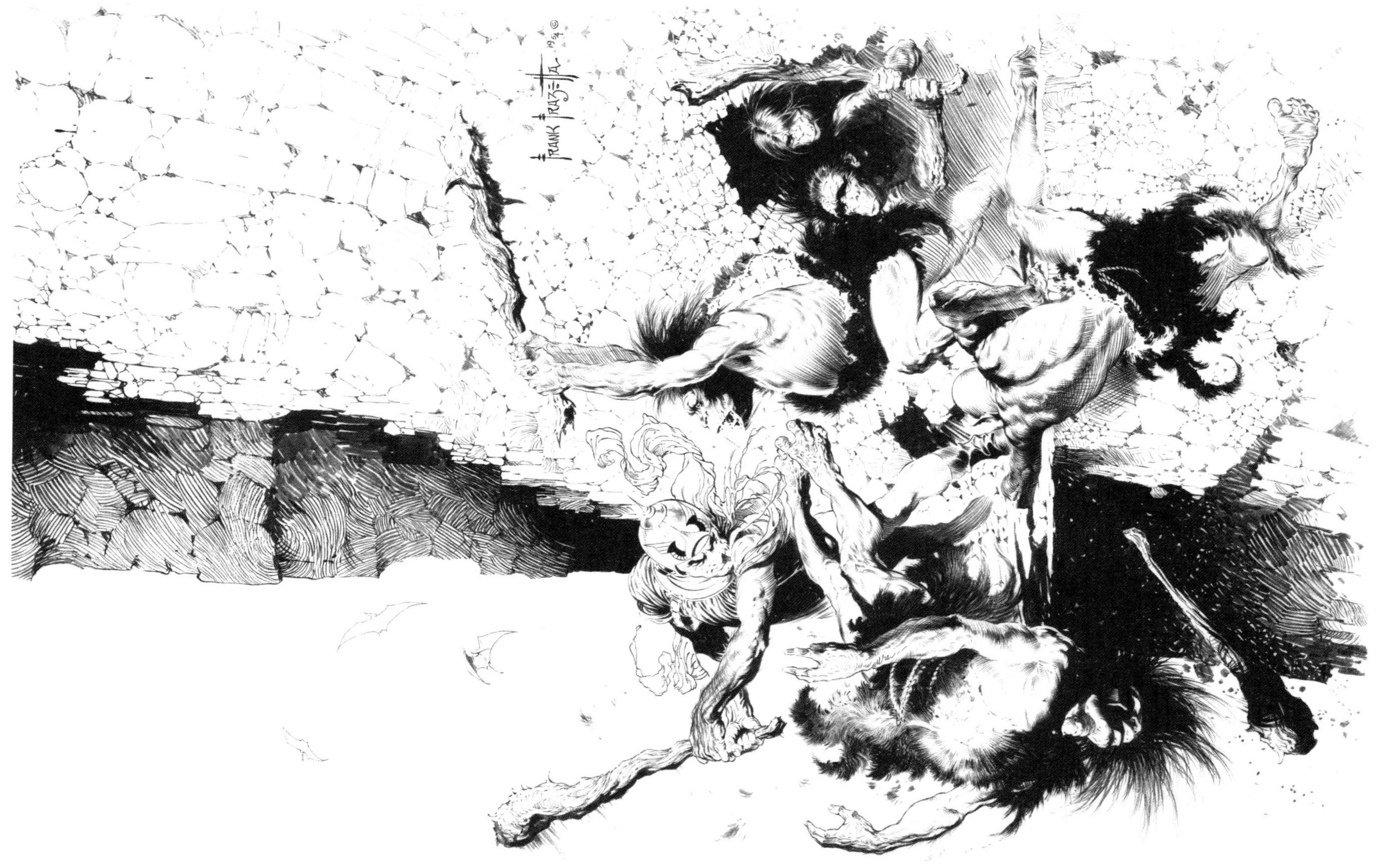

womanizer, guilty Catholic. The character and the artist wore the jeans and T-shirt uniform of the street tough. As Frazetta would later tell publisher Russ Cochran: "I'm very physical minded. Brain, fine, but this body is put here for use. If anybody could jump around like my heroes, it's me. Not many artists are [the] physical type. I've been jumped on by 20 guys in a movie theater and got out alive. In Brooklyn I *knew* Conan, I knew guys just like him." His fellow Fleagles were closer to fan culture—more timid and career minded, and hardly athletic. They were deferential to the material, where Frazetta was not, and all went on to fairly traditional careers in comics and fantasy art.

Frazetta never stuck with a title for very long. He'd make a splash, as with *Thun'da*, fall out with the art director or publisher, and move on. Some of it he would attribute to laziness: "Maybe [Hal] Foster didn't like to play stickball and chase girls and goof off. I know that many artists are totally devoted … they'd rather work than eat or sleep. But my art was something that I 'snuck in' from time to time, between living. I never really thought in terms of just sitting there and devoting my life to it … never. I did it to tickle my fancy from time to time, usually if there was nothing else to do, or if it was raining." Chasing girls was a consuming passion for Frazetta, who fetishized ankles, arms, necks, and liked a big round ass. In 1977, he recounted, "They told me 25 years ago, 'You don't put bras on your girls!' Now, today's women are Frazetta girls, long witchy hair, tits. My tits move, they sway. It's all instinct. I didn't know what I was doing. Crazy. Funny thing about my girls—I'm an ass man. Not a breast man. Oh, I love incredible breasts. But I like ass; that brings out the animal in me. They told me, 'Frank, you paint all those hairs. You just don't have to.' They don't know I separate the camel's hairs on my brush and laid each hair and just swirl on the hair—ha! Lizards, now I'm not vain enough to think I can do better than nature. I *echo* nature, a smidgen of it, trees, leaves, a saurian jaw. People who think I invent all these things, they're crazy. I like *real* women."

In late 1953, he got a call from Al Capp to assist with drawing the hillbilly satire *Li'l Abner*, then among the most popular comic strips in the country. From 1954 to 1961 he penciled the Sunday pages and completed a handful of related assignments for the Capp studio. Capp's strip was bawdy and fun work: ample, and amply proportioned women, slapstick action, and new settings for the restless artist. Frazetta was paid $150 a week for what he said was a day and a half's work, leaving ample time for the aforementioned goofing around. Capp and his studio offered a good landing pad for Frazetta—steady work as a cartoonist was not easy, and he was able to put down roots—he married Eleanor Kelly in 1956 and soon began a family.

But as the 1960s began, Capp's popularity, and payroll, were in decline, so Frazetta struck out on his own again in 1961. He picked up work drawing illustrations for men's magazines *Gent* and *Dude*, and a handful of romance paperbacks, but he had a bit of trouble getting mainstream illustration work. He was still working in his classic style, which a decade later was beloved by fans, but disdained by art directors in thrall to the refined expressionism of Bob Peak or the classed-up deco of Milton Glaser. Fortunately, running alongside the beginning of cultural change in the 1960s was a boom in pop culture nostalgia, as the early generations of comic book, sci-fi, and fantasy fans grew into adulthood and began publishing ventures of their own. Comic strips started getting the reprint treatment and pulp writers and magazines were suddenly coming back in vogue—it helped that pulps offered cut-rate, or even free material for reprinting in cheap paperbacks sold in drugstores across the country, the more eye-catching the covers, the

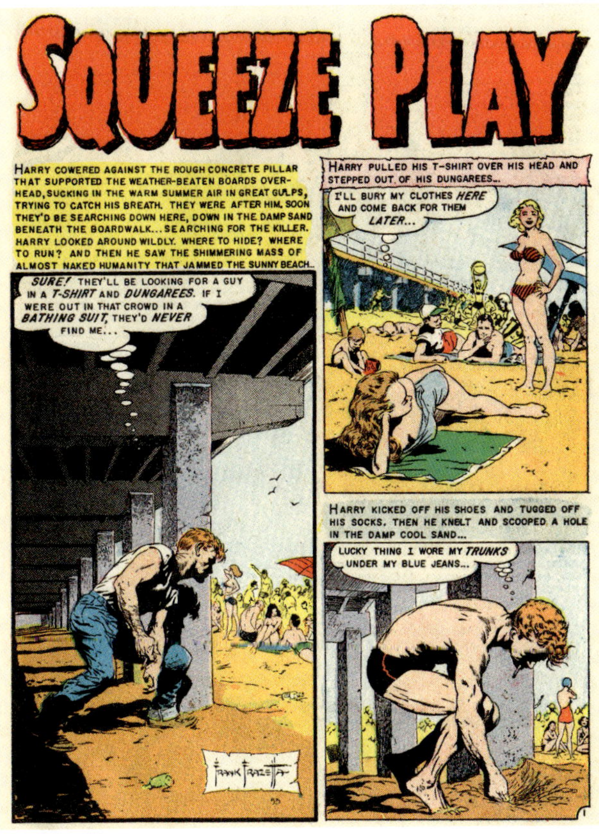

The opening page of "Squeeze Play," Frank's only solo strip for EC. This 7-pager appeared in *Shock SuspenStories* No. 13, 1954. *Courtesy of Heritage Auctions. © William C. Gaines, Agent, Inc. All rights reserved.*

The cover art for EC's *Weird Science-Fantasy* No. 29, 1955. Frazetta originally created this cover for *Famous Funnies'* Buck Rogers series, but it was deemed too violent, making it perfect for EC. Ink on paper, 1955. *© William M. Gaines, Agent, Inc. All rights reserved. Courtesy of James Halperin Collection.*

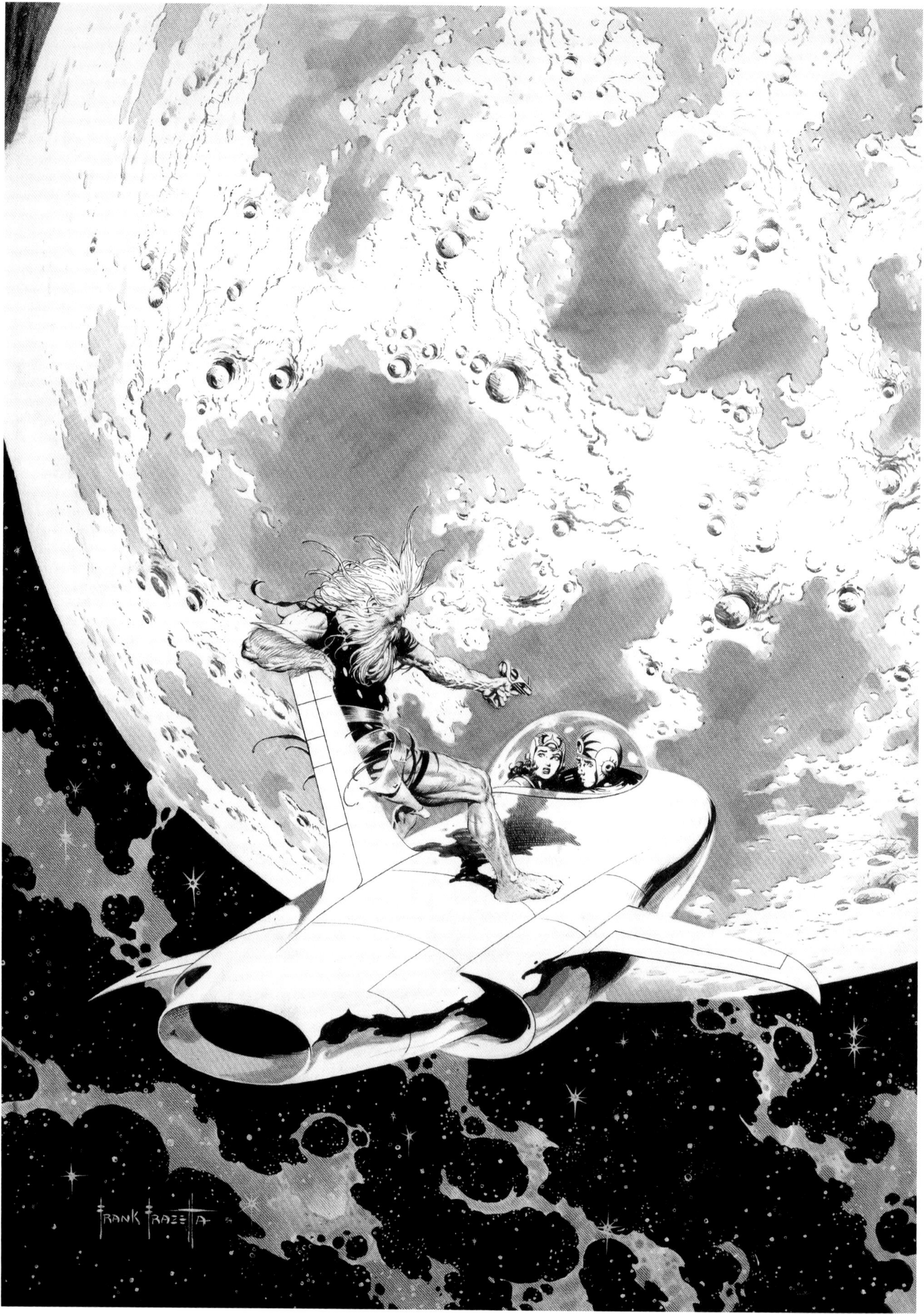

FRANK FRAZETTA

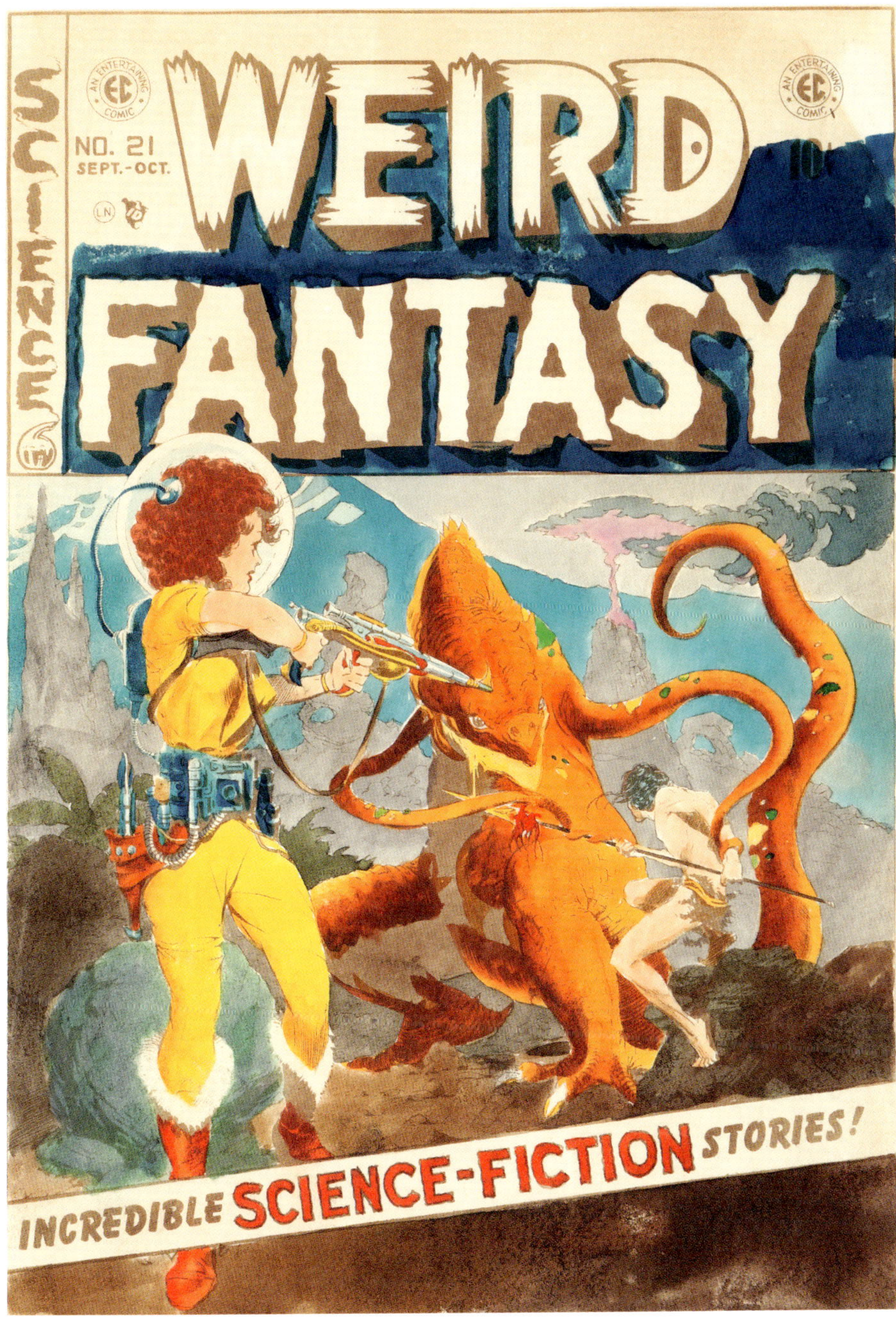

A faded silverprint for EC's *Weird Fantasy* No. 21 cover, a collaboration between Al Williamson and Frazetta. 1953, 26 x 16.8 cm (10.25 x 6.6 inches). *Courtesy of Heritage Auctions. Artwork © William M. Gaines, Agent, Inc. All rights reserved.*

bigger the sales. It was in this old/new world that Frazetta, a virtuosic, wild traditionalist, found his footing.

His old friend Krenkel ("He helped convince me that I could do great things. I didn't really need convincing, but he twisted my arm and pushed me a little. He called me a timewaster and a goof-off, and made me feel guilty about it."), was contracted for Edgar Rice Burroughs's cover illustrations by Ace Books, a dominant paperback publisher in those years. Unable to keep up with the demand, Krenkel put Frazetta forward, and his first cover, *Tarzan and the Lost Empire*, appeared in 1962, leading to many more. Thanks to another Fleagle turned *MAD* staffer, Nick Meglin, his grotesquely funny portrait of Ringo Starr graced the October 1964 back cover of the magazine. It rang a cultural bell like Basil Wolverton's "Beautiful Girl of the Month" cover for *MAD* a decade before, and suddenly Frazetta was in demand again. Movie poster requests came in, first for Woody

The cover for *Buck Rogers Featured in Famous Funnies* No. 214, 1954. Frazetta created the cover in ink over graphite on board and the color was stripped in later for printing.

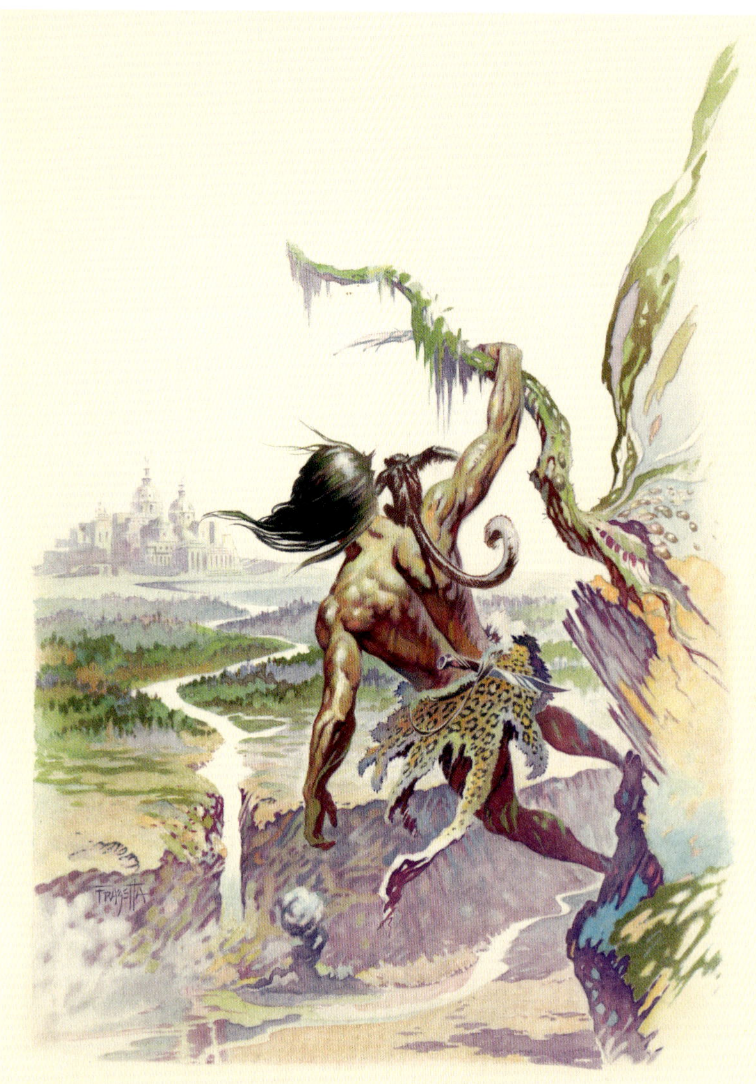

Cover art for Edgar Rice Burroughs's *Tarzan and the Lost Empire*, Frazetta's first cover for Ace Books' Tarzan series. Watercolor on paper, 1962. *Courtesy of Edgar Rice Burroughs Inc.*

Allen's *What's New Pussycat?*, and then many others wanting crowded slapstick scenes à la Al Capp and Jack Davis.

Then, tapping into his old fans, Frazetta began working for James Warren's EC-inspired comic magazines *Creepy*, *Blazing Combat*, *Eerie* and *Vampirella*. He painted what he pleased for those covers, developing what became his mature style. His designs are as clear as 1930s advertising: single focus, deep spaces, and color ways that move the eye through the image without ever straying from the center. He was undistracted by fidelity to gravity, let alone costumes or narrative. Only the feel of the picture itself had to work. The quick brushstrokes he used as shorthand shrunk to barely visible splashes of color, and the whole image was given additional punch by the absorbent paper stock. In a moment of pop gloss, Frazetta offered a hypersexualized, often forbidding fantasy world—energetic, immersive, private. This mode would reach a peak when he left Ace (he felt disrespected) for a smaller outfit called Lancer, run by a couple of refugees from the old-time comic book and pulp magazine world. At Lancer he launched the company's reprint editions of pulp journeyman Robert E. Howard's 1930s tales of Conan, a wandering warrior of little moral character but a voracious lust for life. "Conan came to me at exactly the right time …" he remembered. "I had something to prove … the pay was in a different ballpark, and they treated me fairly and with respect. I was ready to do much better work, which I did. Howard's stories have been around a long while and a lot of artists gave it their best shot. But when I read it, I thought, here's something different, here's something right up my alley, and I'm going to show the world what I can do when I really want to. And I did." Frazetta replicated his own dimples on his Conan's face, and from 1966 through the early 1970s produced a staggering array of nightmarish scenes from the character's life—standing atop a hill of bodies; galloping into a dark pit; chained and defiant astride a deadly serpent; in battle on snowcapped mountains. These are unremittingly dark paintings made first in the family's Long Island home and then in his East Stroudsburg, Pennsylvania, farmhouse, a 67-acre retreat in the Poconos. They were what finally made Frazetta a cultural phenomenon.

Unlike his colleagues, Frazetta didn't traffic in any contemporary styles—he was sui generis. He didn't do the noble costumed pageantry of Krenkel, and neither did he traffic in modernist design tropes like Richard Powers, nor the surrealism-inflected pop of Ed Emshwiller. Frazetta stripped down both figure and image, generous buttocks and flexed forearms, and focused on just the thump of it all, making his work far closer to Tom of Finland than J. Allen St. John. He amplified sexual impulses just awakening in the counterculture but still under wraps at Rexall drugstores. The very stuff of adventure and wonder that was "safe" for kids could be erotic to adults. And, of course, art has been a repository for repressed sexuality for centuries. It was inherent in the classical education Frazetta received *and* his ideals of roughhousing with other men in sports. It's a perfect

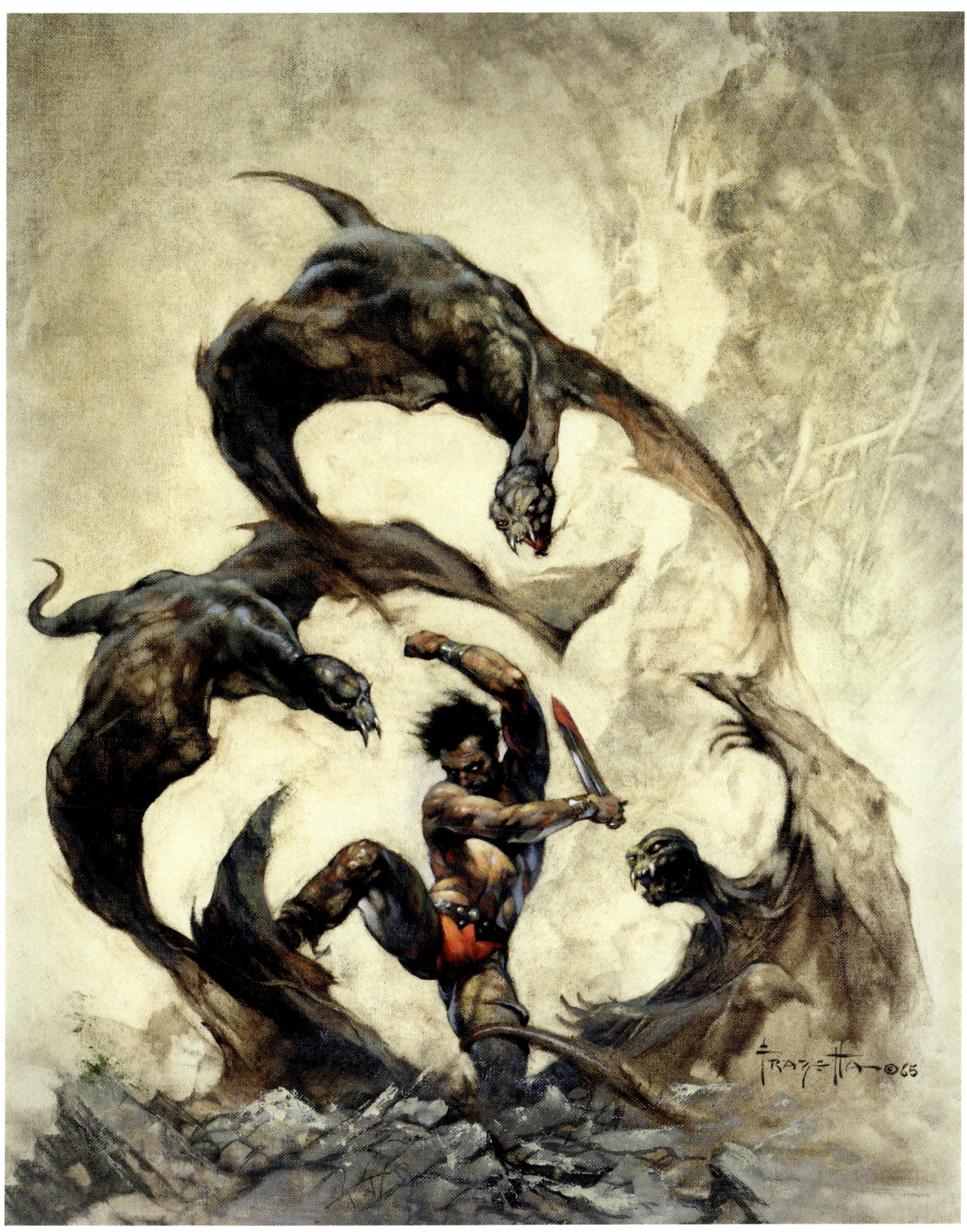

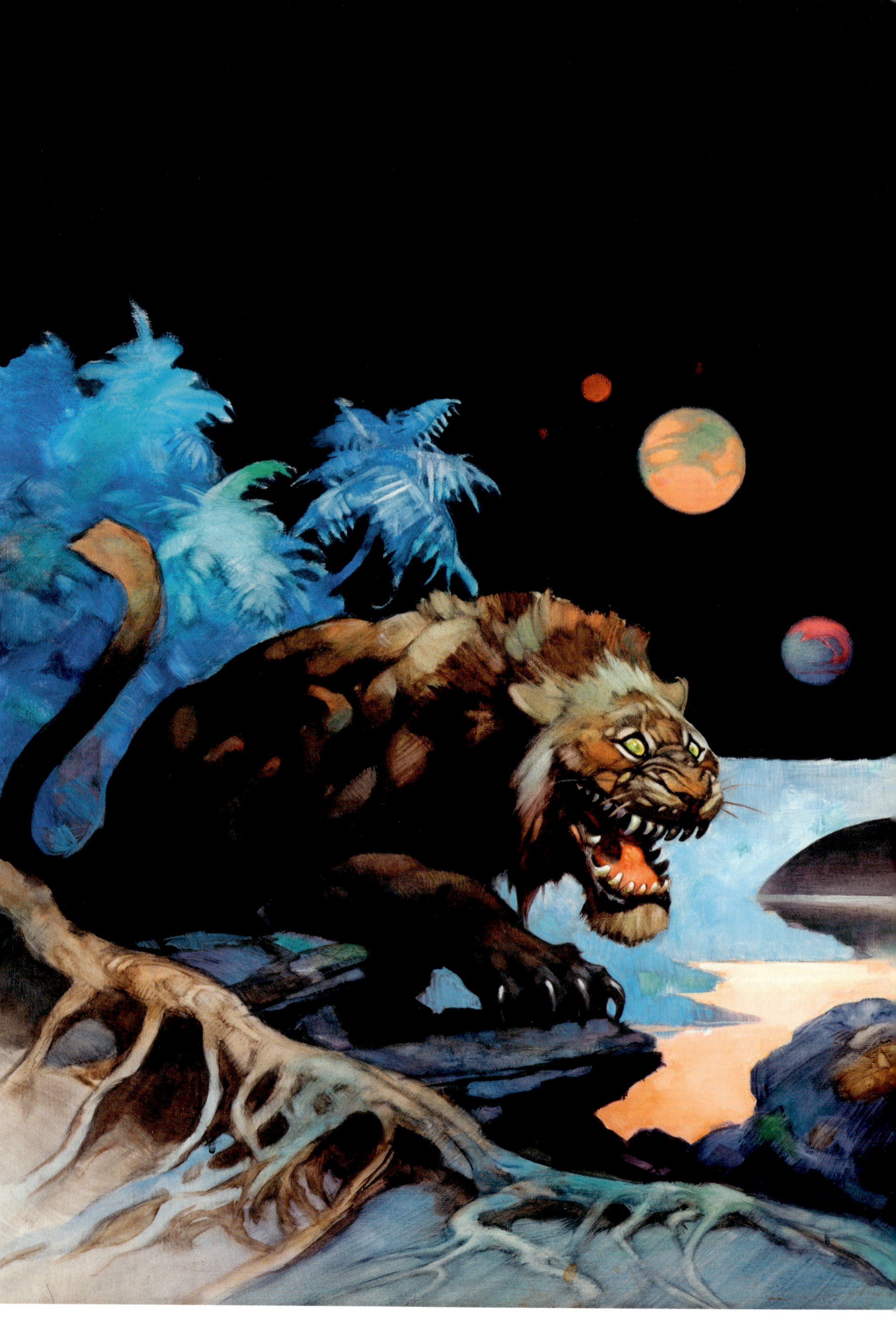

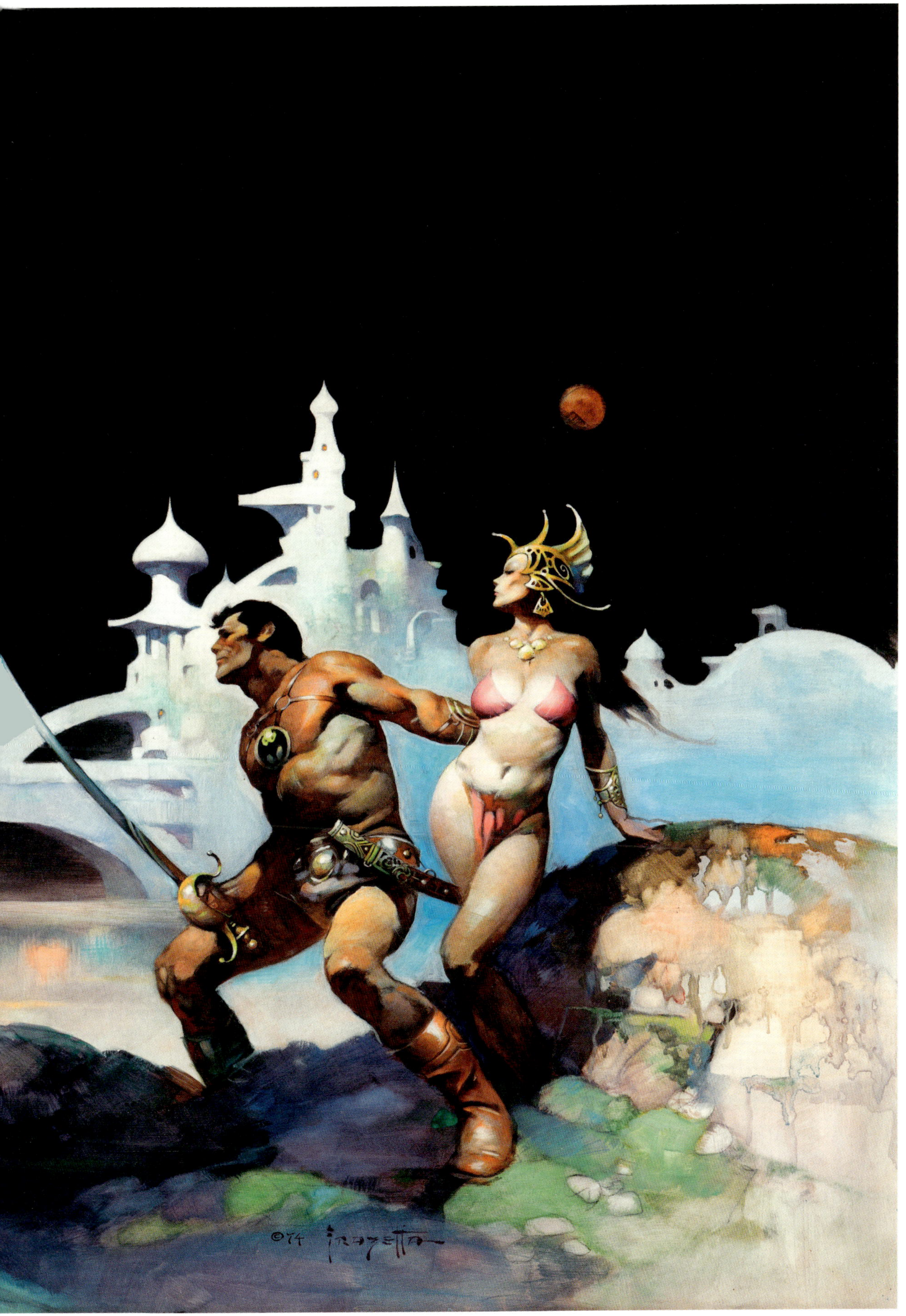

Nobody did female flesh like Frank Frazetta, and no booty was better than Princess Duare's for Edgar Rice Burroughs's *Escape on Venus*. This painting, understandably, was used on several reprints of the novel. Oil on board, 1972, 40 x 50.8 cm (15.75 x 20 inches). *Courtesy of Edgar Rice Burroughs Inc.*

safe space for straight guys to let out their pansexual feelings, and a space for an acid-taking hippie like Rick Griffin to get back to the sweat and grime of the soil.

When heavy metal bands including Dust, Molly Hatchet, and Nazareth used his paintings on their album covers they were signaling a worldview, as surely as the Grateful Dead did with Rick Griffin: the badass virtuosic fantasy of Frazetta was a clear sign to kids everywhere that this was hot, heavy, sexy, and not for parents. The homogeneity and feeling of all-out catharsis at a heavy metal concert was just a massive and public version of the private release experienced by readers in suburban bedrooms across the country. Frazetta's visuals were now part of a larger boom in fantasy filmmaking and merchandise that pushed cinematic possibilities even as it retrenched itself in traditional values after the prolonged hangover of the counterculture's failure. Frazetta fans Sylvester Stallone, George Lucas, and Clint Eastwood came a-calling, Molly Hatchet's 1978 debut album cover made the artist's "Death Dealer" character popular, and "Frazetta" became a brand as much, and eventually more so, than an artist.

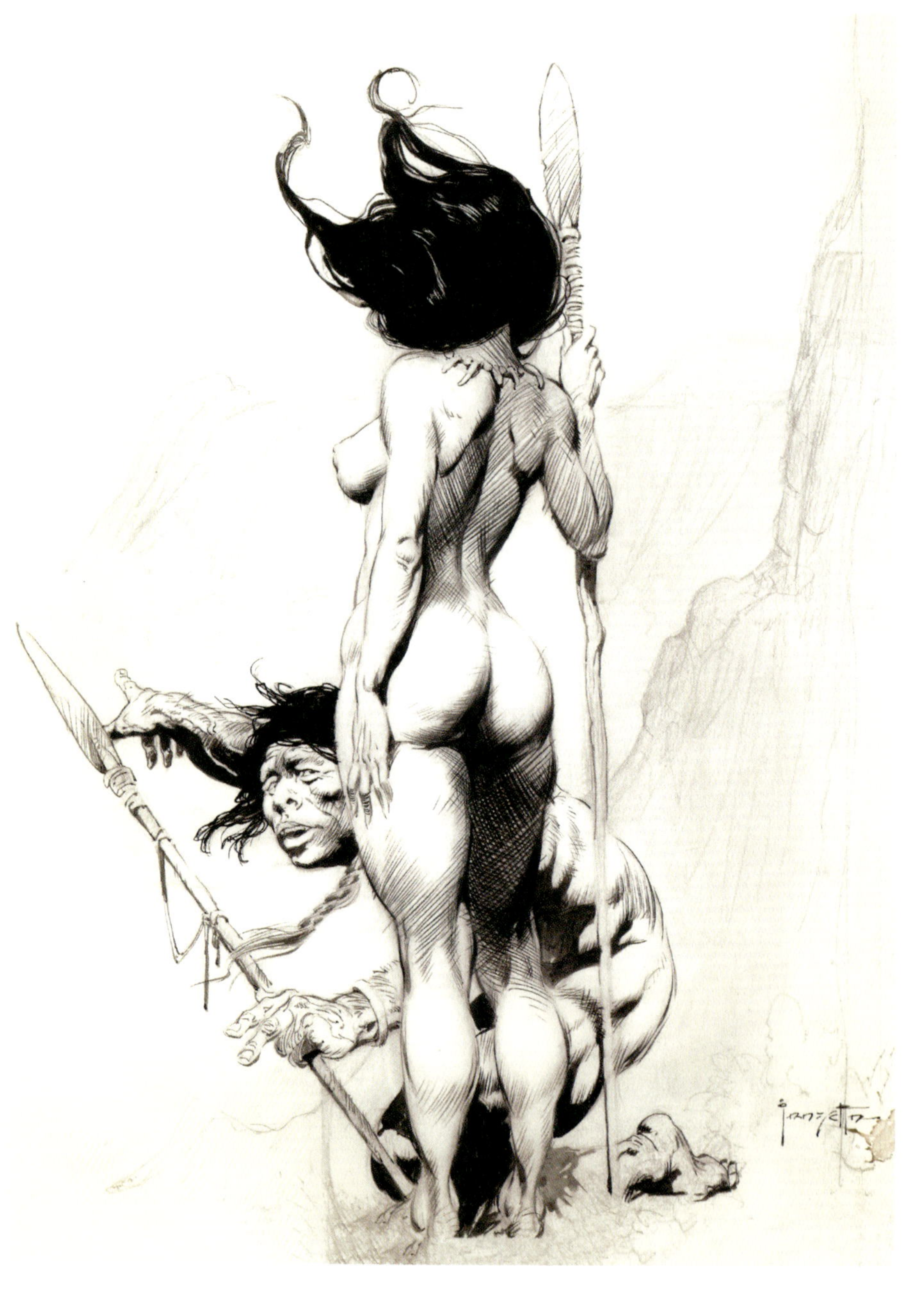

Nude Hunters appeared in *Frazetta: The Living Legend* (1981), one of a few books self-published by Frank and Ellie. Pen and ink with graphite on paper, 1968, 32.3 x 24.1 cm (12.75 x 9.5 inches). *Courtesy of Heritage Auctions.*

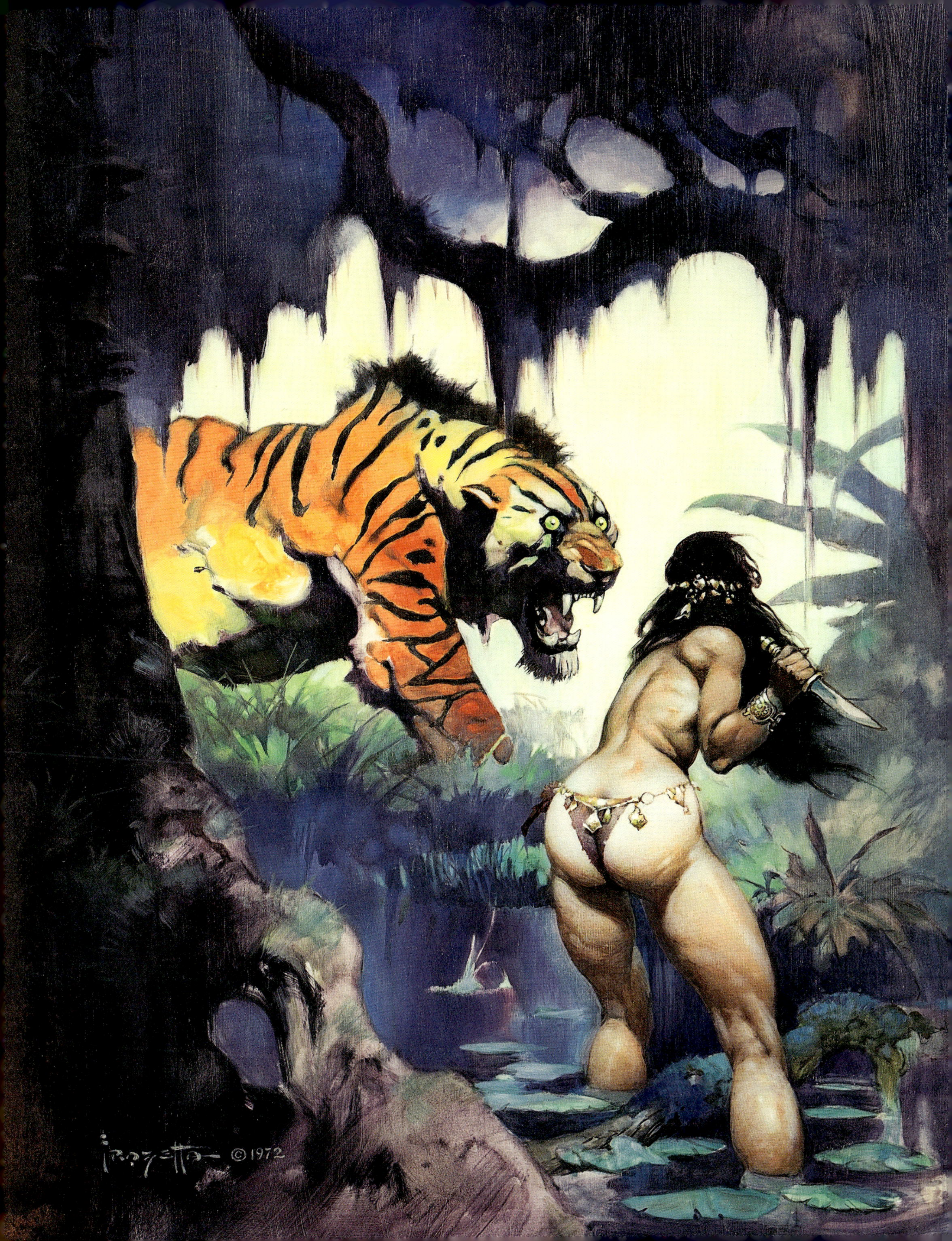

Frazetta ©1972

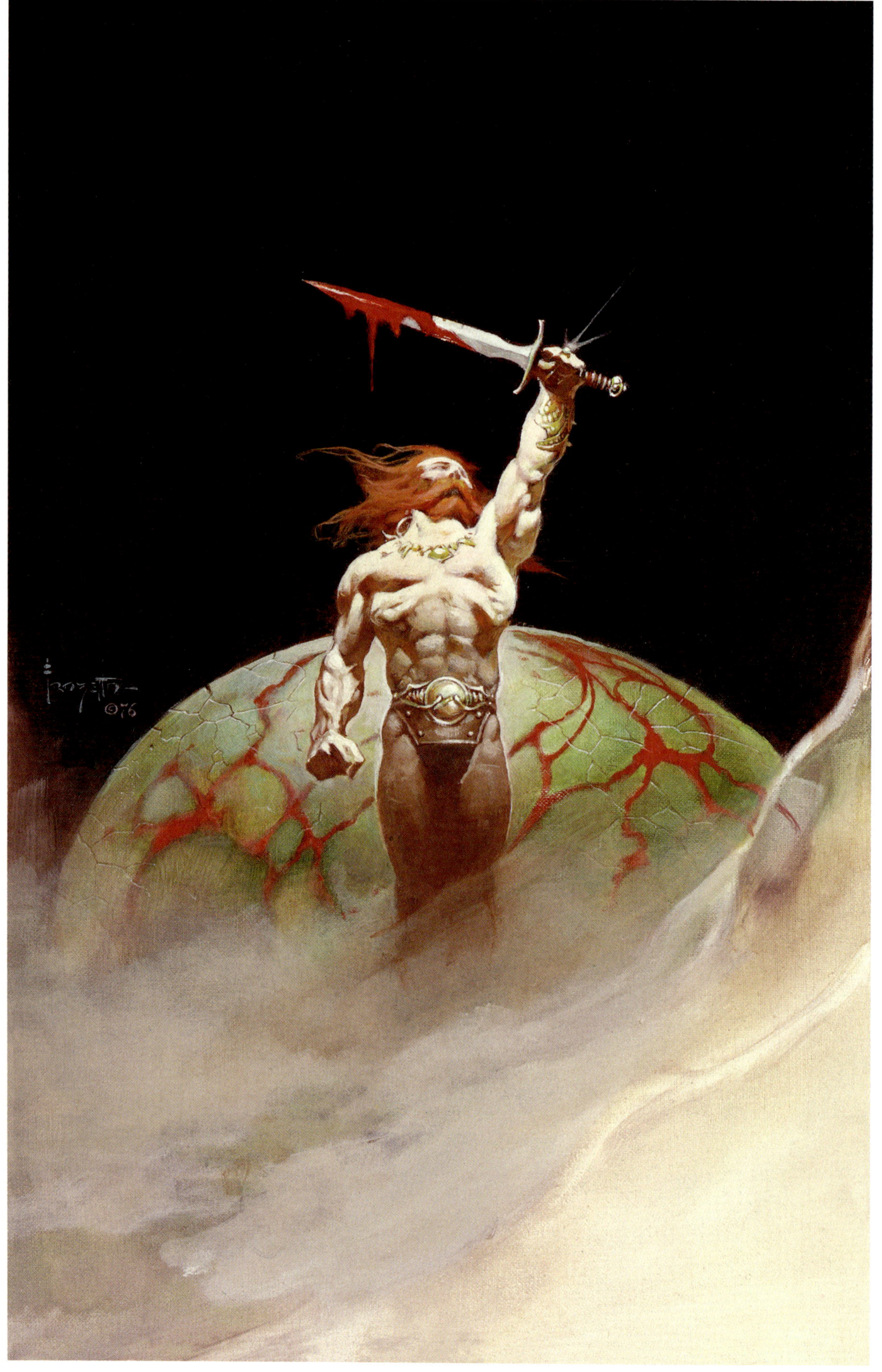

Writer Donald Newlove visited Frazetta for a 1977 *Esquire* profile. *The Fantastic Art of Frank Frazetta* (1975, Peacock Press) was in its sixth printing of 200,000 copies, and that year's Frazetta Calendar had moved 100,000 copies. Frazetta now owned a yellow 1977 black top Coupe deVille, and quite a few cameras and pistols, including a vintage Walther. His drafting table was in the living room—he painted mostly at night, entertained visitors, and enjoyed his notoriety. He didn't read the books he illustrated or listen to the bands who worshiped him. He liked Sinatra on the record player and Robert Mitchum on the screen. His home was festooned with his paintings; Newlove described the bedroom, containing "a fabulously crammed painting of Frazetta nymphs and satyrs copulating in soft red foam, and he has taken his knife to the bedposts and carved an upright phallus into a vagina on each post."

It was every Depression-era Brooklyn boy's dream to get out of the city to a nice parcel of land, create his own space, provide for his family, whittle some dirty images, and live in peace, and that's more or less what Frazetta did. The fantasy he promulgated was nearly the fantasy in which he lived—the old hustler, out in the sticks, master of art and

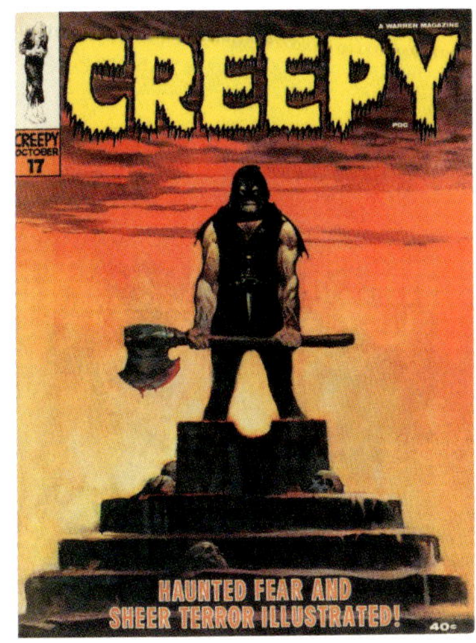

The Executioner cover of *Creepy* No. 17, October 1967. Frazetta claimed his contract allowed him to create the art and a writer would make a story to go with it. The story accompanying this cover was "Heritage of Horror."

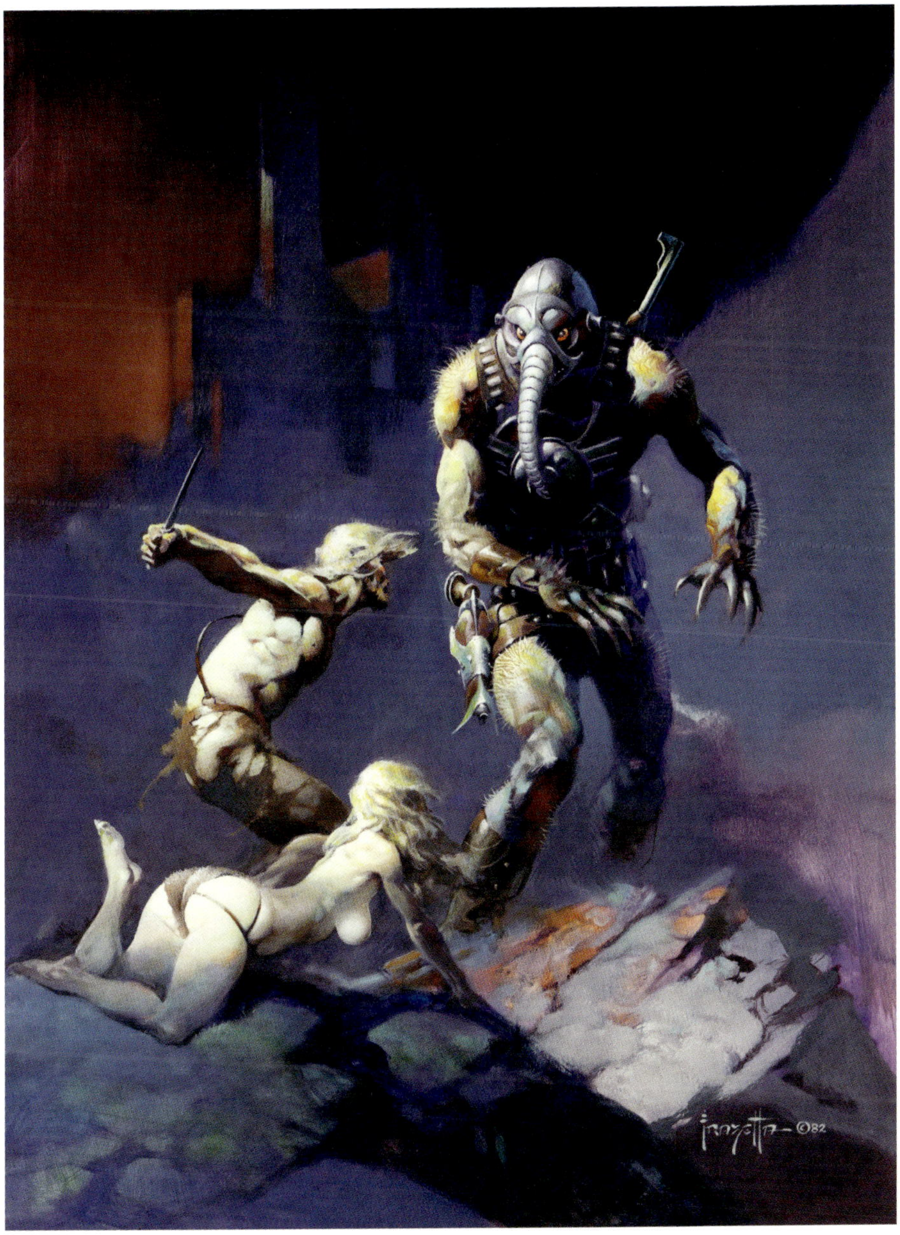

LEFT
Battlefield Earth, for the L. Ron Hubbard novel originally titled *Man: The Endangered Species*. The sci-fi writer turned Scientology cult founder called Frazetta the King of Illustrators and commissioned him for several projects in the 1980s. Oil on canvas board, 1982.

OPPOSITE
Bloodstone, for the Karl Edward Wagner hardcover novel of the same name. Oil on canvas board, 1976, 47 x 30.4 cm (18.5 x 12 inches). *Courtesy of Heritage Auctions.*

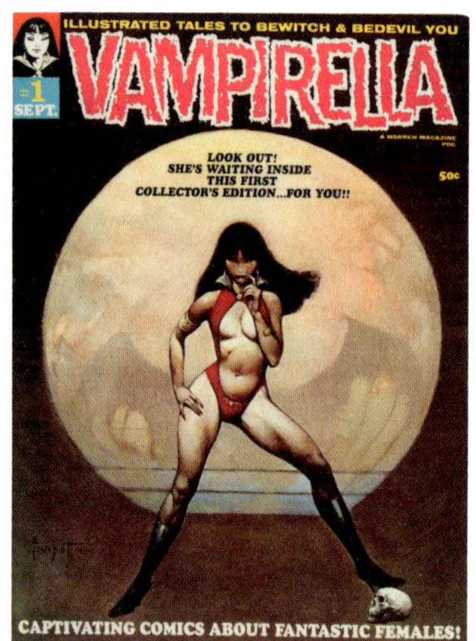

commerce. There were oodles of licensing deals, his own museum, and a steady stream of visiting fans. And, of course, more paintings followed until his death in 2010.

The art has endured for precisely the reason it first really succeeded: it is virtuosic but not impenetrable. It forever promises both tradition and transgression, dominance and submission. A liberation from self, but with both feet on the ground. It's a heady overlay on old pulp fiction, but the very antiquated nature of those stories allowed Frazetta a place to jump off. He performs alongside those narratives, offering startlingly contemporary and emotionally piercing atmosphere and mental space to get into, get lost in, and find wonder, power, sex, and some measure of freedom.

Warren Publishing kicked off its new magazine, *Vampirella*, in 1969 with a cover by Frazetta, who defined the character's look for all artists to follow.

Ghoul Queen, a magnificent cover for the August 1973 issue of *National Lampoon*. Watercolor on board, 1972, 53.3 x 40.6 cm (21 x 16 inches).

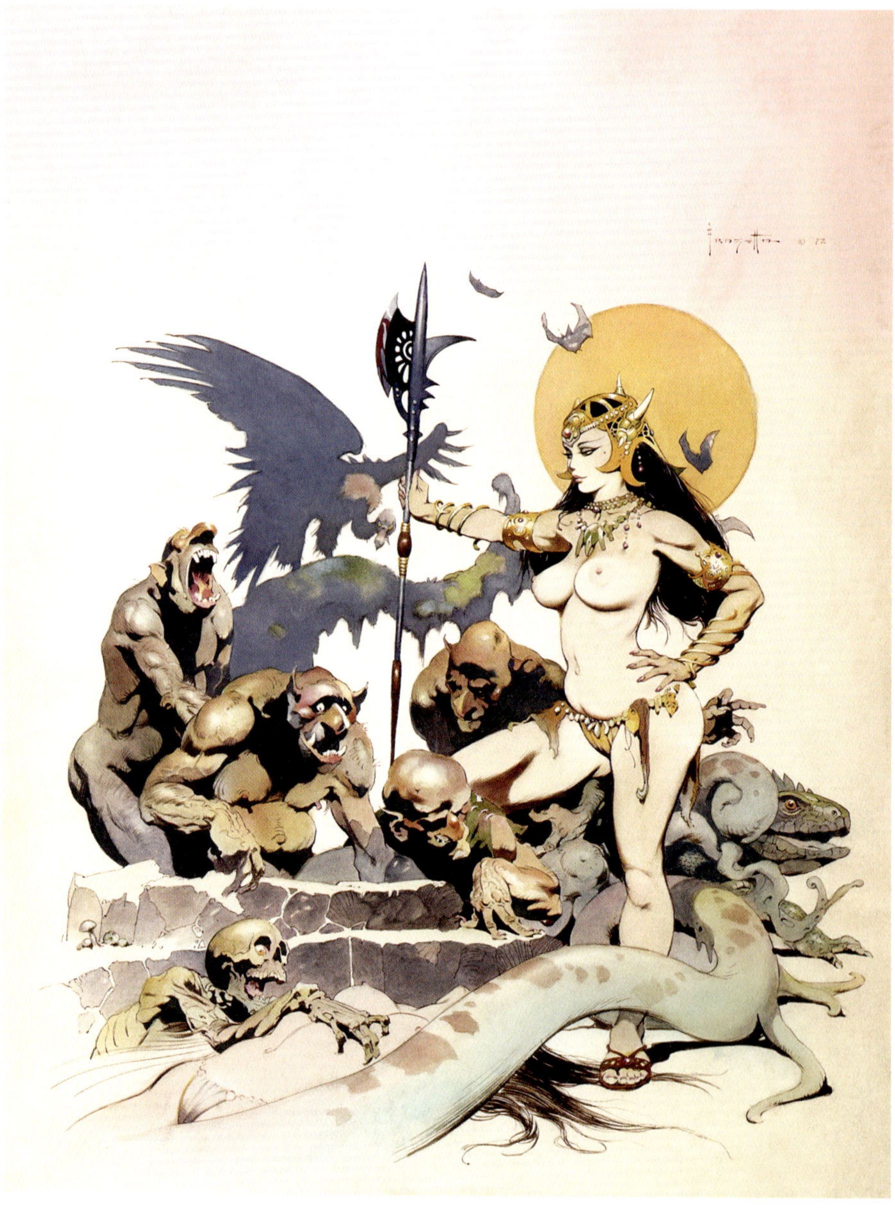

OPPOSITE
Queen Kong, for the cover of *Eerie* No. 81, 1977. Oil on Masonite, 1976, 50.8 x 40.6 cm (20 x 16 inches).

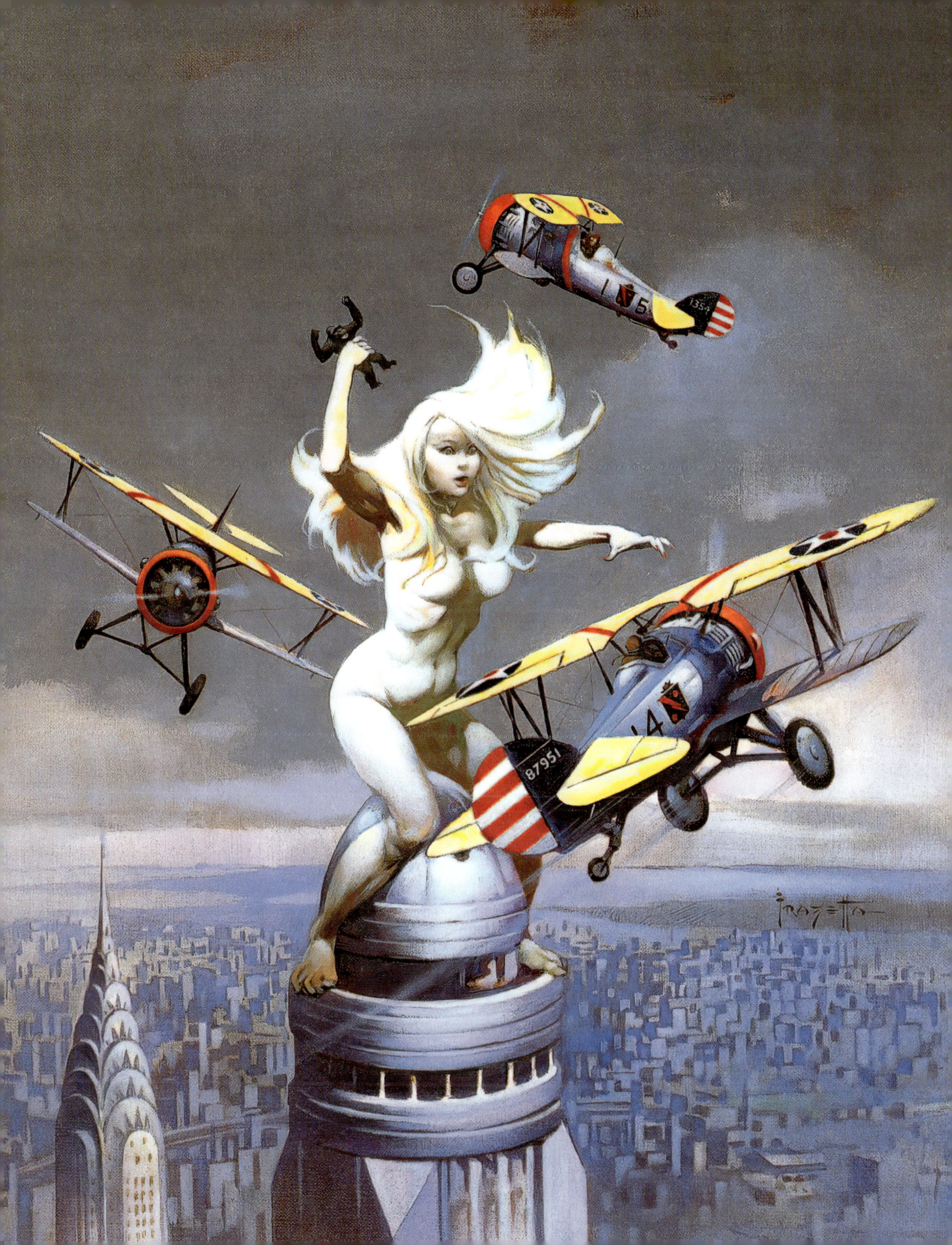

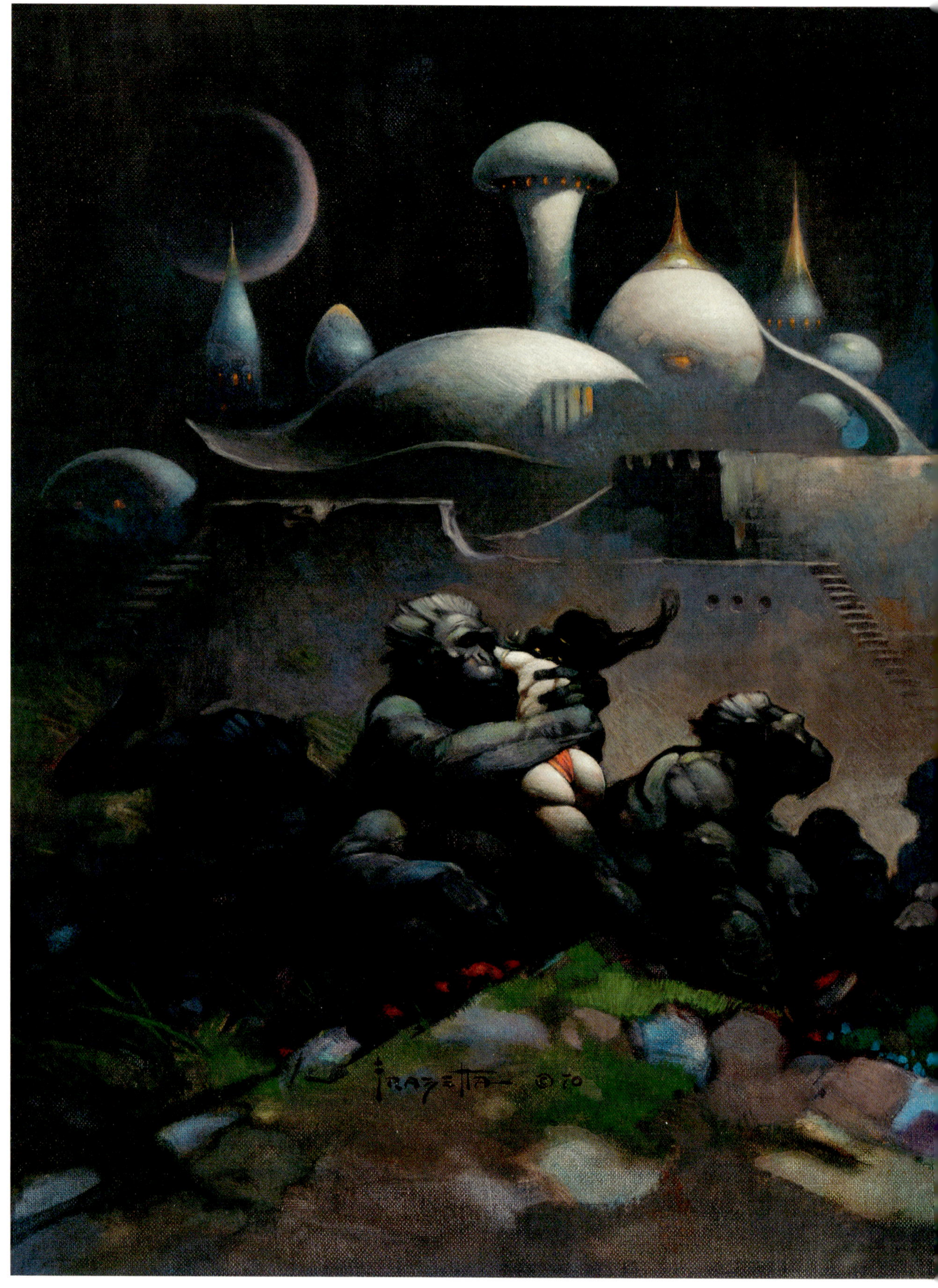

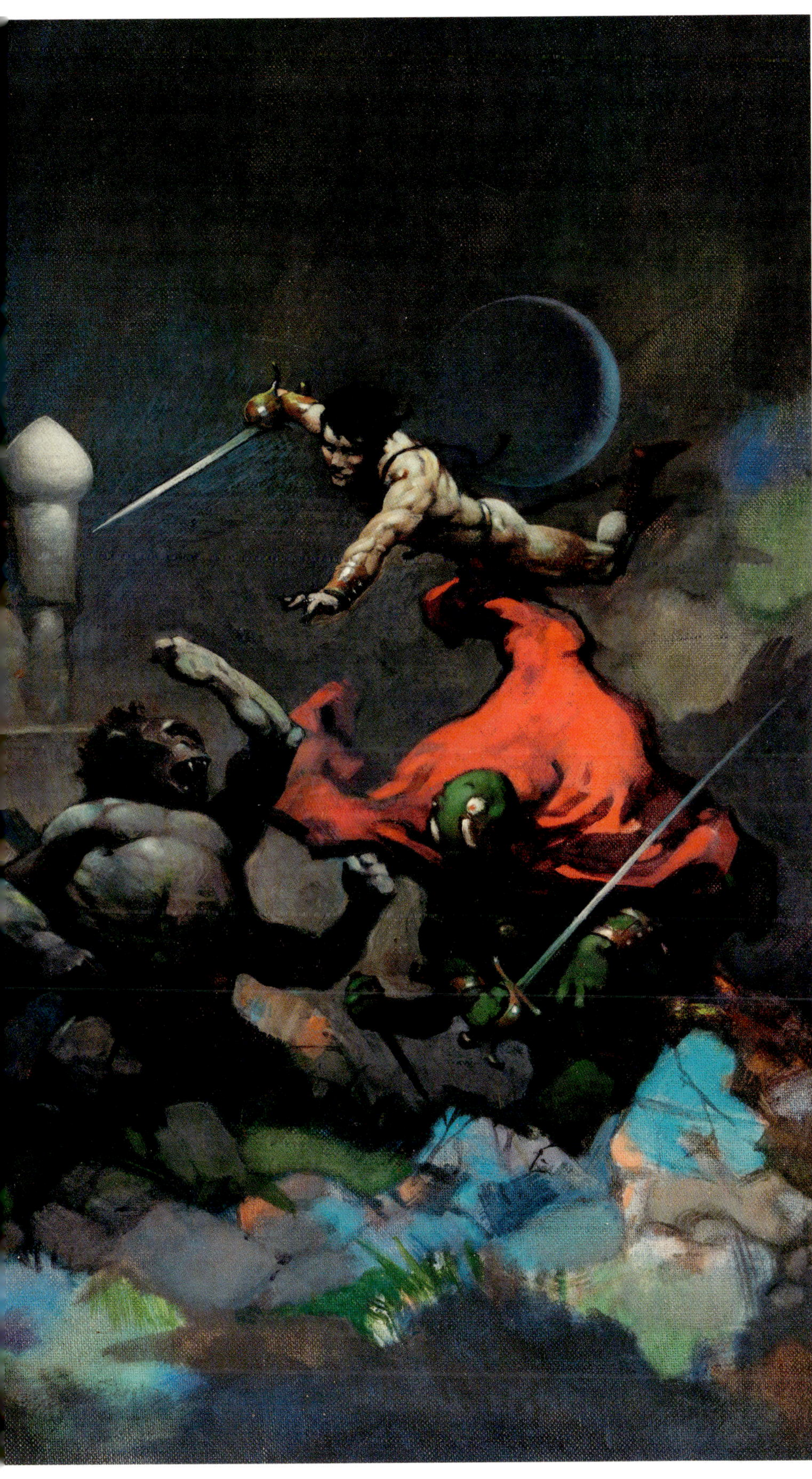

John Carter and the Savage Apes of Mars, wraparound cover for the Doubleday Book Club hardcover Burroughs novels *The Gods of Mars* and *The Warlord of Mars*. Oil on canvas board, 1970. *Courtesy of Edgar Rice Burroughs Inc.*

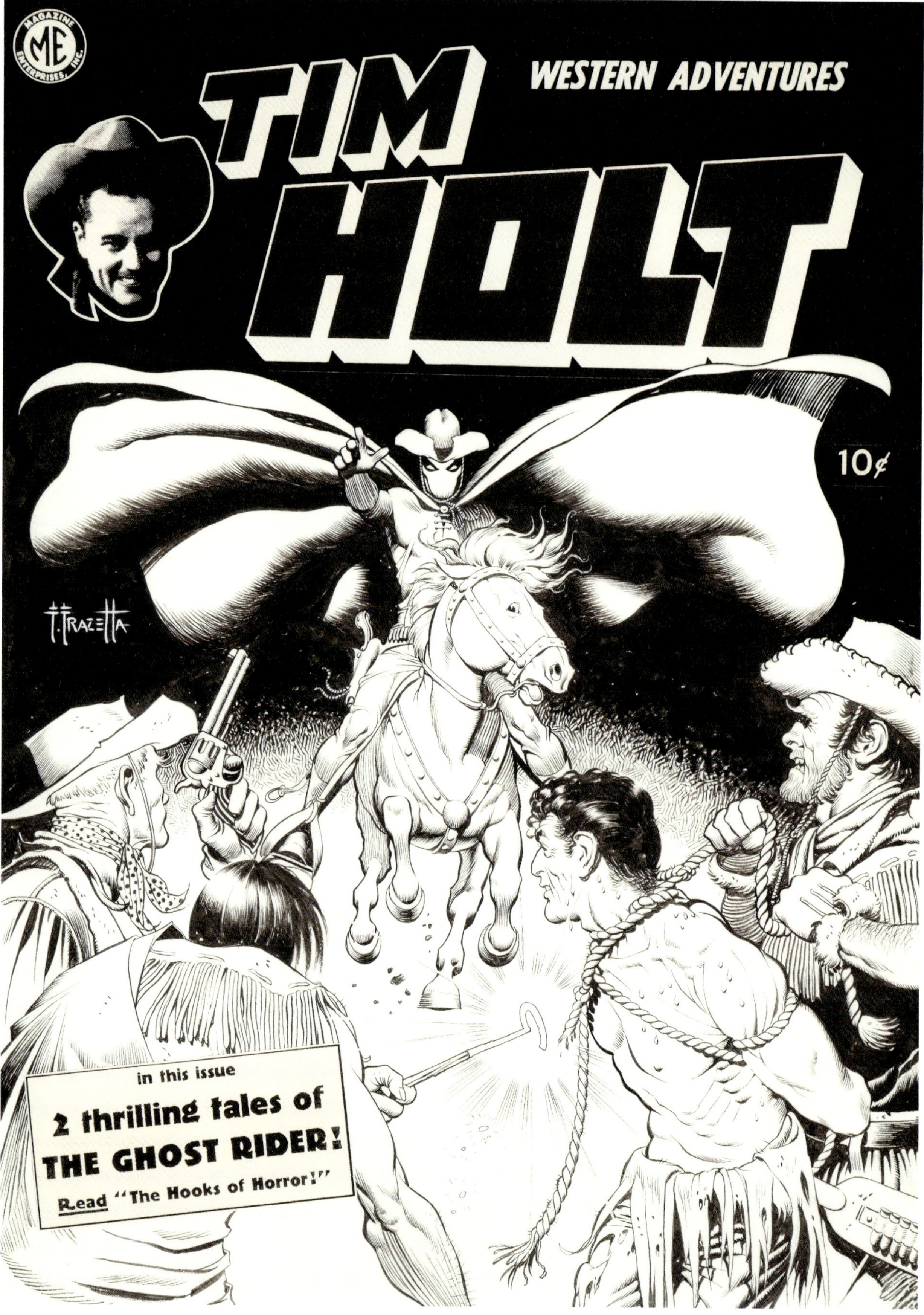

MAGAZINE ENTERPRISES, INC.
ME
WESTERN ADVENTURES
TIM HOLT
10¢
in this issue
2 thrilling tales of
THE GHOST RIDER!
Read "The Hooks of Horror!"

Anthropomorphic Animals and Li'l Abner
1944–1959

"The Bold Little Antelope," "The Just-the-Same Mouse," "Busy Billy Beaver," "Playful Bear," "Strong Little Elephant," "Abbott the Rabbit"—if it had fur and said "Gee whiz!" during the Truman administration, Frank Frazetta drew it and signed it "Fritz." Hints of what would become known as vintage Frazetta occasionally crept in around the edges: "The Elephant Who Wouldn't Help" in *Happy Comics* No. 28 is drawn falling face first into a lake in front of some distinctly fantastic and alien trees. Aside from the occasional buxom lass or menacing big cat, the most Frazettian element in all this early work is how landscapes warp and abstract to frame the characters: waves, branches, roofs, and mushrooms inflate, curve, and silhouette to make whatever the pigs and squirrels are doing more dramatic, while—within the constraints of the genre and the hand-me-down character models—the animals' hands, legs, beaks, and tails flare out from a central core like exploding popcorn.

Everyone with an interest in American comic books knows Frank Frazetta, yet almost no one knows his comics. Once he graduated from funny animals, his career was of a kind all too familiar to fans: the perfect-pitch draftsman whose best work is obviously done on the longest deadlines, who streaks from book to book almost at random until he settles into nothing but covers, single-page features, and other short-form work, leaving no long, series-defining runs behind him.

Nevertheless, the range of characters and genres Frazetta essayed before drifting off was impressive, including Westerns, sci-fi, teen comedy, fantasy, horror, and romance. About the only comic genre he didn't do from 1944 to '52 was sports—ironic considering that when he wasn't drawing he was playing baseball for the Coney Islanders and Brooklyn Bombers sandlot teams. The same year he won a Certificate of Merit at the Scholastic Art Awards he also won the Triple Crown for the Marine Park League. At the age of 19 he was not only four years into a burgeoning comics career, he was MVP of the Parade Grounds League with a batting average in the 400s. He would later say he'd turned down working at Disney and playing for the New York Giants' farm team for the same reason: he didn't want to leave home.

Of the latter decision he said, "I remember that going to another state seemed like going to the end of the world. They bus you back and forth and it was just one big disgusting hassle. So, I said maybe next year … time went by and before you know it, I'm too old."

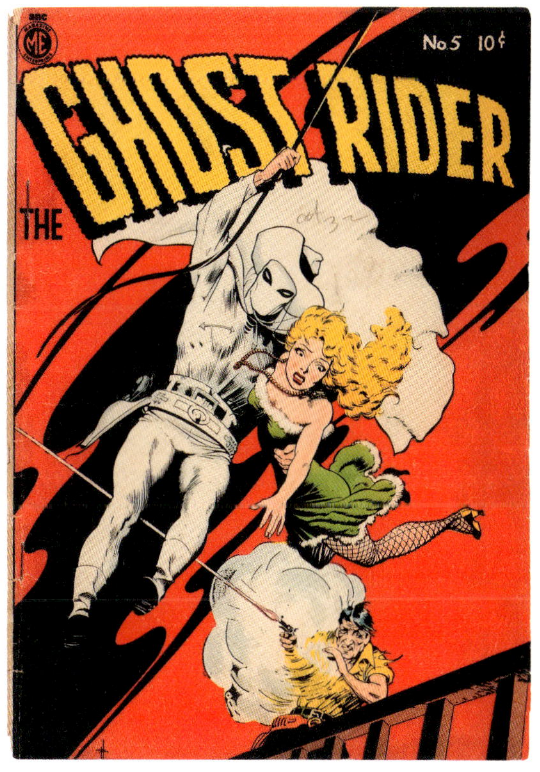

Frazetta produced seven Ghost Rider covers for Magazine Enterprises in the early 1950s, including Ghost Rider for *B-Bar-B* and *Tim Holt* comics. Here, *The Ghost Rider* No. 5, 1951.

Cover art for *Tim Holt* No. 17, featuring the Ghost Rider, as well as actor Victor Mature. Ink over graphite on board, 1950, 47 x 33 cm (18.5 x 13 inches). *Courtesy of Heritage Auctions.*

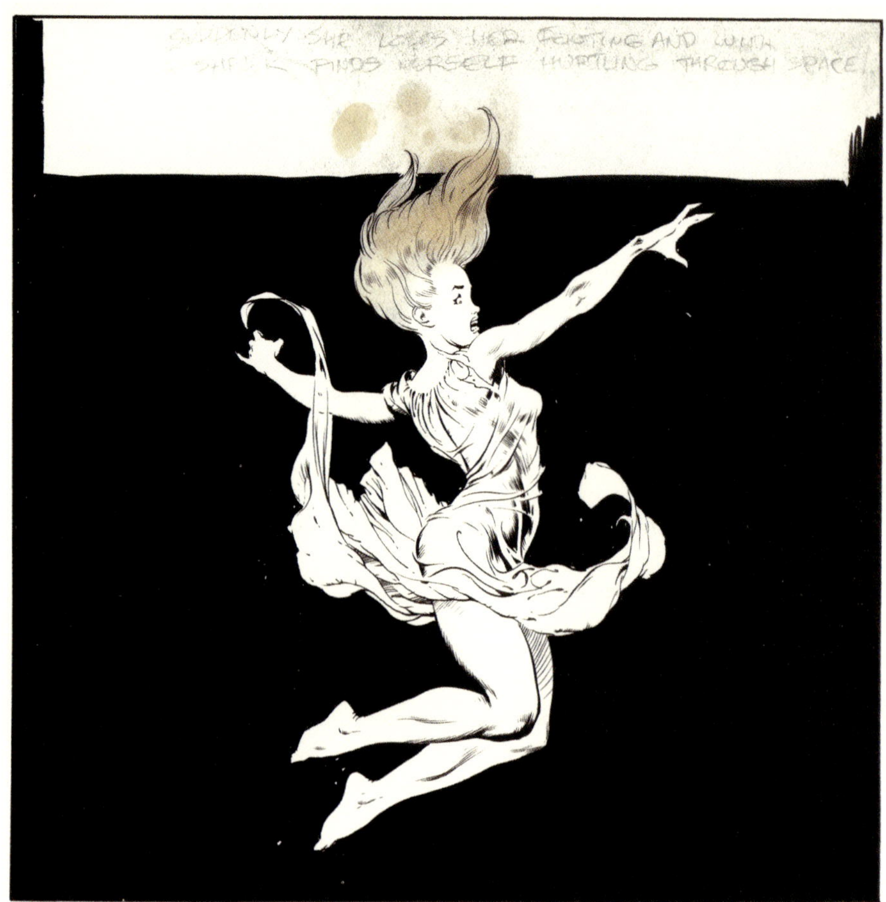

RIGHT AND OPPOSITE BOTTOM
Frazetta created his spec newspaper strip
Nina in 1950/51. When no paper showed
interest, Frank sat on it until Wally Wood
printed the five panels, along with an
unshown opener, in his 'zine *Witzend*
No. 8, Summer 1971, accompanied
by an Edgar Allan Poe poem. Ink over
graphite on paper, 1950/51.

Athletic, handsome, mischievous, marred only by a scar allegedly resulting from
a shotgun blast of rock salt after he pulled a prank on an irate farmer (there were still
farms in Sheepshead Bay then), the young Frazetta didn't look or act like a comic book
artist: "I was a loner and I knew that if I didn't stand up for myself I'd have nothing but
trouble, so one day I threw a rock at the leader of this gang of punks and he came swag-
gering over and said, 'Did you hit me with this rock?' I said, 'Yeah, what are you gonna
do about it?' and just as he was starting to tell me, I was on him! Bam! Like that! He
was down and hollering for help and all of his buddies were running for cover. All I had
to do was take on the leader and suddenly I had a reputation all over Brooklyn. I went
looking for fights after that, hoping that someone would provoke me. It was only for a
short period of time between the ages of 15 and 19. If anybody is going to be tough, that's
the period. I was sort of a confused kid between adolescence and adulthood and I acted
like a jerk. But I felt good, I didn't give a damn. I wanted those cowardly bullies to fear
me. I thought that was great, and I grew up and realized how incredibly stupid that was.
What a waste of time!"

In 1952, he finally got a sports comic—a newspaper daily about crime and racing
penned by journeyman Earl Baldwin, but allegedly written by Indianapolis 500 champion
Peter DePaolo. "Johnny Comet" was a devil-may-care hero who wore black T-shirts,
had a heavy dark curl hanging over his handsome forehead, and bore more than a pass-
ing resemblance to the man who drew him—though Frazetta was more excited about
the steady paycheck than rendering race cars. The gig had come about after someone at
McNaught Syndicate came across advance copies of *Thun'da* No. 1—a Tarzan-like hero
(likewise with Frazetta's wavy black hair, dark brow, and high cheekbones) that turned
out to be the only complete front-to-back comic Frank ever produced.

These two strips introduced the 24-year-old Frazetta to yet more dubious traditions of a creative career, specifically, having something you create become a film for which you are paid nothing, then being hired to secretly ghost a more successful artist's work for peanuts. *Thun'da* was adapted to a 15-chapter movie serial starring Buster Crabbe, and *Johnny Comet*, though short-lived, brought Frazetta to the attention of *Li'l Abner* creator Al Capp—for whom Frazetta would draw strips, uncredited, for the next nine years.

1952 also brought a less mixed blessing in the form of one Eleanor Kelly. "Frank and I first met at Coney Island one night. He was with one of his buddies and they were giving me the eye and whispering to each other and nudging each other and laughing. So, I walked right over to them with my hands on my hips and said, 'Hey, are you two talking about me?' And Frank said, 'Well, yeah,' and asked if I was the girl from the skating rink with the purple panties—I had this skating outfit with the short skirt and the purple pants—and I said that I was. And he was gorgeous! Like a movie star! And I knew there was something special between us right from the start."

Depending who you ask, she either met him while he was sitting on a Harley, or she soon convinced him to buy one. Four years later she would become Ellie Frazetta and the year after that their first child, Alfonso (aka "Frank Jr." or "Frankie"), would be born.

The *Li'l Abner* job required only one day of work a week and allowed Frazetta more time to pick and choose his projects. His most refined comic work appeared during this time: science-fiction covers for *Weird Fantasy* and *Famous Funnies* with beautifully lilting lines (influenced by and influencing his friend Wally Wood, maestro of bubble helmets); "Squeeze Play," a crime story for *Shock SuspenStories* set in Brooklyn's very own Coney Island; and "Untamed Love" for *Personal Love* No. 32—a fantastically well-drawn romance-and-safari story (with a familiar dark-haired hero) told in richly detailed panels with a level of attention to line and shadow seldom seen in any comic before or since. Another intriguing piece—a reworking of a Wally Wood *Shock SuspenStories* thriller called "Came the Dawn" for Bill Gaines's *Shock Illustrated* #4—was never published. Gaines was forced to close the magazine

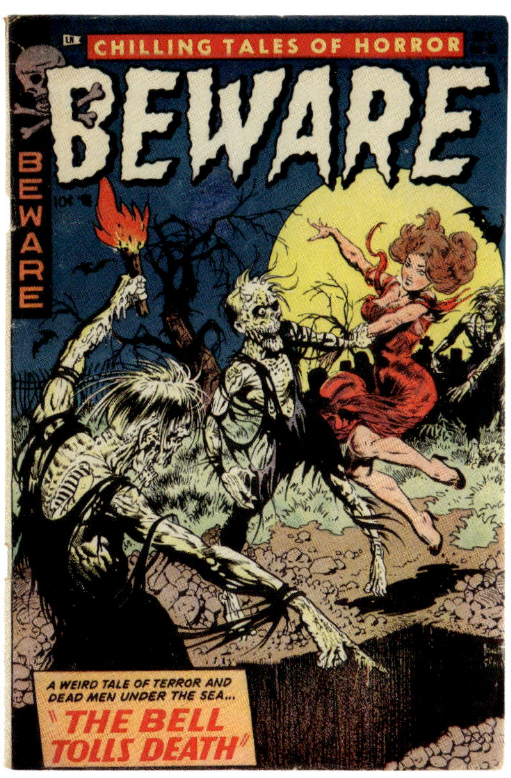

Beware No. 10 from Trojan Magazines, 1954, with a stunning cover by Frazetta and Sid Check.

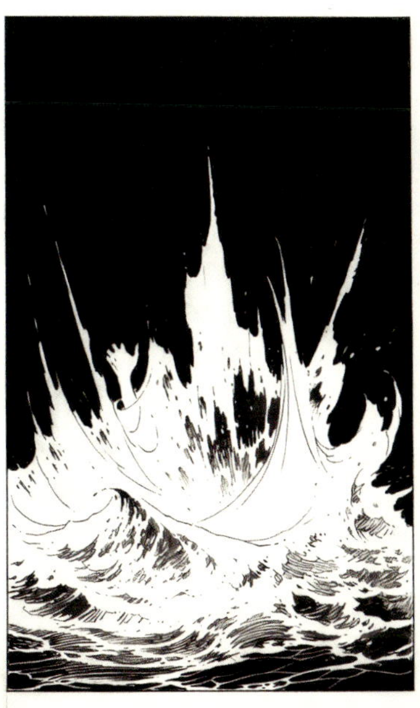
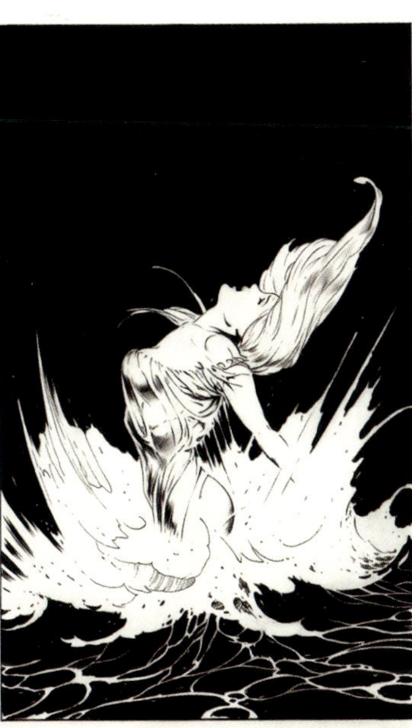
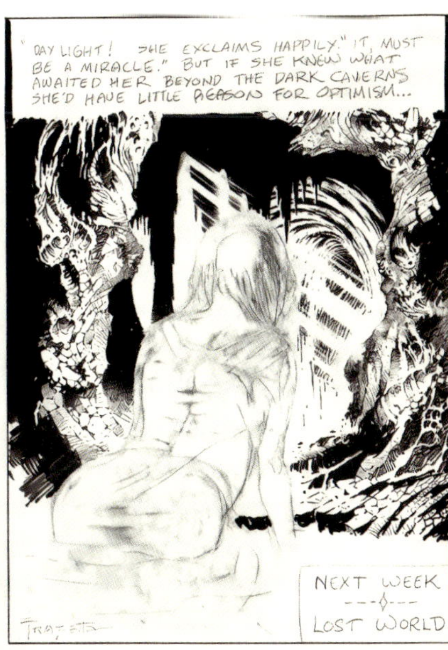

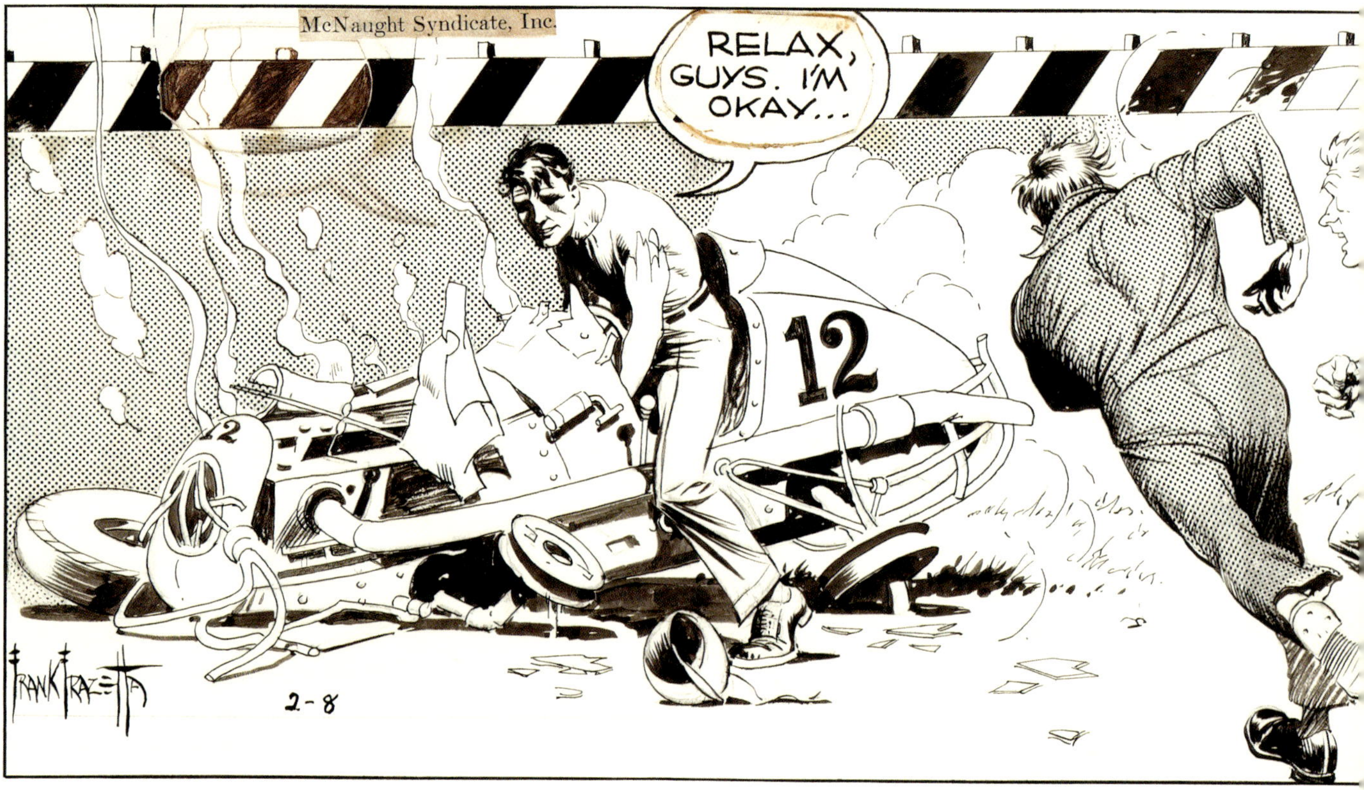

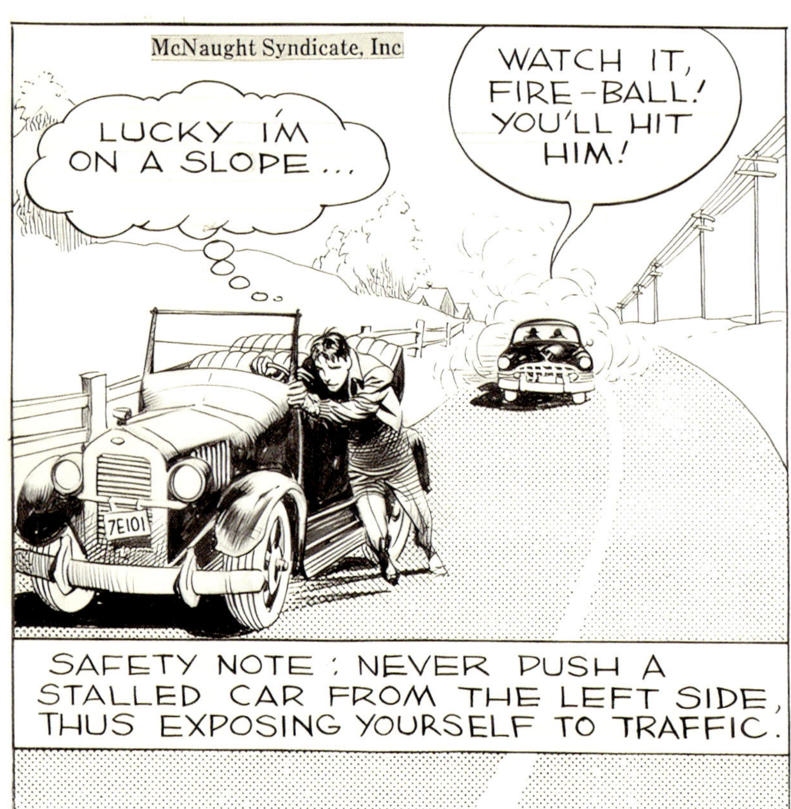

McNaught Syndicate, Inc.
RELAX, GUYS. I'M OKAY...
12
2
FRANK FRAZETTA
2-8

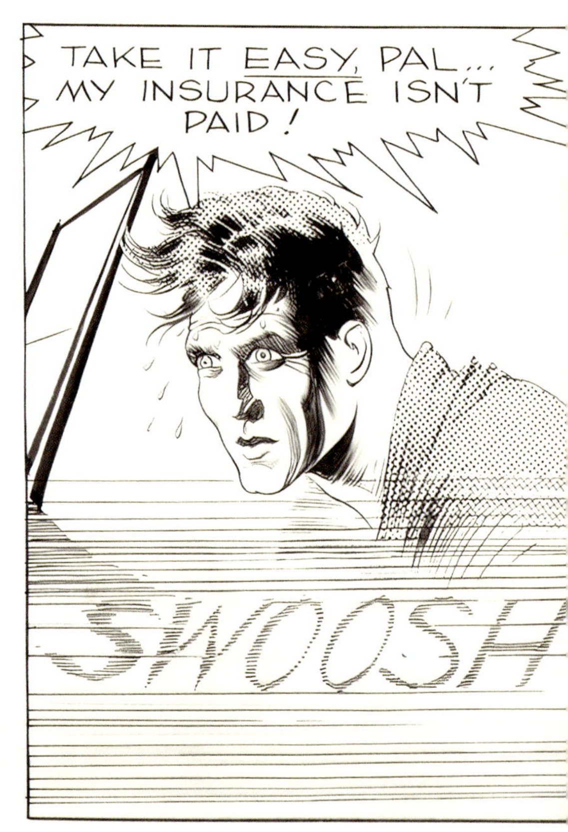

McNaught Syndicate, Inc
LUCKY I'M ON A SLOPE...
WATCH IT, FIRE-BALL! YOU'LL HIT HIM!
TAKE IT EASY, PAL... MY INSURANCE ISN'T PAID!
7E101
SWOOSH
SAFETY NOTE: NEVER PUSH A STALLED CAR FROM THE LEFT SIDE, THUS EXPOSING YOURSELF TO TRAFFIC.

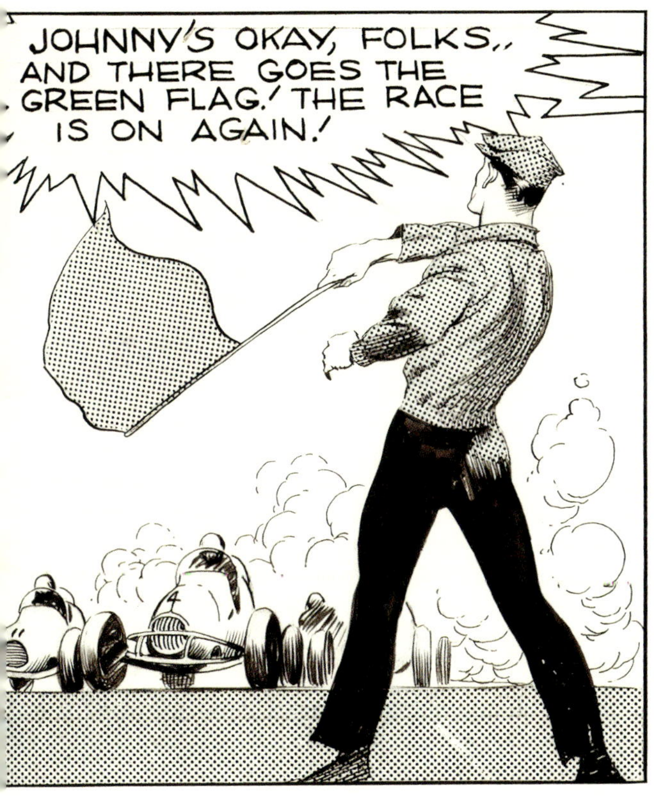

JOHNNY'S OKAY, FOLKS,, AND THERE GOES THE GREEN FLAG! THE RACE IS ON AGAIN!

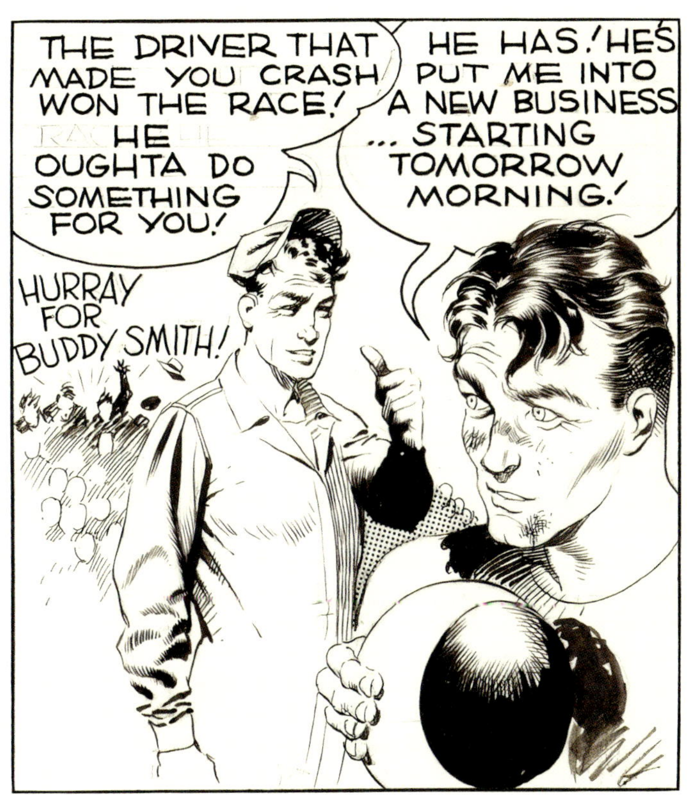

THE DRIVER THAT MADE YOU CRASH WON THE RACE! HE OUGHTA DO SOMETHING FOR YOU!
HE HAS! HES PUT ME INTO A NEW BUSINESS ...STARTING TOMORROW MORNING!
HURRAY FOR BUDDY SMITH!

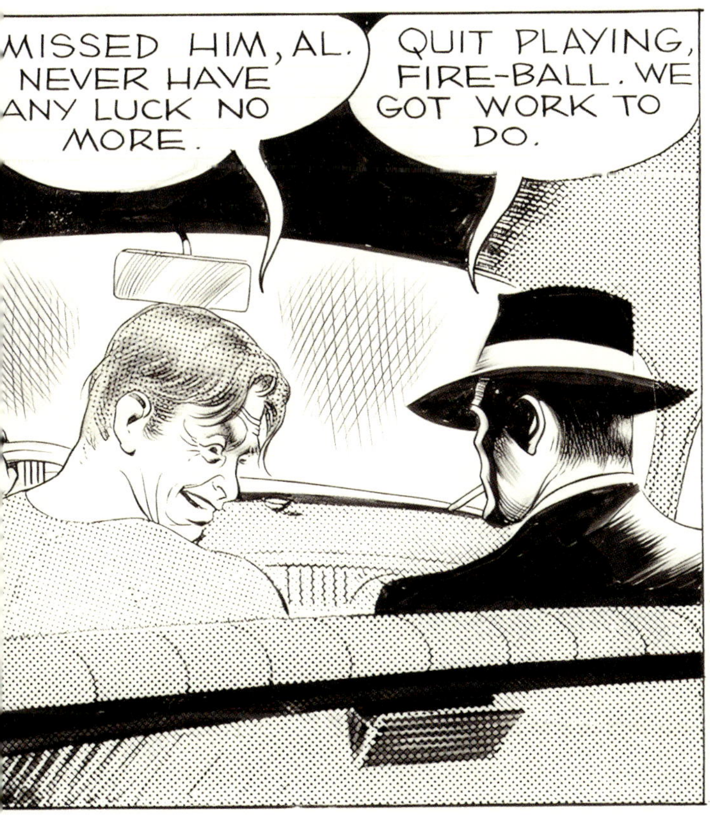

MISSED HIM, AL. NEVER HAVE ANY LUCK NO MORE.
QUIT PLAYING, FIRE-BALL. WE GOT WORK TO DO.

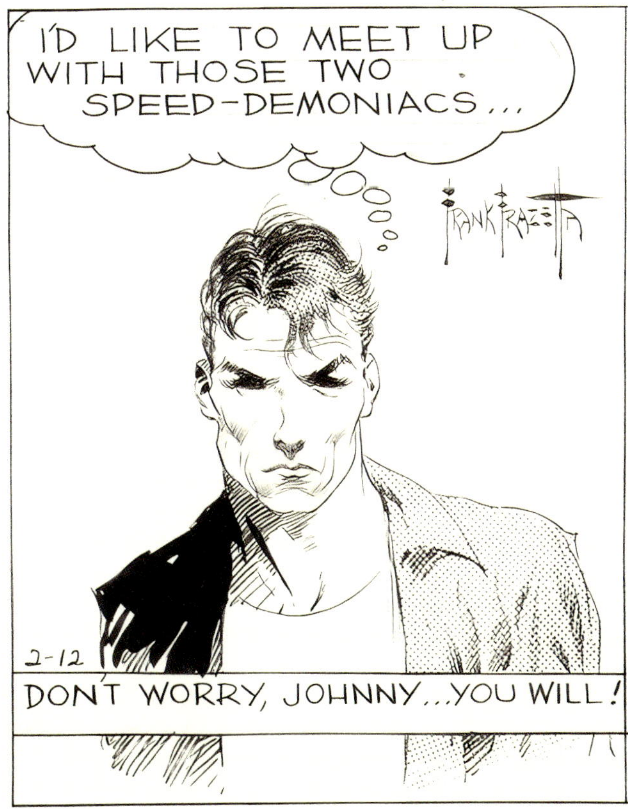

I'D LIKE TO MEET UP WITH THOSE TWO SPEED-DEMONIACS...
FRANK FRAZETTA
2-12
DON'T WORRY, JOHNNY...YOU WILL!

These daily *Johnny Comet* strips are from the hopeful, early days in February 1952. Ink and Zipatone over graphite on board, 1952, 14.6 x 53.9 cm (5.75 x 21.25 inches). *Courtesy of Heritage Auctions.*

in the wake of the 1954 congressional hearings, spearheaded by Senator Estes Kefauver and later-discredited child psychologist Fredric Wertham, linking comics to juvenile delinquency. The story was among Frazetta's favorite works from this period: "I was trying something new in that story. I was using a lot of strong blacks. The story would have been filled with mood and atmosphere. I think it really would have been my best work if I had finished it."

Nevertheless, as Frazetta continued to work for Capp his outside comic work tapered off—by the late '50s he wasn't doing anything else. He spent most of his spare time with the Fleagles playing ball, goofing off around Brooklyn, and delaying adulthood as long as possible.

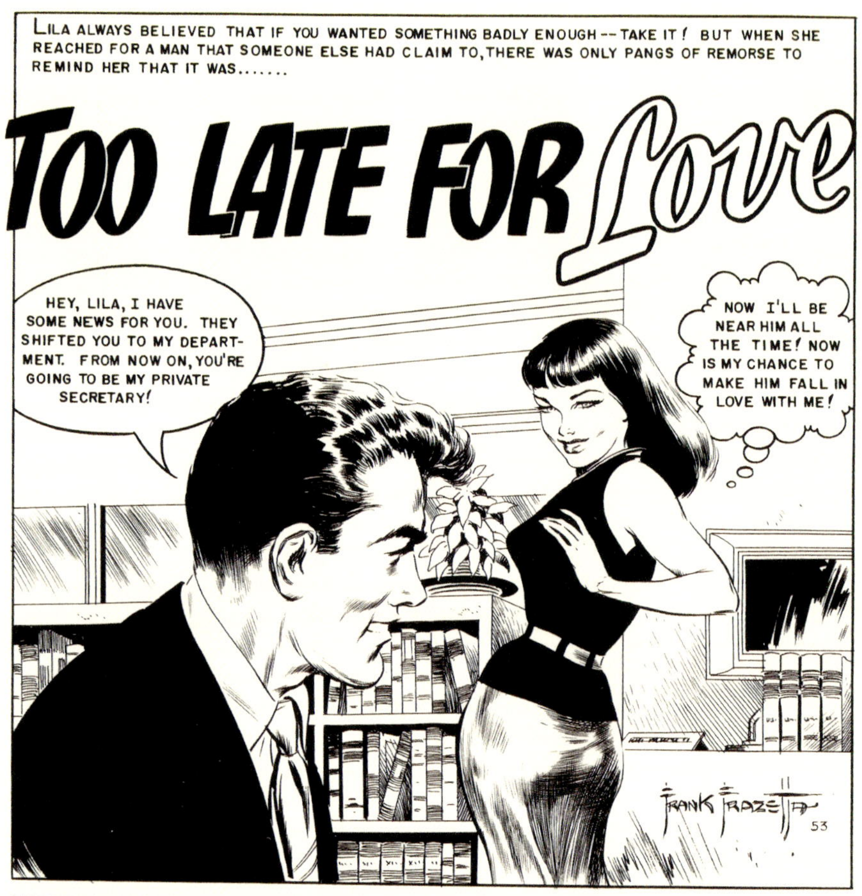

Frazetta took any work he could get in the beginning, including this moralistic love story for *Personal Love* No. 25, aimed at women, but starring Frank's signature sexy femmes fatales. Ink over graphite on board, 1953.

Frazetta ghosted Al Capp's *Li'l Abner* newspaper comic strip from 1954 to 1961. He faithfully copied Capp's style for the figures, though showing more of notable figures like Moonbeam McSwine, here, and her high-society doppelgänger Gloria Van Welbilt. That tree is pure Frazetta. Ink over graphite on board, 1954, 65.4 x 53.3 cm (25.75 x 21 inches). *Courtesy of Heritage Auctions.*

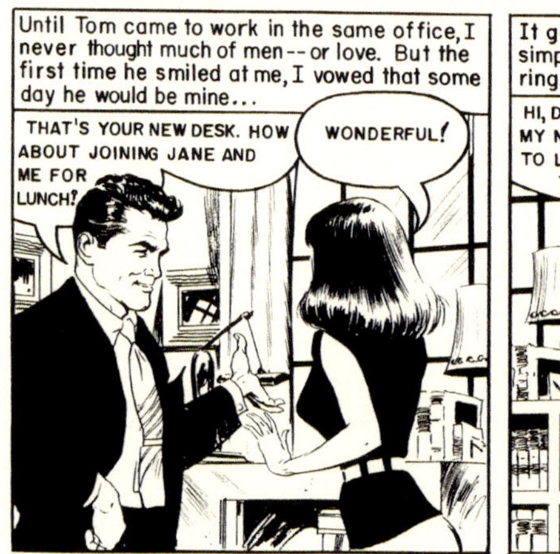

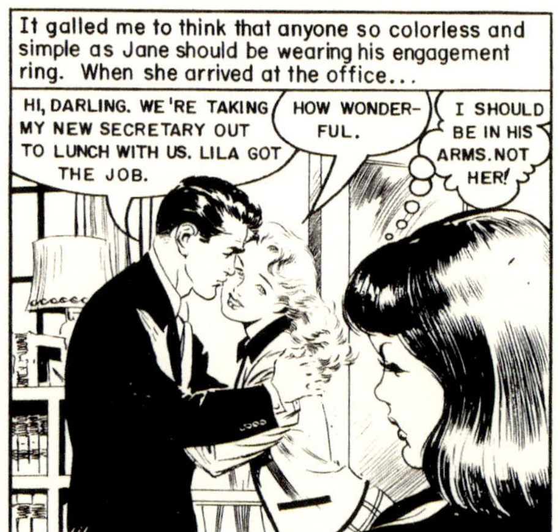

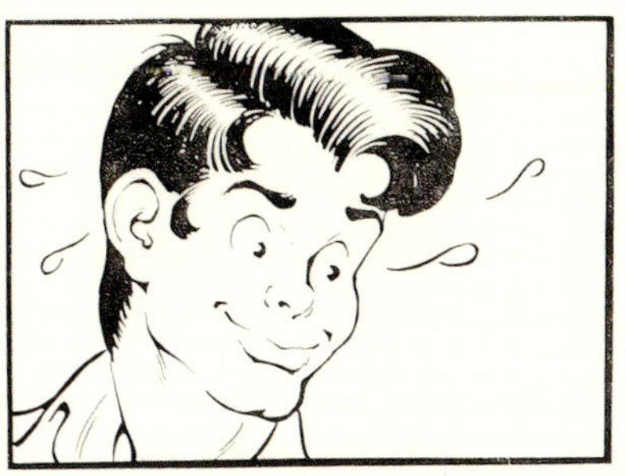

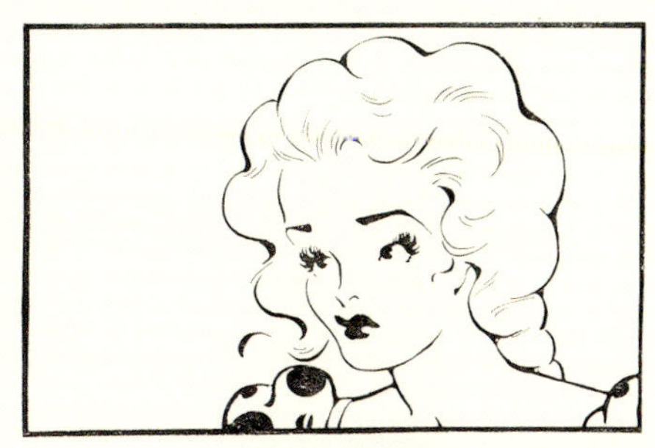

LI'L ABNER
by AL CAPP

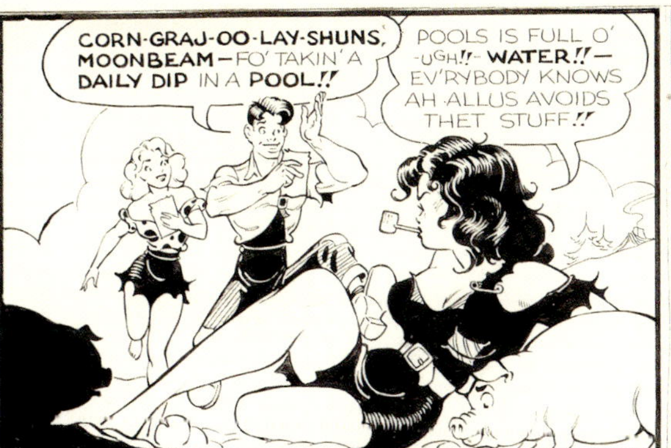

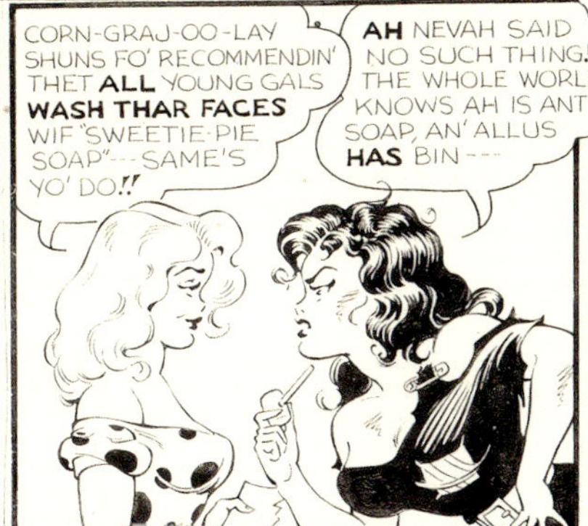

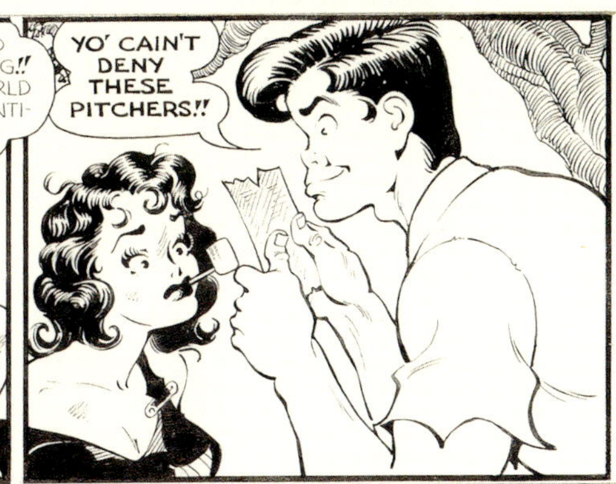

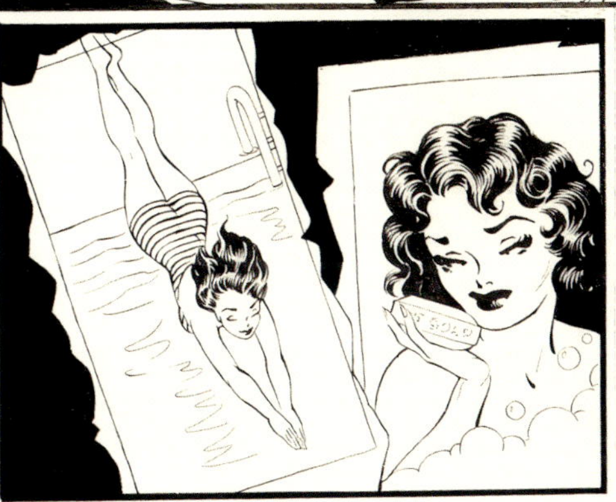

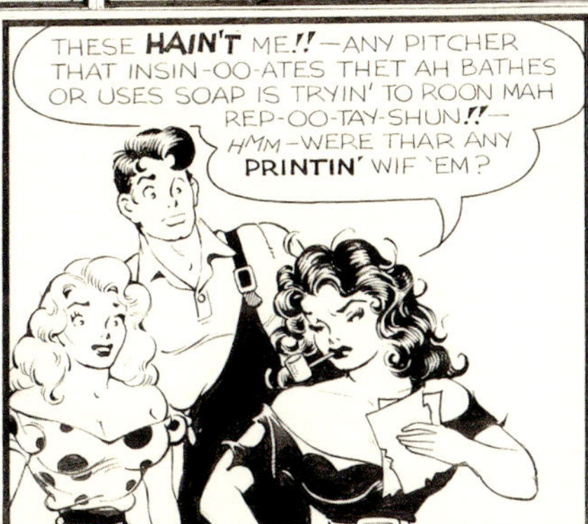

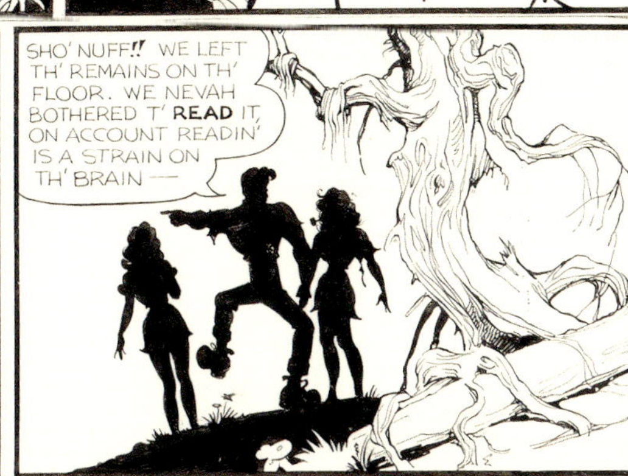

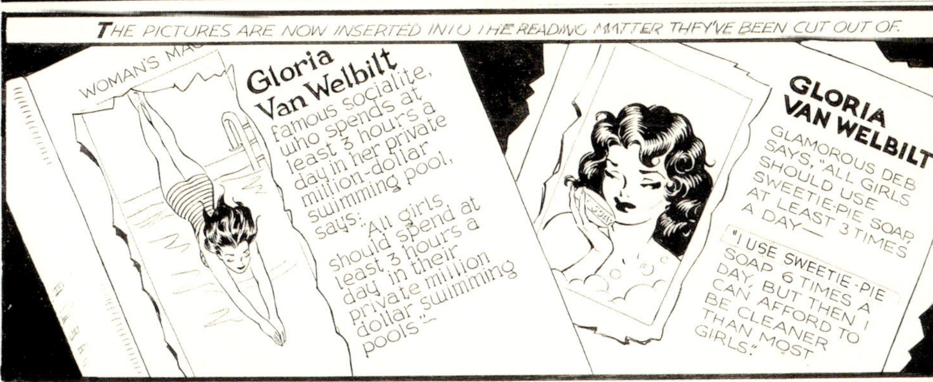

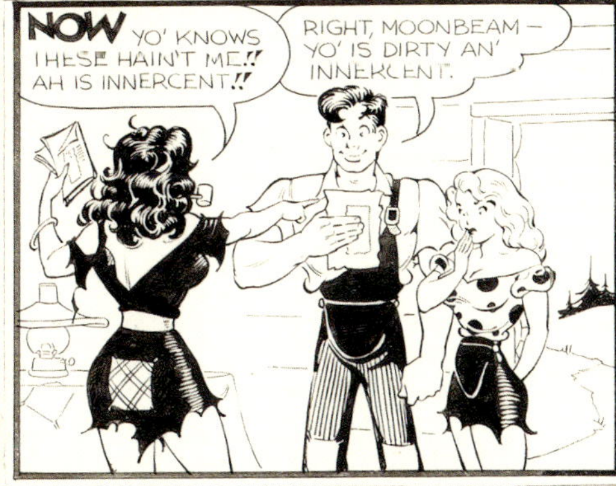

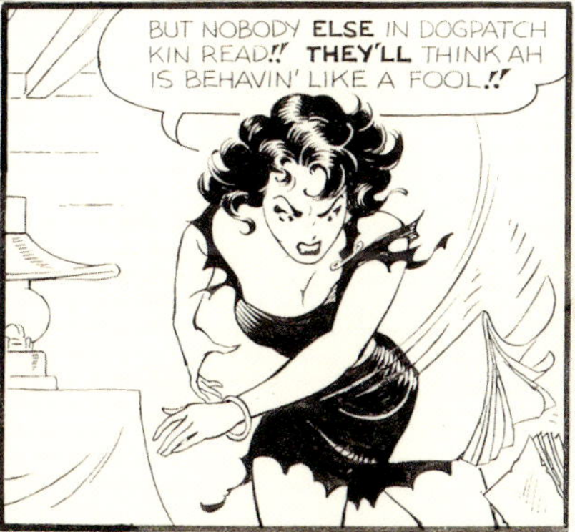

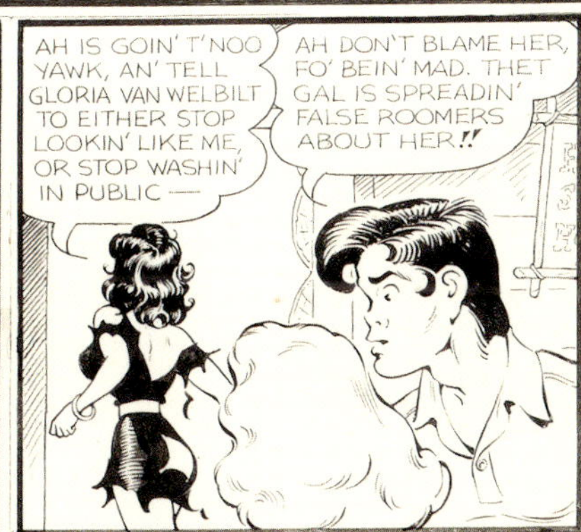

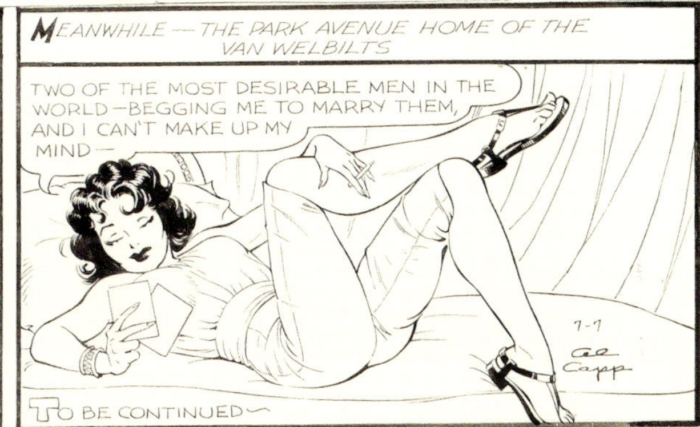

Two's Company...

Every night, before sleep crept in upon us and closed our tired eyes, Velda and I would lie beside each other in the stillness and gaze up at the planetoid's sky and watch for the finger of flame that would mean the rescue ship had finally come to take us back to Earth. And every night, as we searched among the stars and waited, I would *TELL* Velda of Earth. I would tell her of Earth's *FORESTS*, and its *RUSHING SILVER RIVERS*, and its *GLEAMING CITIES*. I would tell her of the *SOLAR RANCH HOUSE* we'd build and the *COMFORTS* we'd have. And Velda would smile at me, and squeeze my hand to let me know she understood, and she would turn away again to look up into the heavens...

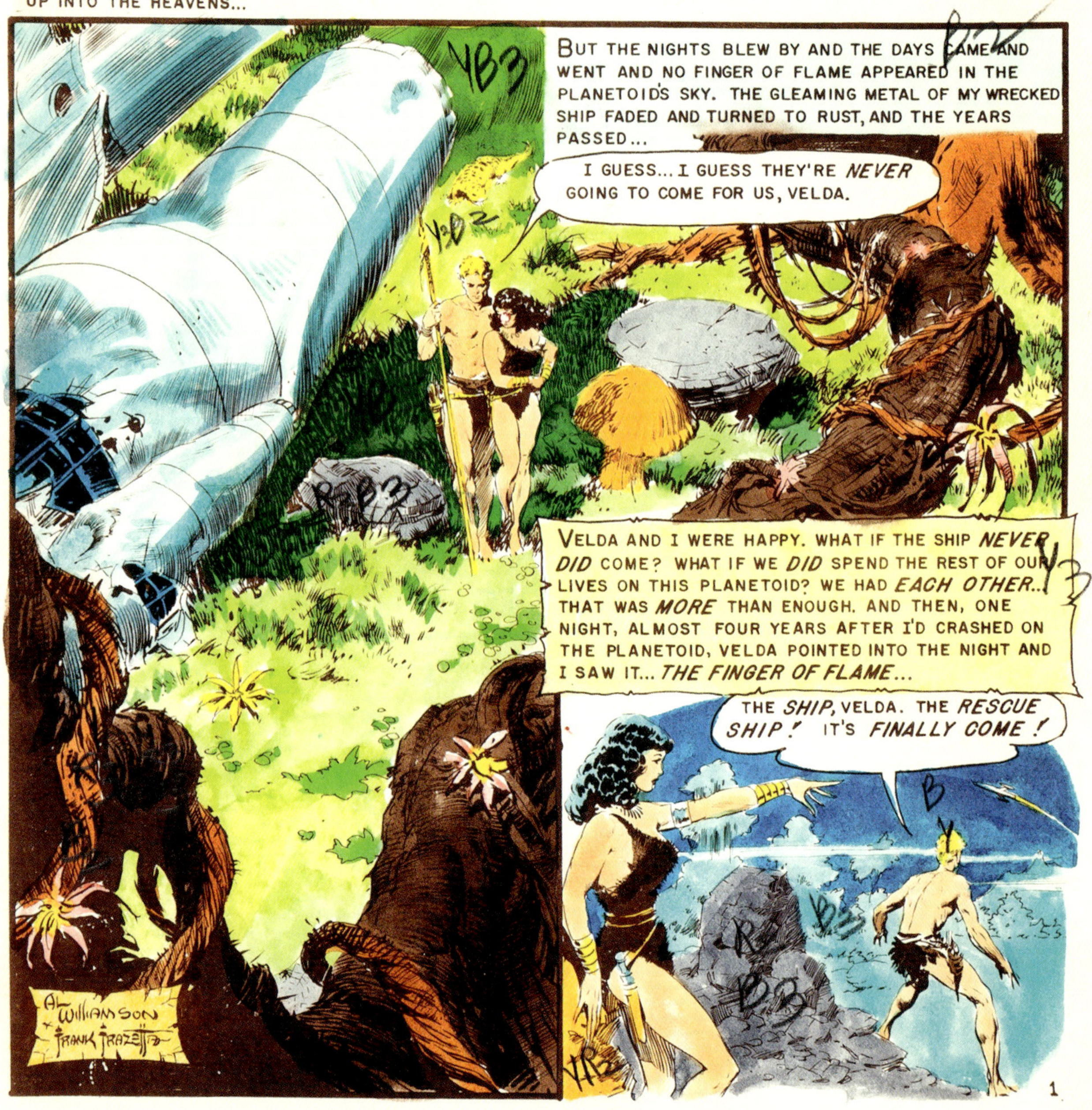

1

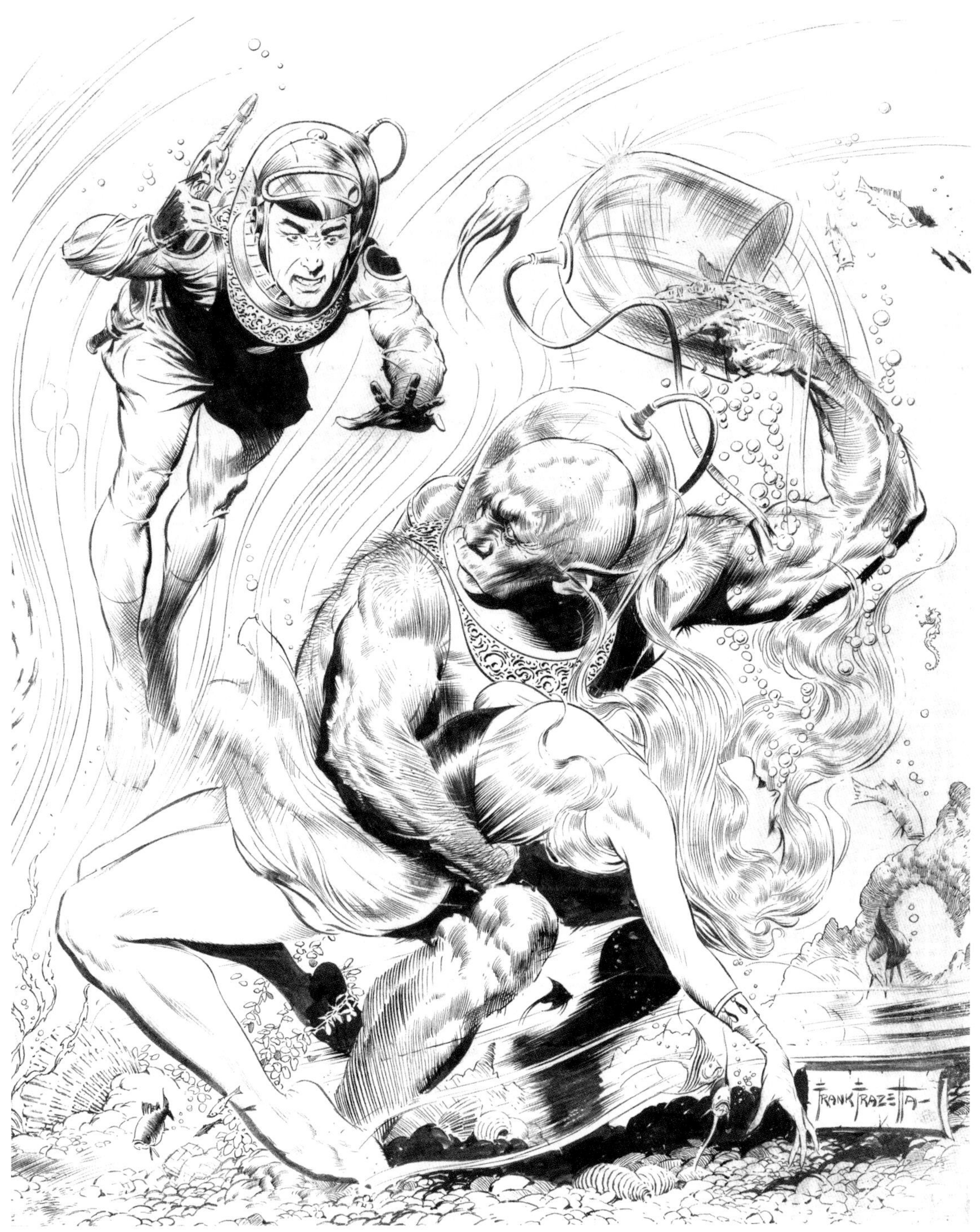

"Two's Company," splash page silver-print proof for EC's *Weird Science* No. 21, a Frazetta/Williamson collaboration. Colored ink over print, 1953, 26.4 x 17.2 cm (10.4 x 6.8 inches). *Courtesy of Heritage Auctions. Artwork © William M. Gaines, Agent, Inc. All rights reserved.*

Frazetta produced four covers for *Famous Funnies Featuring Buck Rogers* and four covers for *Buck Rogers Featured in Famous Funnies*. Here we have No. 210, including the holy trinity of sci-fi: a hero, a monster, and a maiden in distress. Ink over graphite on board, 1954, etc. *Courtesy of James Halperin Collection.*

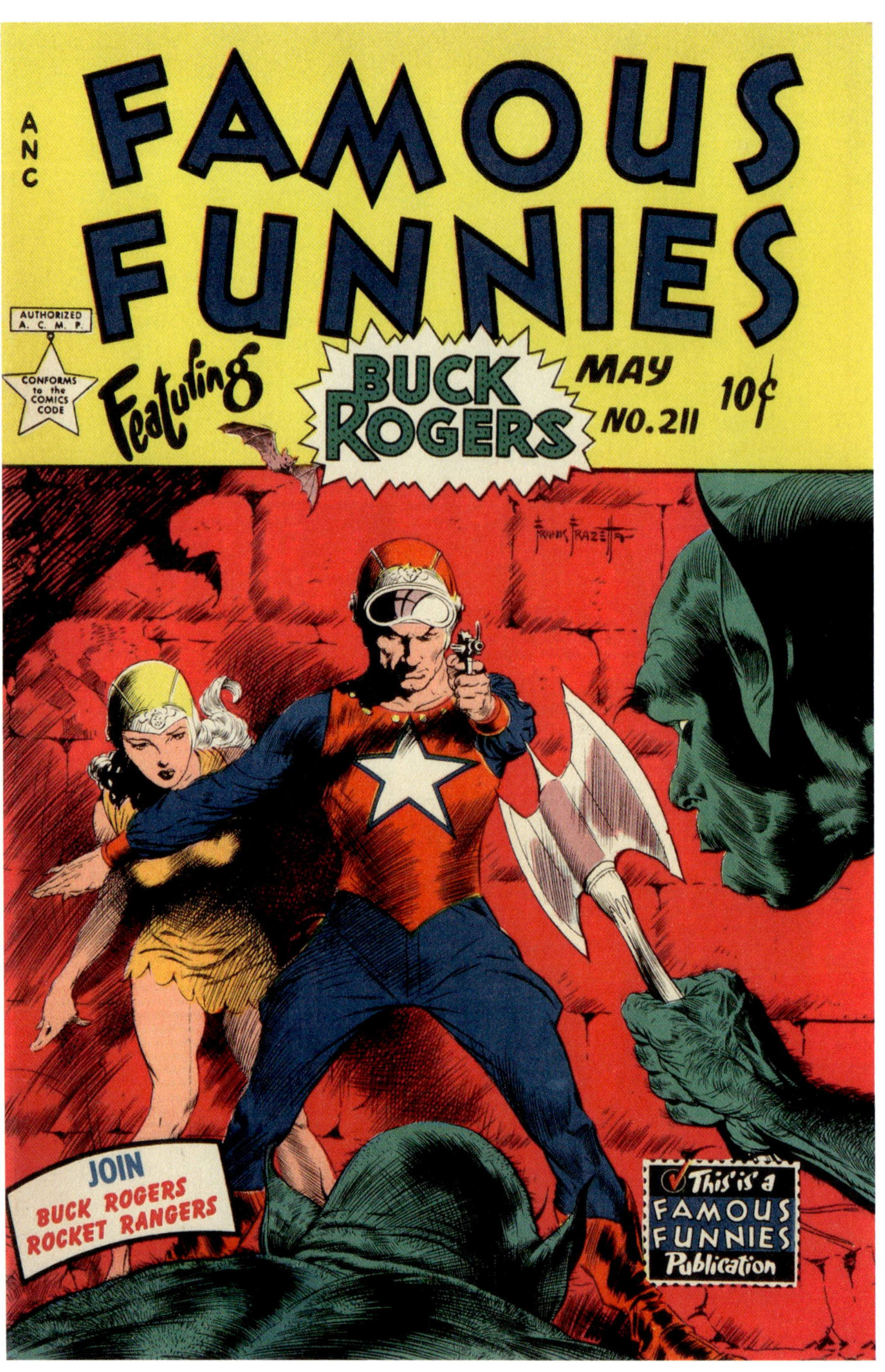

OPPOSITE
Another *Buck Rogers* cover; this one No. 209, once again including the hero, the monsters, the maiden. It never got old. Ink over graphite on board, with logo recreation, 1953, 36.8 x 35.5 cm (14.5 x 14 inches). *Courtesy of Heritage Auctions.*

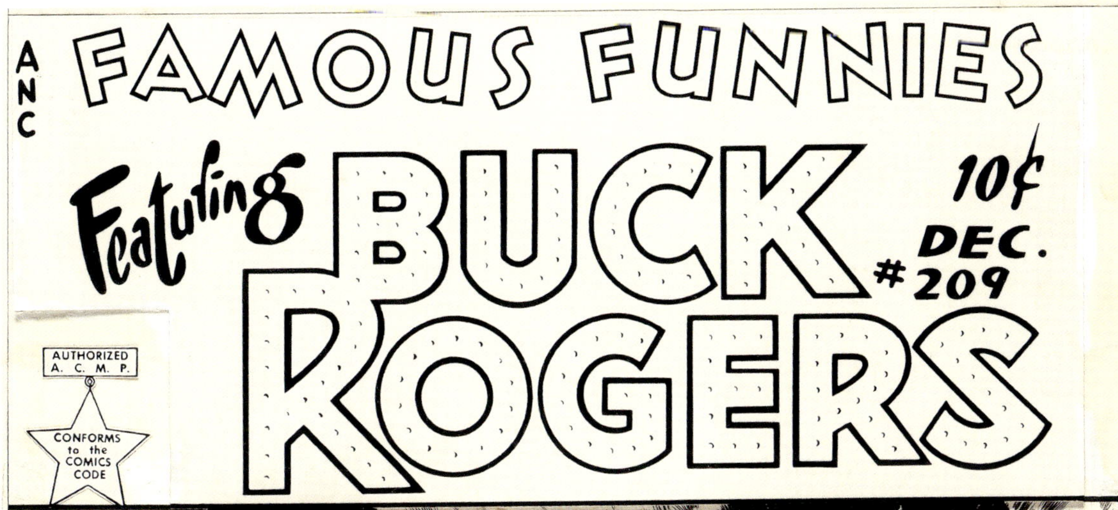
ANC
FAMOUS FUNNIES
Featuring BUCK ROGERS
10¢
DEC.
209
AUTHORIZED A. C. M. P.
CONFORMS to the COMICS CODE
FRANK FRAZETTA

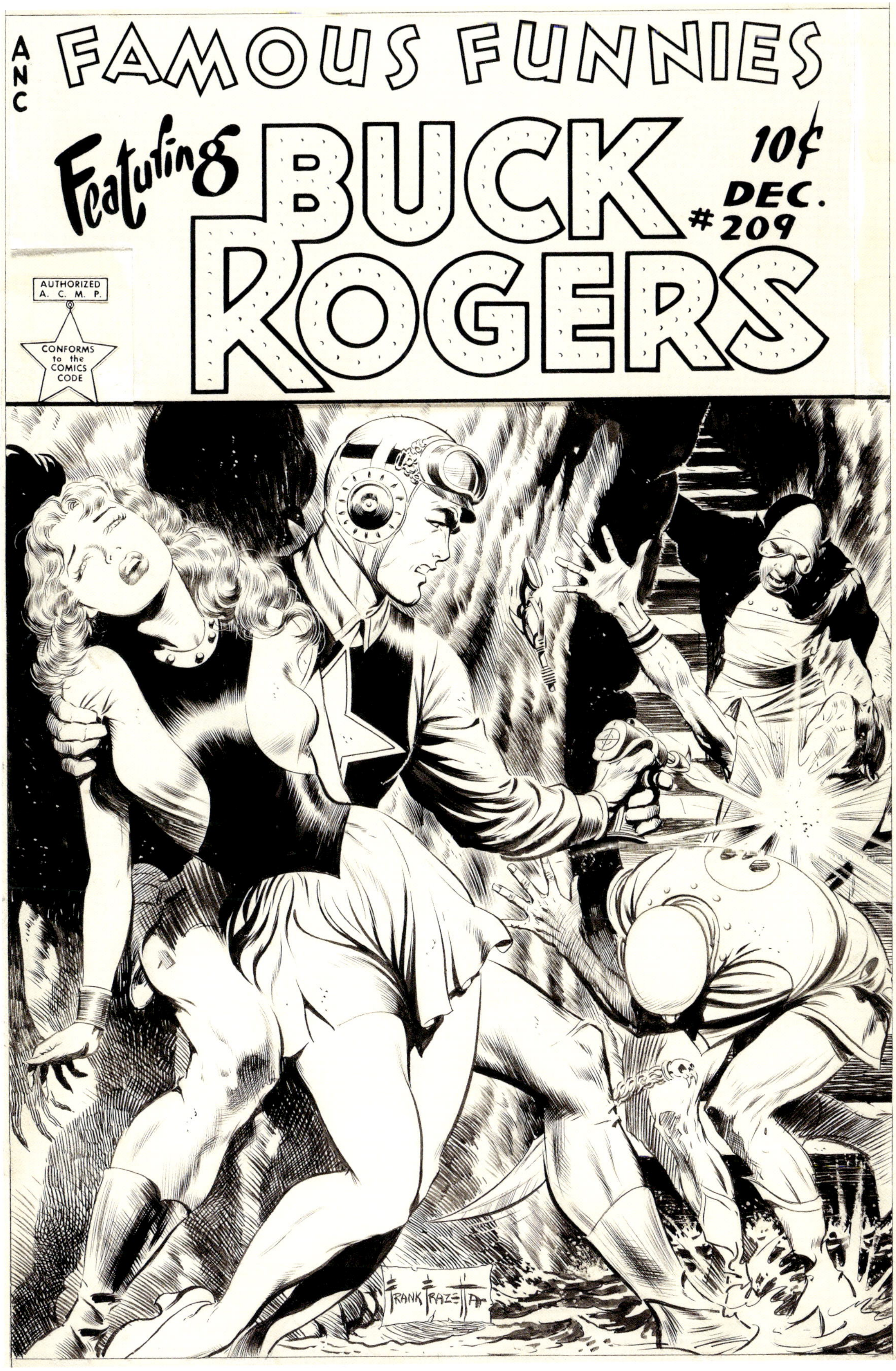

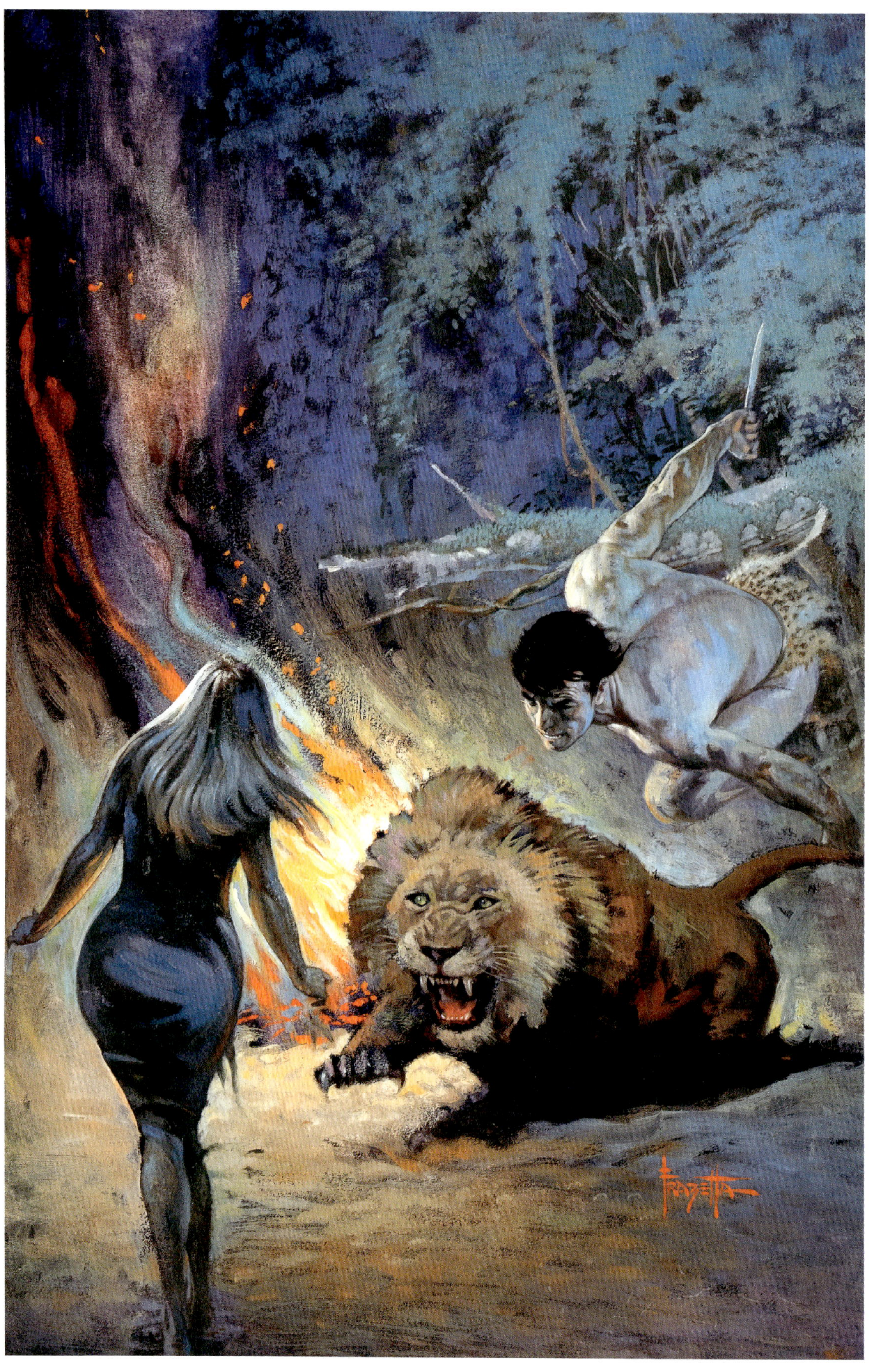

Tarzan, Conan, and Ringo Starr
1960–1969

In 1961, Al Capp ordered Frank to move to Boston, where he lived, and become Capp's full-time ghost. When Frazetta refused, Capp tried to cut his salary in half and Frank walked out, assuming he could pick up with comics where he left off. Whether tastes had simply changed when the feathered figurework of the late '40s gave way to the design-conscious, pop-arty Silver Age of comics (as he was told), or because Capp had him blacklisted (as he suspected), Frazetta wore holes in his shoes visiting ad agencies all over Manhattan, but still couldn't find work.

George Evans helped him through these lean times with pages to ink for his *Frogman* and *Twilight Zone* comics, and there were a few illustration jobs for soft-core romance magazines aimed at women. This led to work for post-*Playboy* "men's sophisticates," including *Cavalcade, Gent,* and *Dude* and then, most notoriously, to interior drawings for four cheap erotic double paperbacks from Midwood Books: *The Wild Week* and *Imitation Lovers*; *Perfumed* and *Pampered*; *The Dangerous Age* and *Bad By Choice*; and *Perfumed* and *The Wild Week*. These literally "throwaway" pulps are now some of the most sought-after pieces in Frazetta fandom precisely because no one cared about them at the time.

It was another pair of old friends who helped lift him out of the rut entirely: fellow Fleagle Roy Krenkel and, perhaps Frazetta's oldest friend, Tarzan, the Edgar Rice Burroughs jungle adventurer he'd followed in Hal Foster's newspaper strip since he was a child. "To me," Frank reminisced, "Foster's Tarzan was *it*. I *loved* Tarzan, I wanted to *be* Tarzan, just like all my friends. Let me tell you—Foster was a *fine* artist and that's what I wanted to do."

Krenkel had been commissioned by Ace Books to do a series of Tarzan covers but was daunted by the idea of taking on the task alone. Frazetta started by helping Krenkel, and eventually Ace let Frazetta—fresh off creating some drawings for the Canaveral Press version of *Tarzan at the Earth's Core*—do some covers of his own. But while Frazetta turned out increasingly muscular, action-packed images with dynamic Hal Foster shadows and Hollywood angles, Ace editor Donald Wollheim wanted to recreate the fairy-tale poise of the classic pulp-era Tarzan produced by J. Allen St. John. "Wollheim looked down his nose at me and, yeah, that hurt my feelings, especially in the beginning when I was trying to give them good work. Look at *Tarzan and the Jewels of Opar*—he

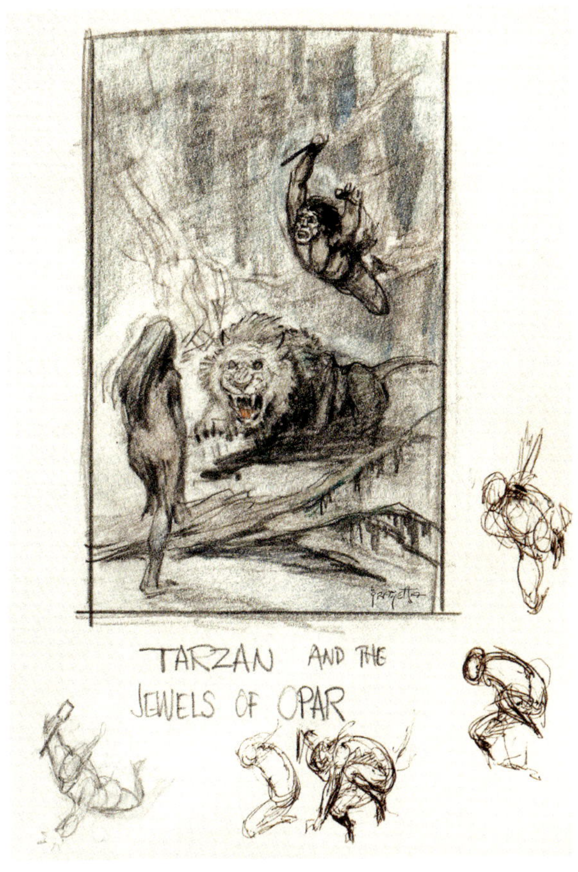

Preliminary sketch for *Tarzan and the Jewels of Opar*. Graphite and colored pencil on paper, 1963, 23.4 x 16.5 cm (9.25 x 6.5 inches). *Courtesy of Heritage Auctions* and *Edgar Rice Burroughs Inc.*

Cover illustration for the 1964 Ace paperback edition of *Tarzan and the Jewels of Opar*. Watercolor and ink on paper.

actually *sneered* at that one! Though that didn't keep Ace from keeping my originals and selling them to fans!" After a while his heart wasn't in it. Frazetta is straightforward in his assessment of these early paintings: "The *Jungle Tales of Tarzan* painting is bad. I painted it and *City of Gold* and *Lion Man* all in a single weekend—and they really look it. And that wasn't two solid days of painting, either; I did some goofing around as well."

While it's clear why the anatomy-conscious Frazetta might wince at the way his *Jungle Tales* Tarzan isn't quite standing on the branch he's anchored to, the snapshot way the jungle king is braced to receive the slightly abstracted ape propelling down on him is pure Frazetta, and the suffused green and purple of the overhanging canopy foreshadows his more fully developed color work to come. Even with time and technique stripped away, a unique set of instincts holds the picture together, and the Frazetta covers sold well.

In 1965, his poverty waning, Frazetta's classic period began, enabled by a pair of disparate commercial developments. First, his caricature of Ringo Starr for *MAD* magazine brought him to the attention of United Artists, which commissioned him to paint the poster for *What's New Pussycat?*, followed by *The Secret of My Success*, *The Fearless Vampire Killers*, *The Night They Raided Minsky's*, *The Busy Body*, *Mixed Company*, *Hotel Paradiso*, *After the Fox*, *Luana*, and *Mad Monster Party*, as well as album covers for comedians Jonathan Winters and political impression tag team Earle Doud and Alen Robin. Ironically, the very dynamics that would eventually end the print illustration boom were now working in Frazetta's favor: by 1964 most American households had a television set, and home viewing cut significantly into book and magazine sales, but also movie profits. Studios knew a provocative poster could put butts in the theater seats, but a suggestive photo could also get a film banned. Frazetta's movie star caricatures were sexy, but also funny, a perfect balance. And with these bigger chins—and other parts—came bigger paychecks; Frazetta would make a year's salary off a single painting. The best of these contain echoes of Frazetta's comic art—the jiggle physics of the

Lost City, a spectacular personal work, and one of the many reasons Frazetta's granddaughter Sara says he was a "sex maniac." Watercolor on board, 1960s, 22.8 x 30.4 cm (9 x 12 inches). *Courtesy of Arnie Fenner.*

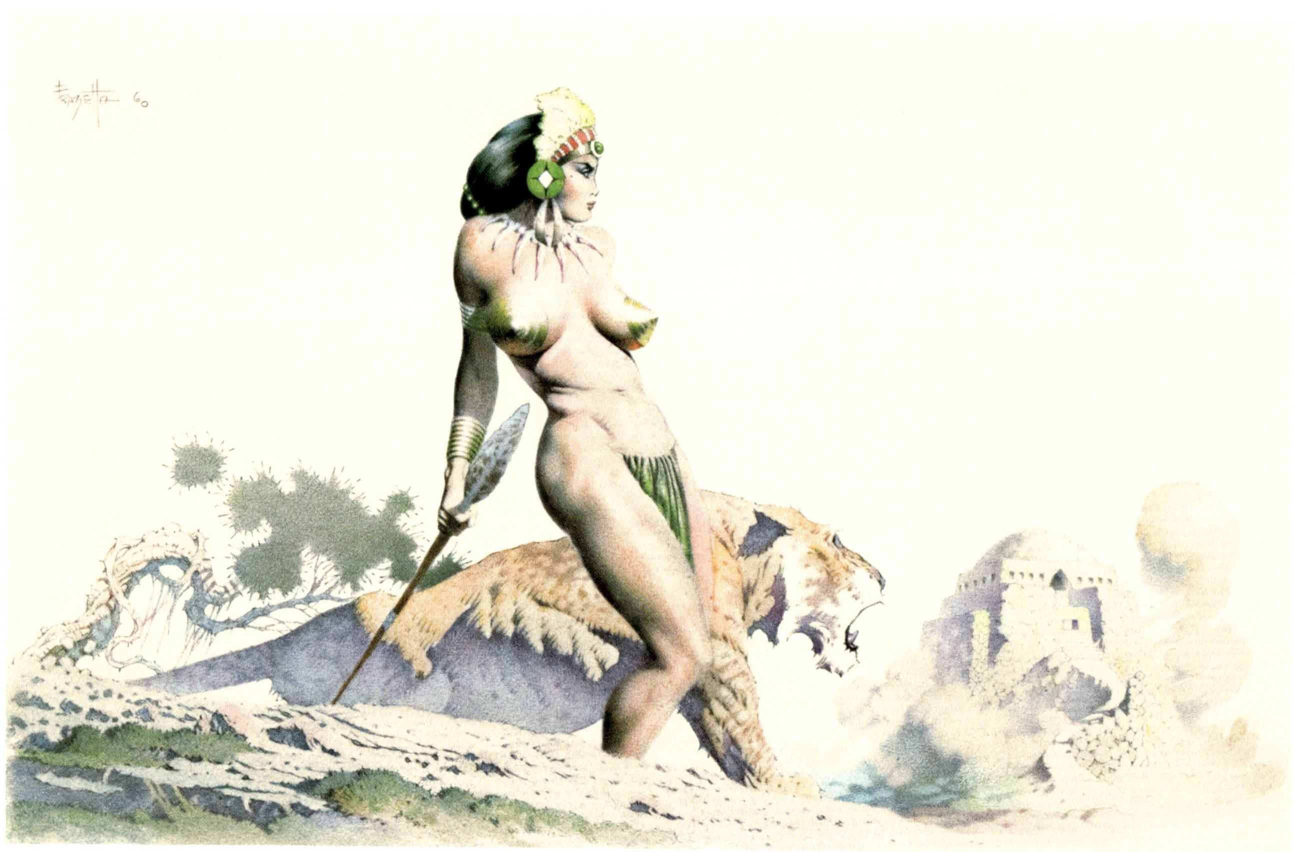

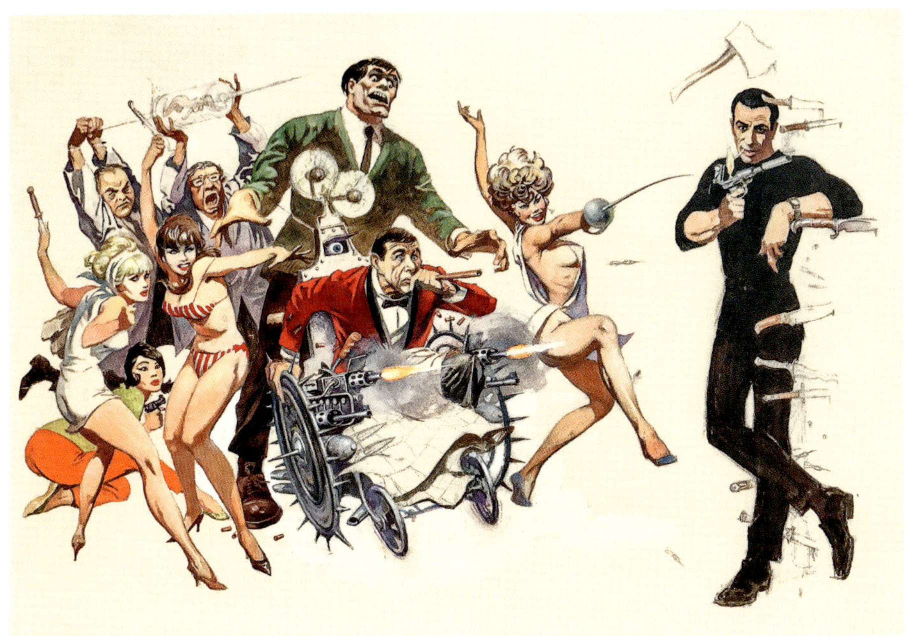

Film poster art for *A Man Called Dagger*, one of many 1960s movies styled after James Bond, this starring long forgotten Paul Mantee as Dick Dagger. Mixed media on board, 1968.

What's New Pussycat? soundtrack cover, the unexpected color and efficient design in the *Mrs. Pollifax–Spy* poster—but there's no doubt he would've rather been painting monsters.

Fortunately, monster magazine magnate Jim Warren asked him to do exactly that. The *Famous Monsters of Filmland* publisher was starting a new line of magazines inspired by EC Comics. He invited Frazetta to do whatever he liked for the covers, starting with the first issue of *Creepy*, late in 1964, expanding to *Blazing Combat* the next year and *Eerie* the year after that. He would then commission an interior story to match. Ellie insisted Frank also be allowed to keep his originals—unheard of in the work-for-hire publishing model of the time—and Warren agreed. Frazetta took full advantage of the situation, producing iconic work like *Neanderthal*, *Cat Girl*, *Sea Witch*, *The Brain*, and *Egyptian Queen* for Warren. On the strength of these early Warren covers, and his earlier Tarzan work for Ace and Canaveral Books, Lancer Books approached him about doing eight covers for their Robert E. Howard Conan paperbacks in 1966.

The Lancer Conans were bigger, sexier, and more carefully conceived than the Tarzans he'd done for Ace, perhaps because Lancer's offer was likewise bigger, sexier, and more carefully conceived: it paid Frazetta twice as much as Ace and allowed him to keep his originals. In exchange, Frazetta changed fantasy illustration forever.

Many artists had drawn the barbarian for the pulps before Frazetta, but none of their Cimmerians would be recognizable as Conan today. Frazetta's images were definitive: brutal, muscular, totally uninterested in costume drama or symbolism, using the fantasy setting as little more than a staging ground for struggle and death. "I liked the energy of the stories, and I think I just really cut loose," he said. "I'm not saying Howard was a great writer, but he was very illustratable." The primal quality of Howard's stories allowed Frazetta to paint things he liked—muscular anatomy, action, weapons, ferocious creatures, sexy girls—but it also allowed him to leave out or shorthand things he didn't respond to—machines, straight lines, architecture, patterns, realistic interiors, period detail, clothing. His

MAD magazine was launched by EC publisher William Gaines, so of course he employed some of his best EC artists. This caricature of Ringo Starr for a 1964 *MAD* back cover led to a movie poster commission for *What's New Pussycat?*, launching a lucrative new career.

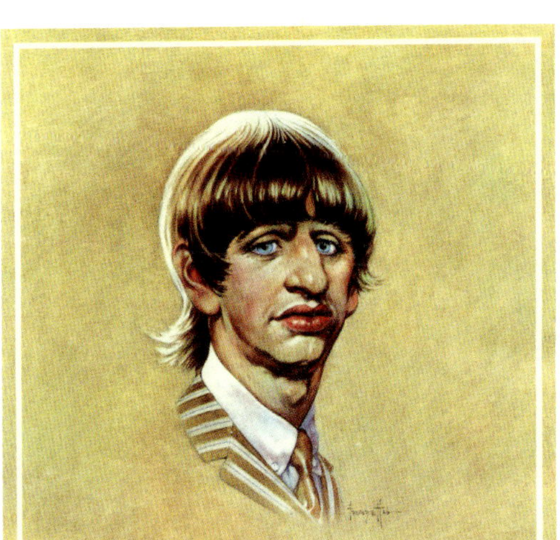

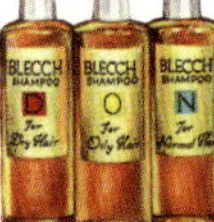

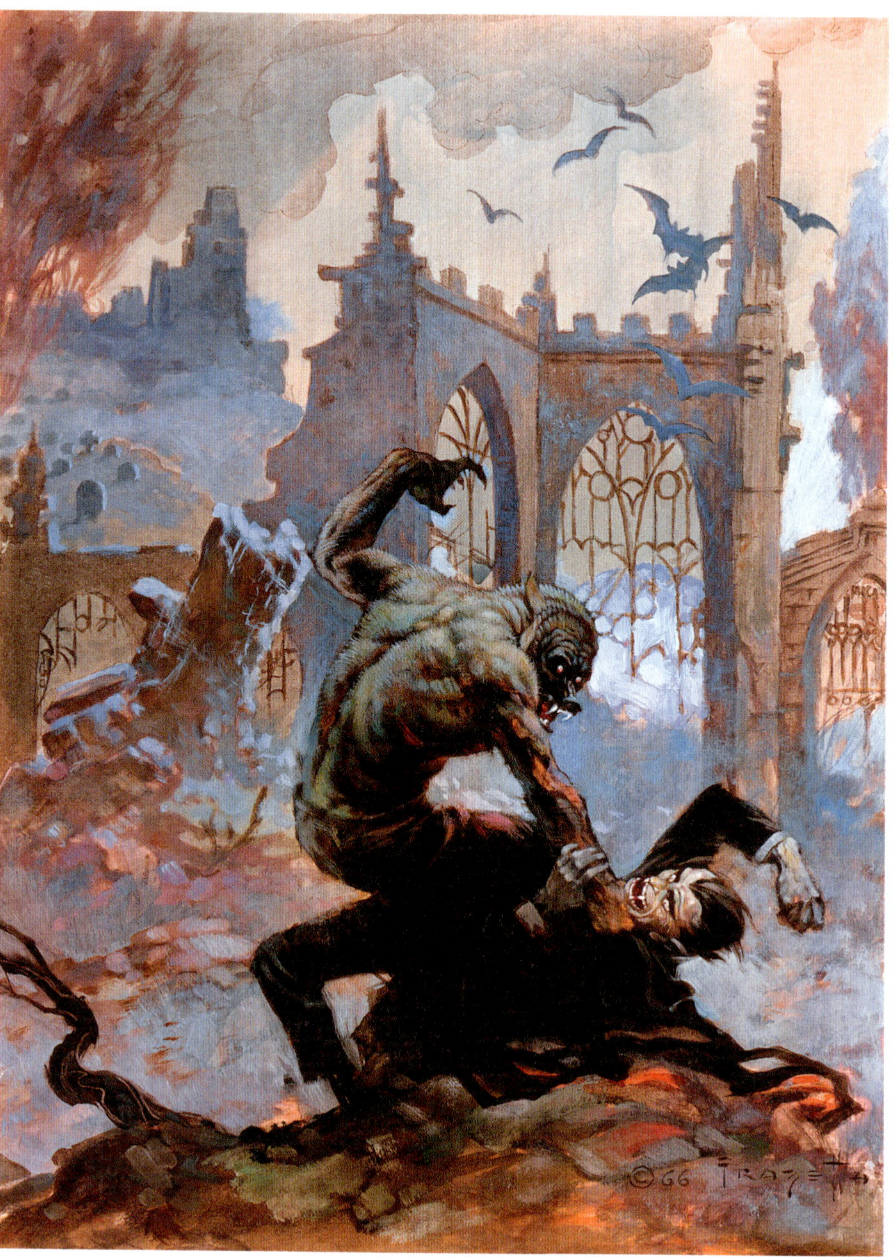

Conan (first seen on the cover of *Conan the Adventurer* in 1966) is also the first ongoing Frank Frazetta male protagonist whose face is definitely *not* modeled on Frank Frazetta's. Except for the dimples.

Most of Frazetta's later heroic imagery—his second go-round at Canaveral with 1965's *Tarzan and the Castaways*; David Innes for the 1968 *Pellucidar* portfolio; *Bran Mak Morn* (1969) for Dell; John Carter for five hardbacks (1970–73) from Doubleday Book Club; five covers for Karl Edward Wagner's Kane (1975–78) from Warner Books; and his own Death Dealer and *Fire and Ice* characters—would be recognizable as tweaked versions of the visual formulae he perfected for Conan.

Frazetta had arrived.

Cover art for *Creepy* No. 4, Frazetta's third and most accomplished cover for the first Warren title. Mixed media on board, 1965, 48.2 x 36.1 cm (19 x 14.25 inches). *Courtesy of Heritage Auctions.*

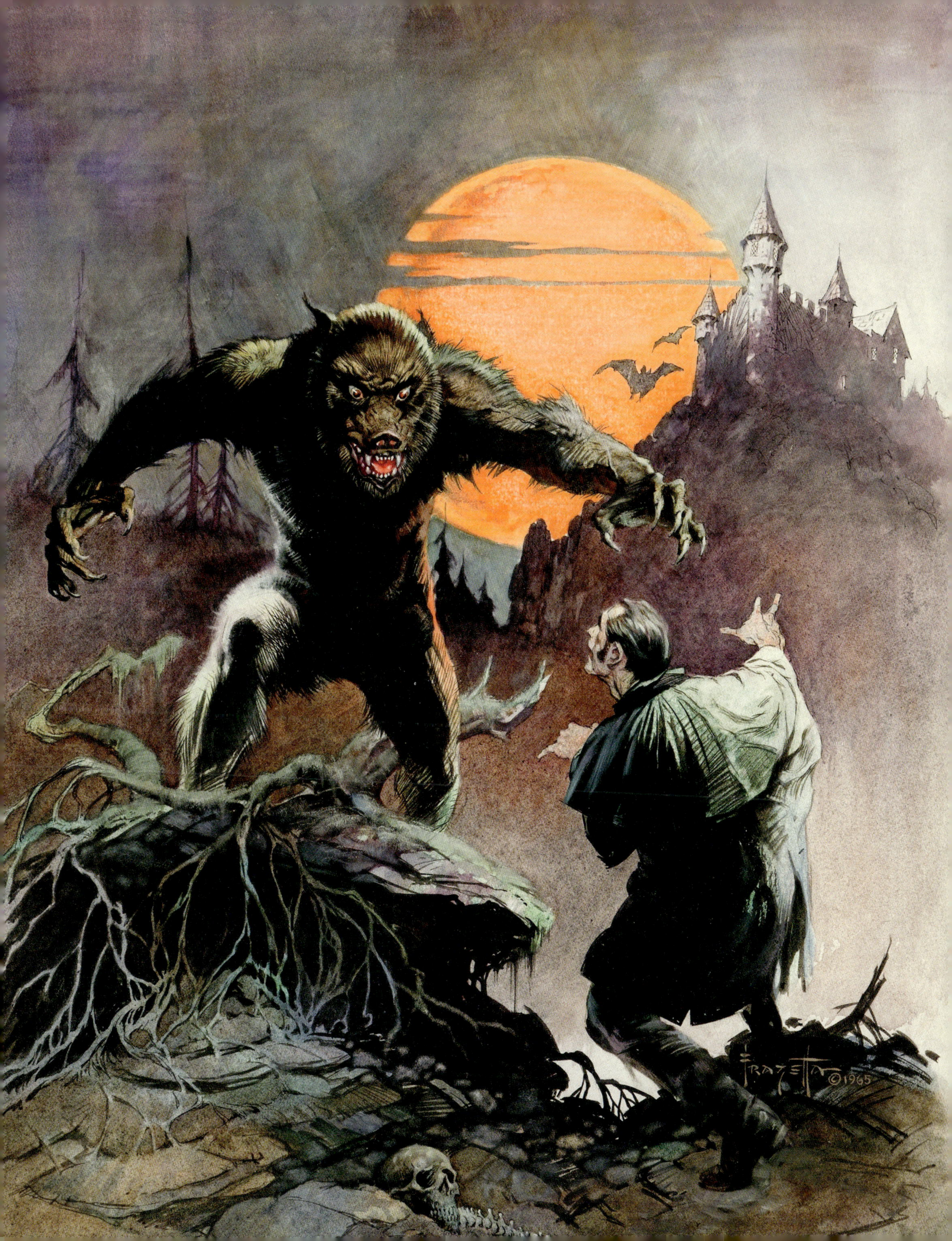
Frazetta ©1965

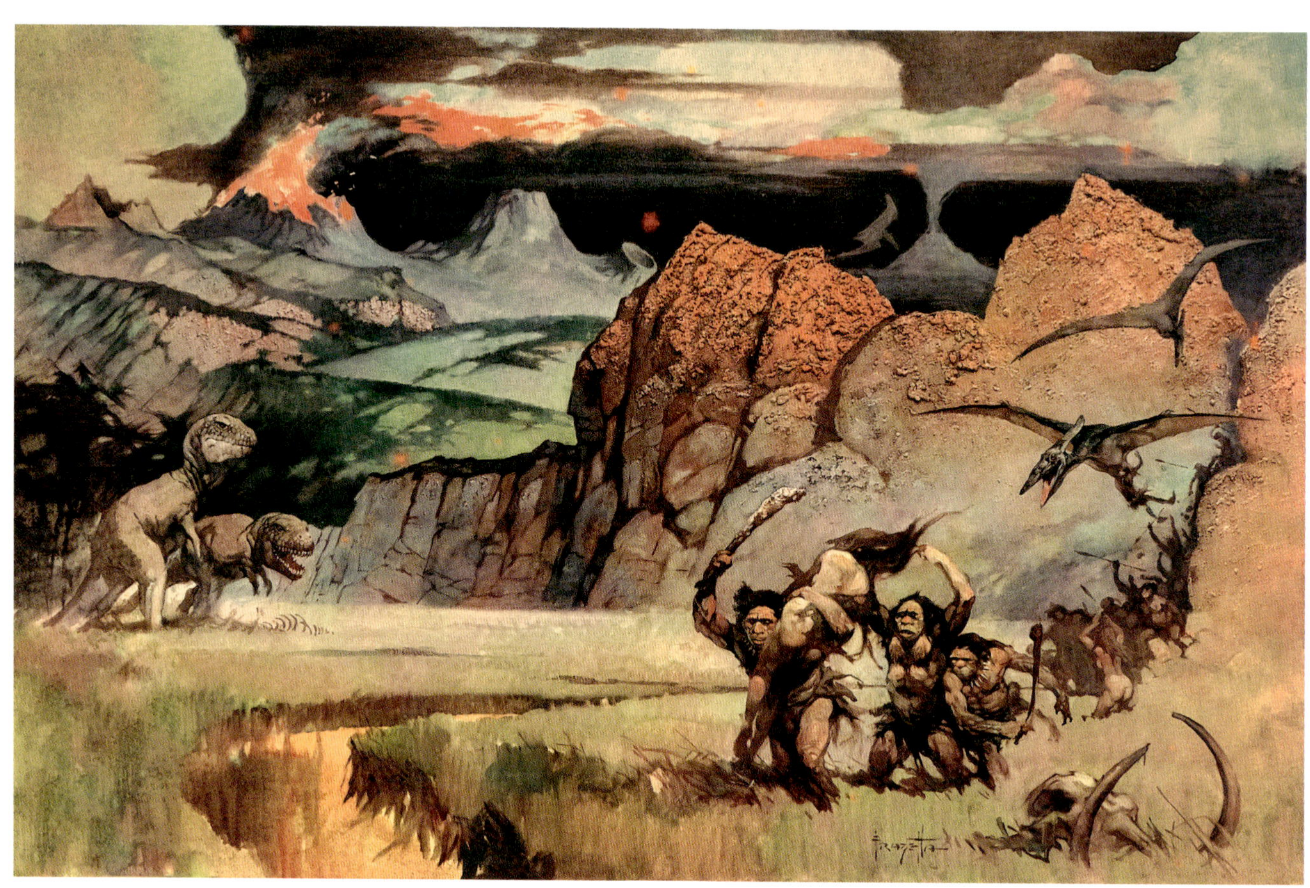

ABOVE

Young World, revision of the wrap-around cover of *Monster Mania* No. 2, "Tribute to Hammer [horror films] Issue." Mixed media on board, 1966, 57.1 x 88.9 cm (22.5 x 35 inches).

OPPOSITE

Jongor Fights Back, for the cover of Robert Moore Williams's Popular Library novel of the same name. Frazetta painted covers for three Jongor novels, with this perhaps the best. Oil on Masonite, 1967, 60.3 x 39.3 cm (23.75 x 15.5 inches).

46

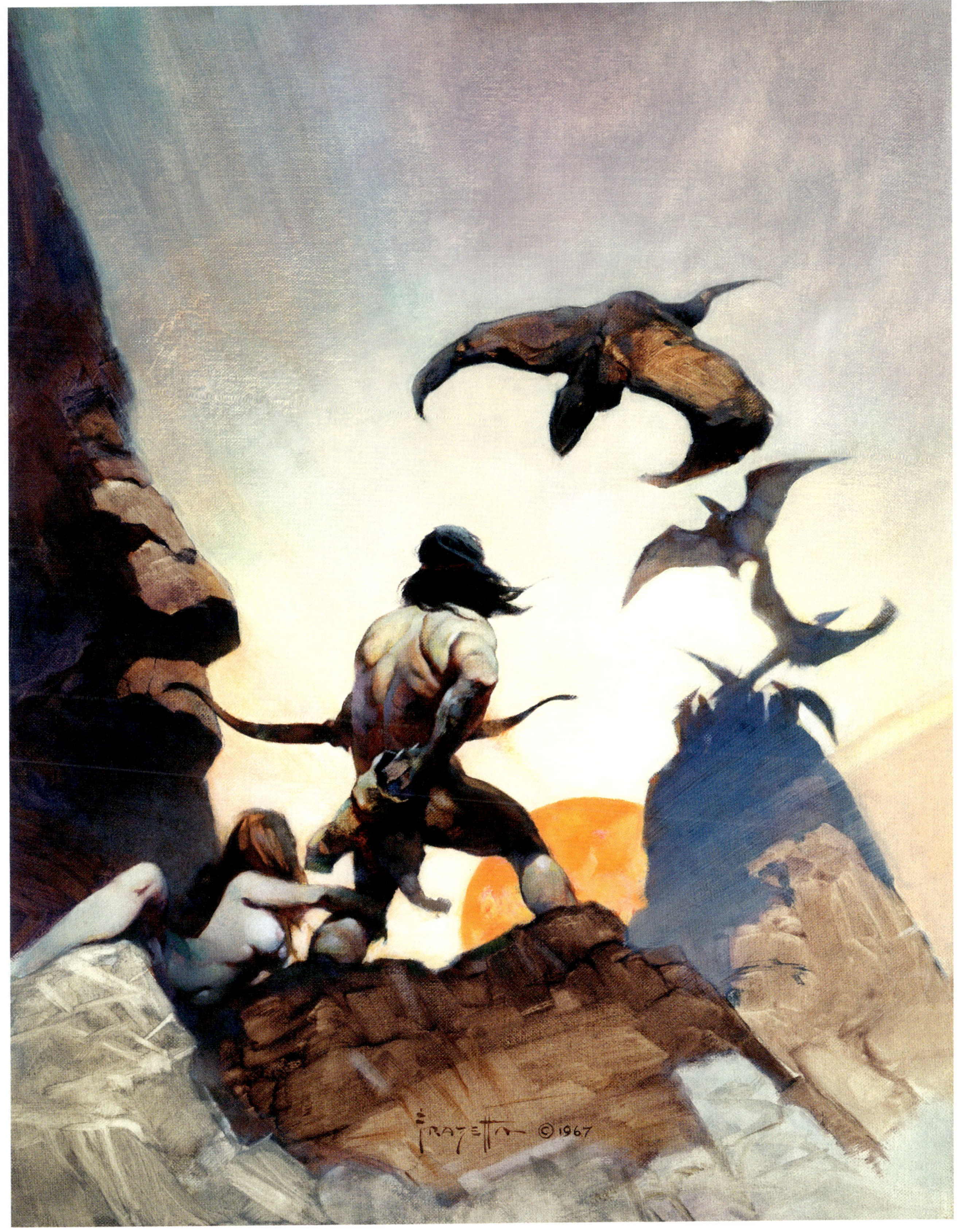

FRAZETTA ©1967

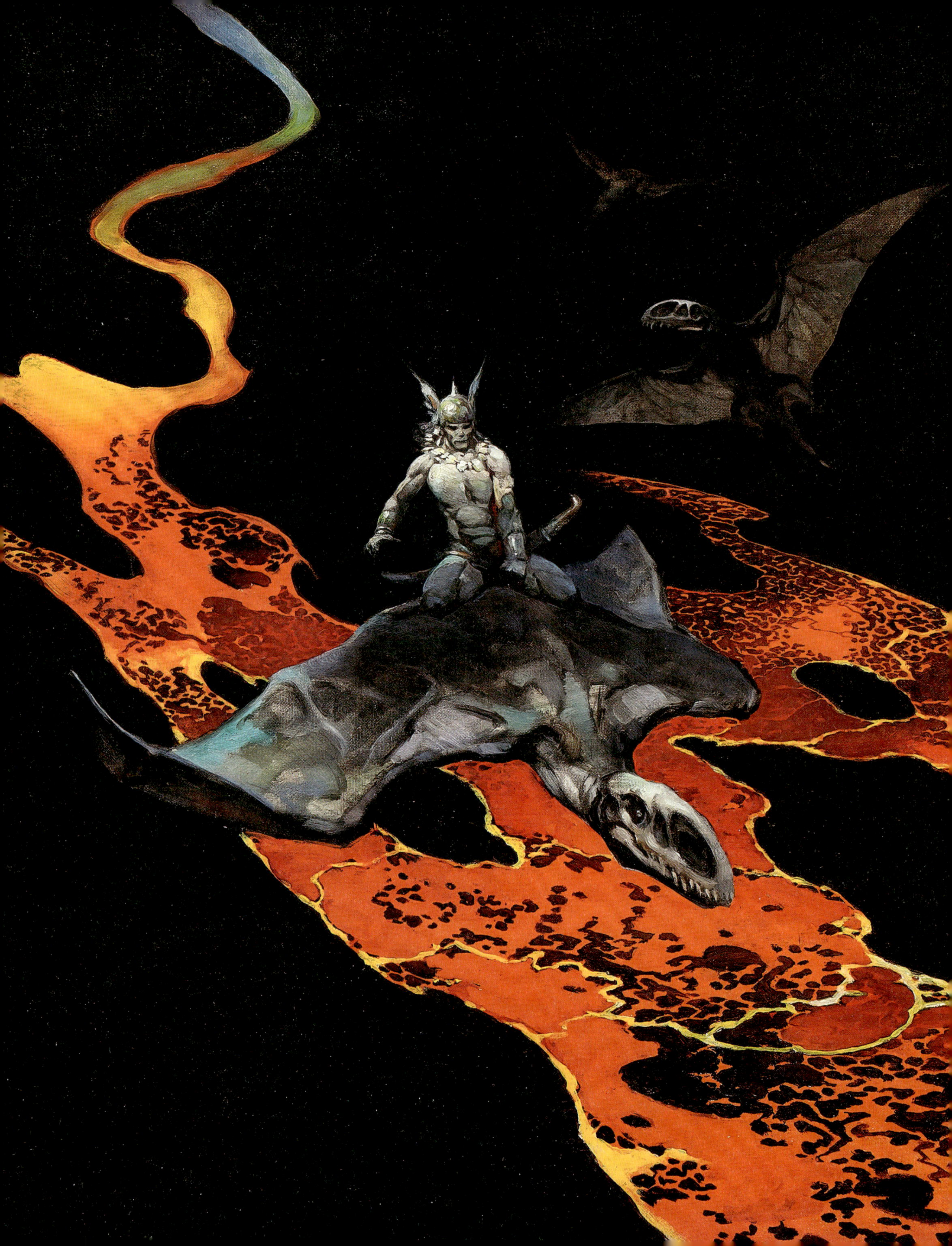

OPPOSITE
Thor's Flight, for the cover of Lin Carter's *Thongor in the City of Magicians*. Oil on canvas board, 1968, 60.9 x 50.8 cm (24 x 20 inches). *Courtesy of Heritage Auctions.*

RIGHT
Cover artwork for Ace Books' *Beyond the Farthest Star*, 1964, a lesser known Burroughs work consisting of two novellas. The art was reprinted as the cover of Ace's *The Land That Time Forgot* in 1970. Watercolor and gouache on board, 1964, 30.4 x 22.8 cm (12 x 9 inches). *Courtesy of Edgar Rice Burroughs Inc.*

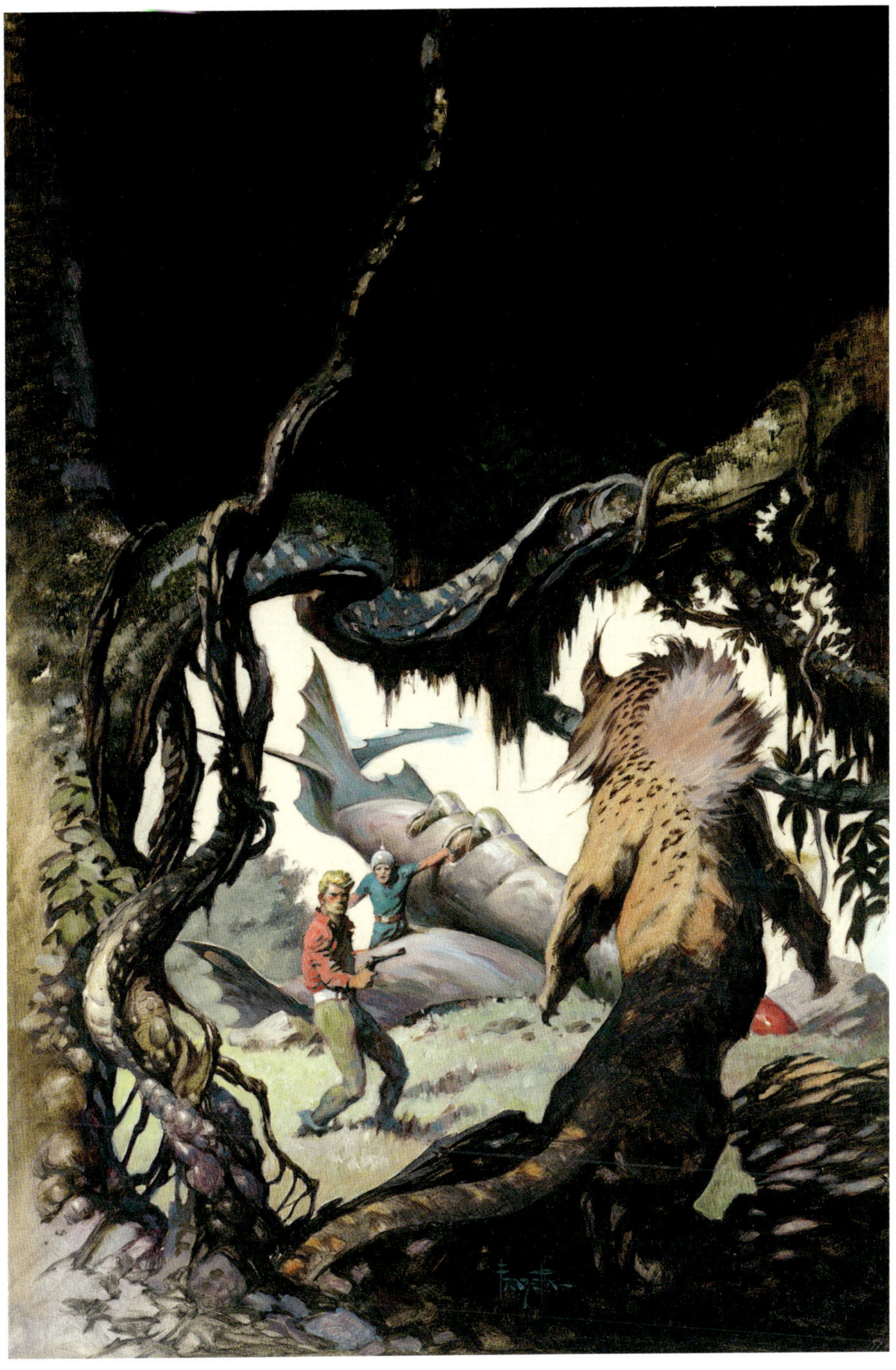

PAGE 50
The iconic cover painting for *Conan the Adventurer* was reprinted on Sphere Books' edition in 1973, and on the Ace edition in 1977, before Dino De Laurentiis chose it as the advance poster for his film *Conan the Barbarian*, starring Arnold Schwarzenegger, in 1980. Oil on canvas board, 1966.

PAGE 51
Berserker, for the cover of Robert E. Howard's *Conan the Conqueror* from Lancer Books was the first Frazetta painting to bring $1,000,000, selling to Kirk Hammett of Metallica in 2012. Oil on board, 1967, 60.9 x 45.7 cm (24 x 18 inches).

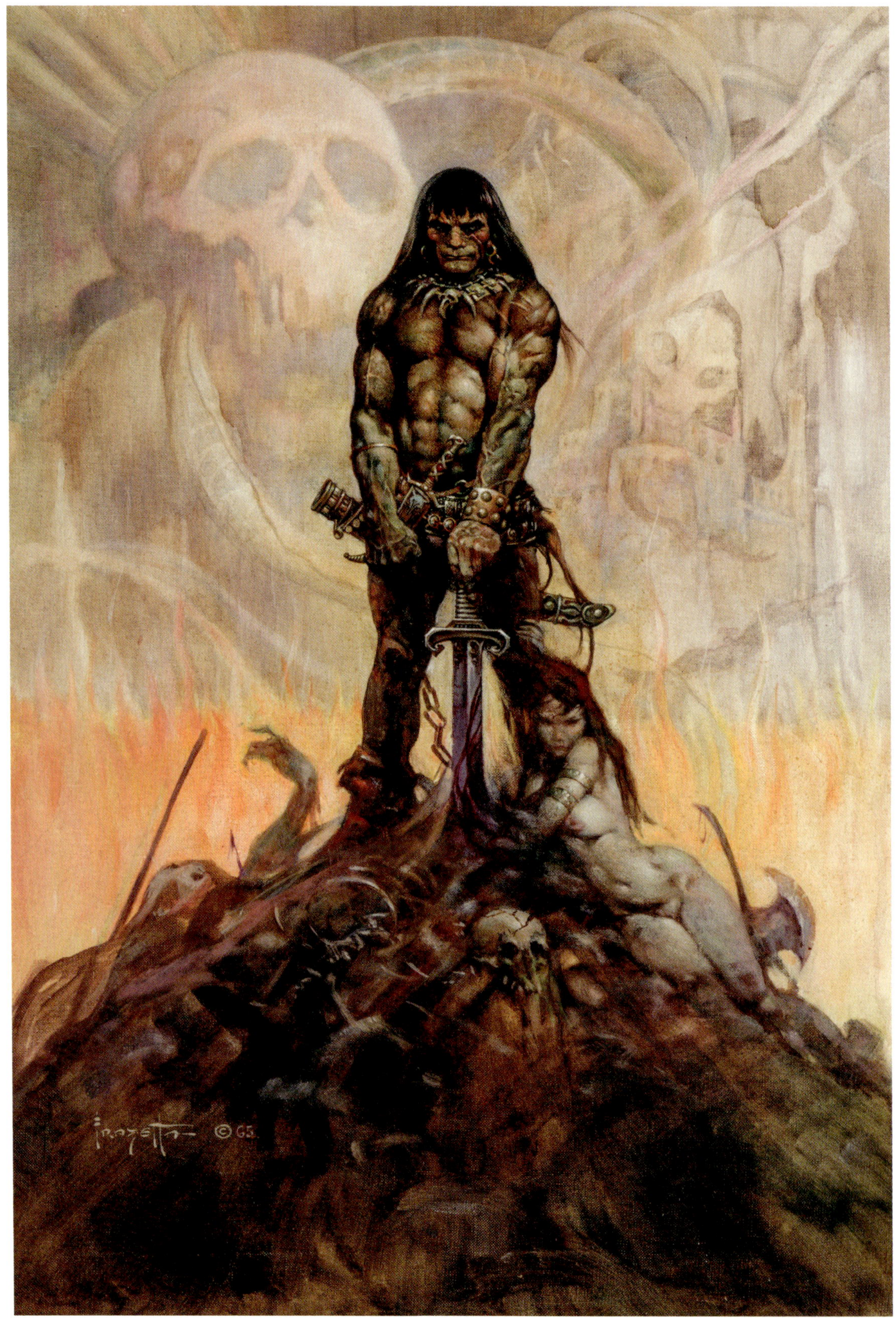

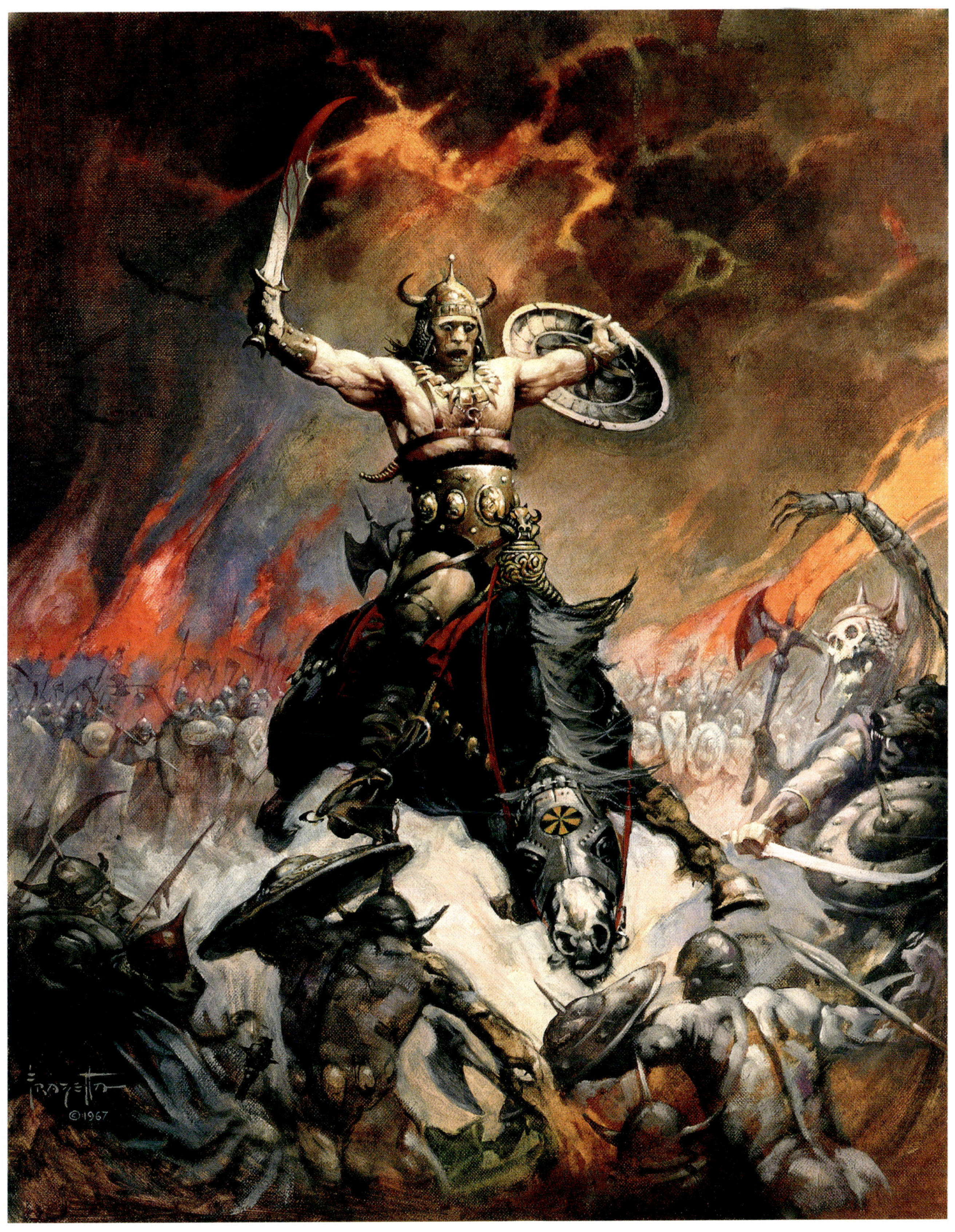

FRAZETTA
©1967

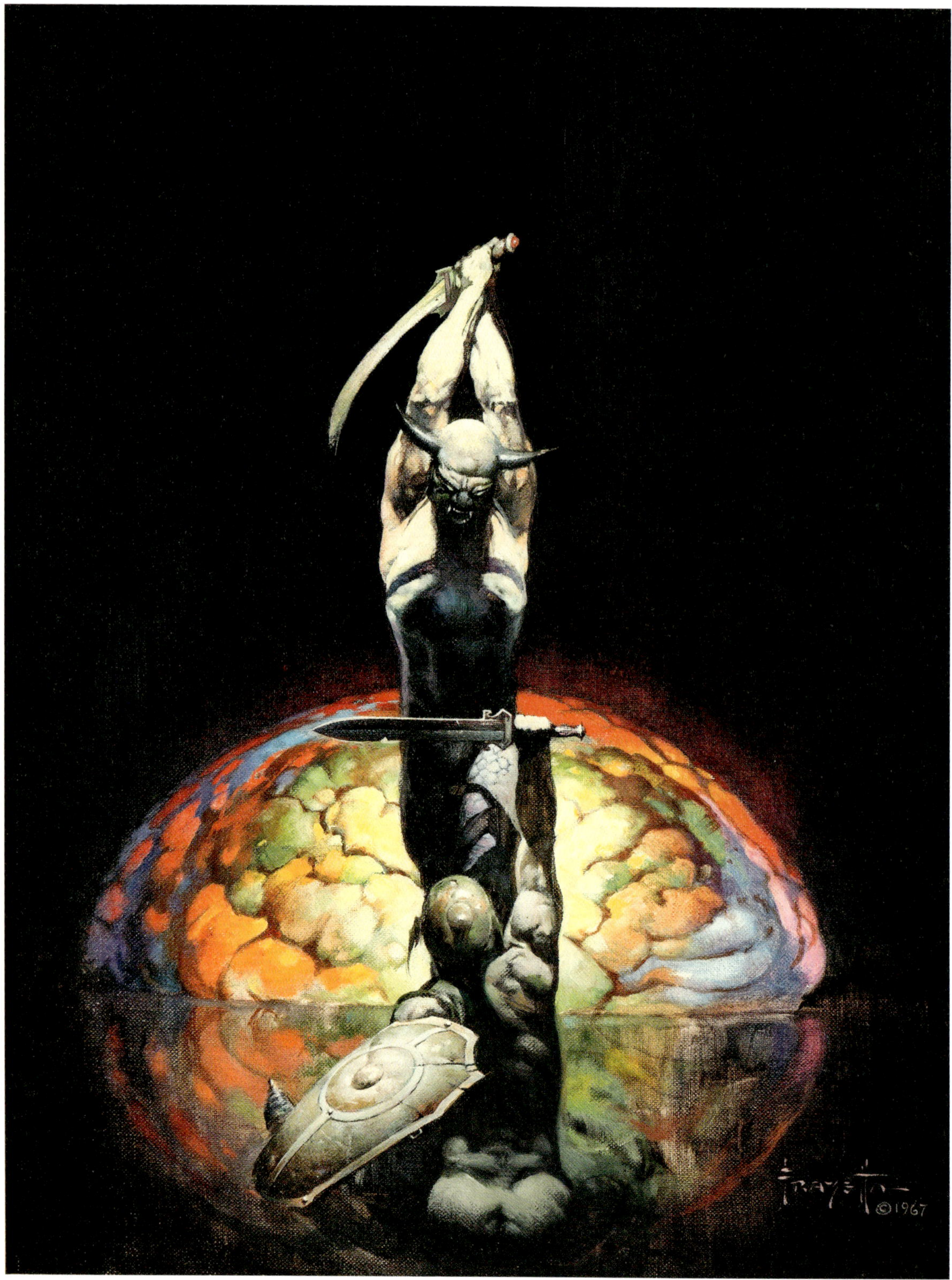

The Brain, for the cover of *Eerie* No. 8; later repurposed for the cover of Nazareth's *Expect No Mercy* album cover. Oil on canvas board, 1967, 58.4 x 43.1 cm (23 x 17 inches). *Courtesy of James Halperin Collection.*

OPPOSITE

Woman with Scythe, completed artwork for the cover of *Vampirella* No. 11. The combination of sexuality and horror make this female "Death" particularly disturbing. Oil on board, 1969, 71.1 x 60.9 cm (28 x 24 inches). © 2021 Dynamite. All rights reserved.

PAGES 54/55

Sea Witch, a revised version of the cover for *Eerie* No. 7 created for the cover of *Seademons,* 1977, by Lawrence Yip. Oil on Masonite, 1966, 50.8 x 91.4 cm (20 x 36 inches).

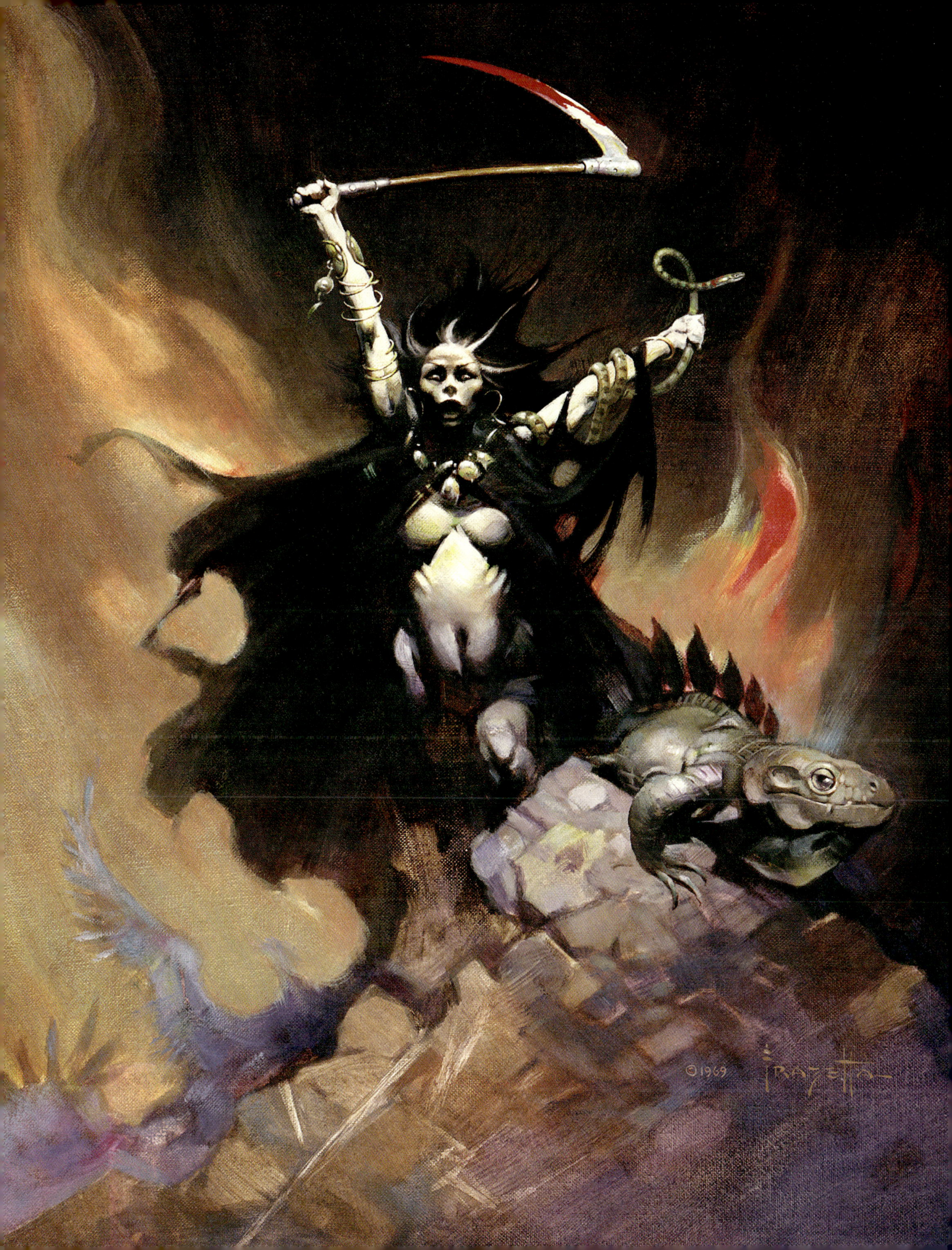

©1969
FRAZETTA

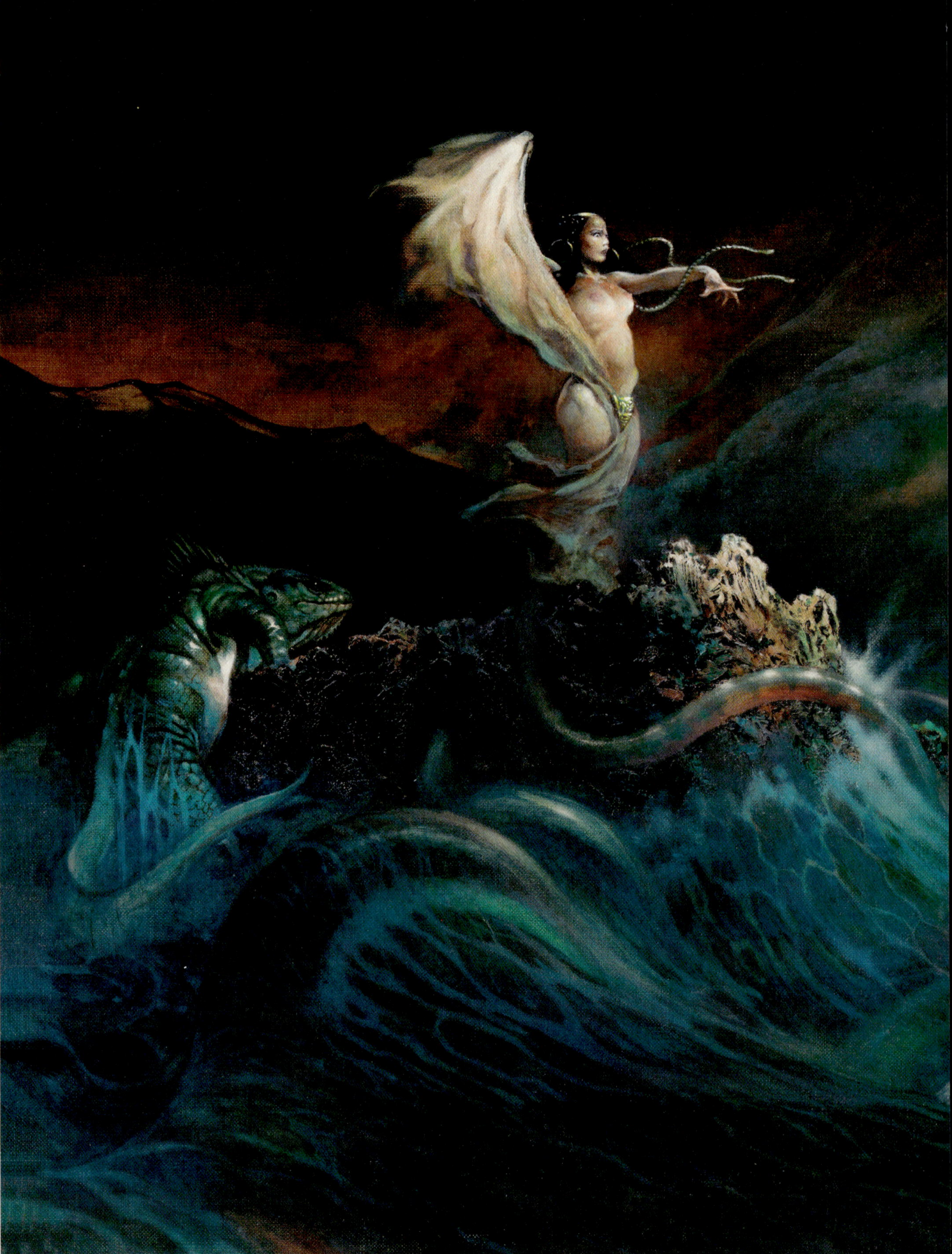

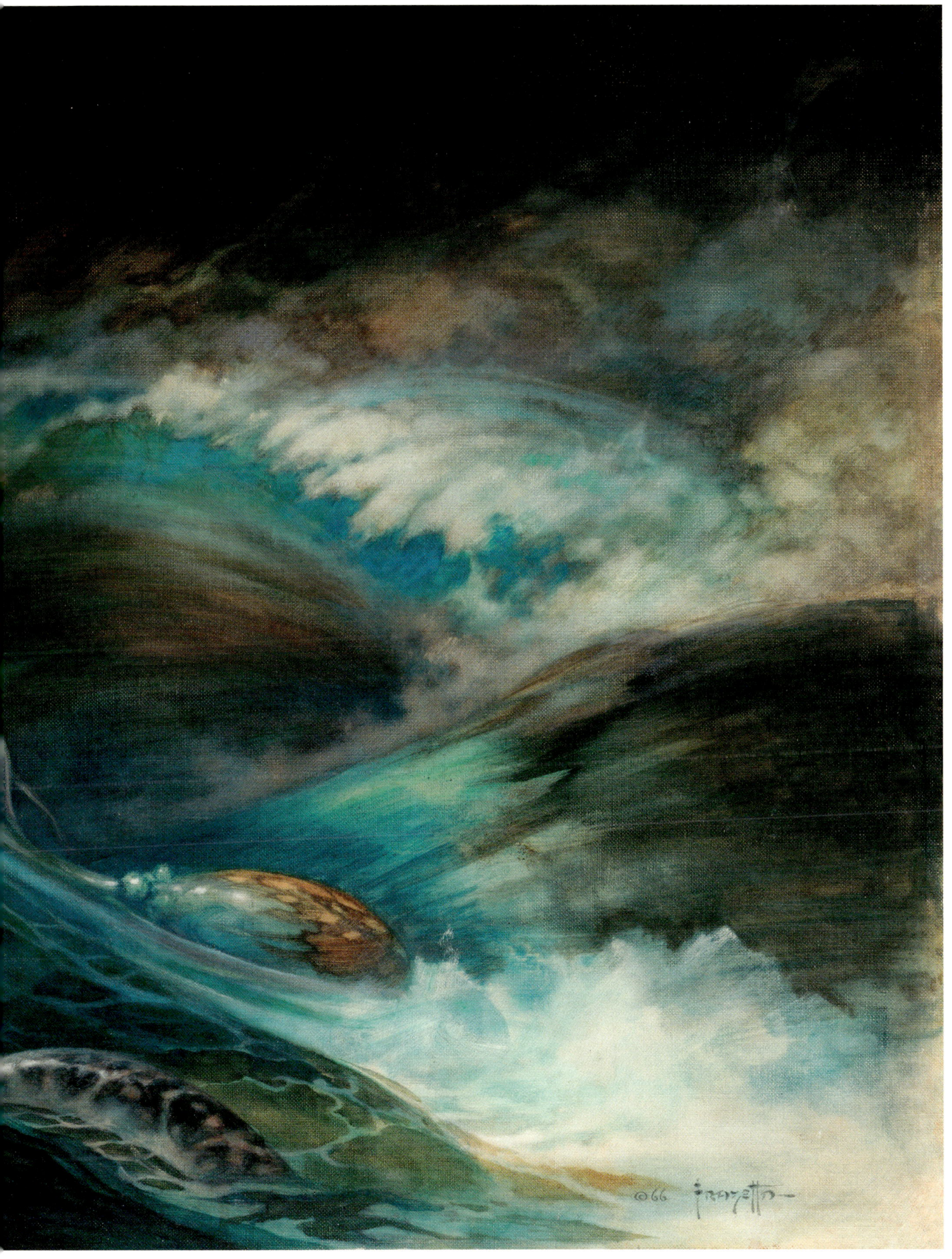
©66 Frazetta

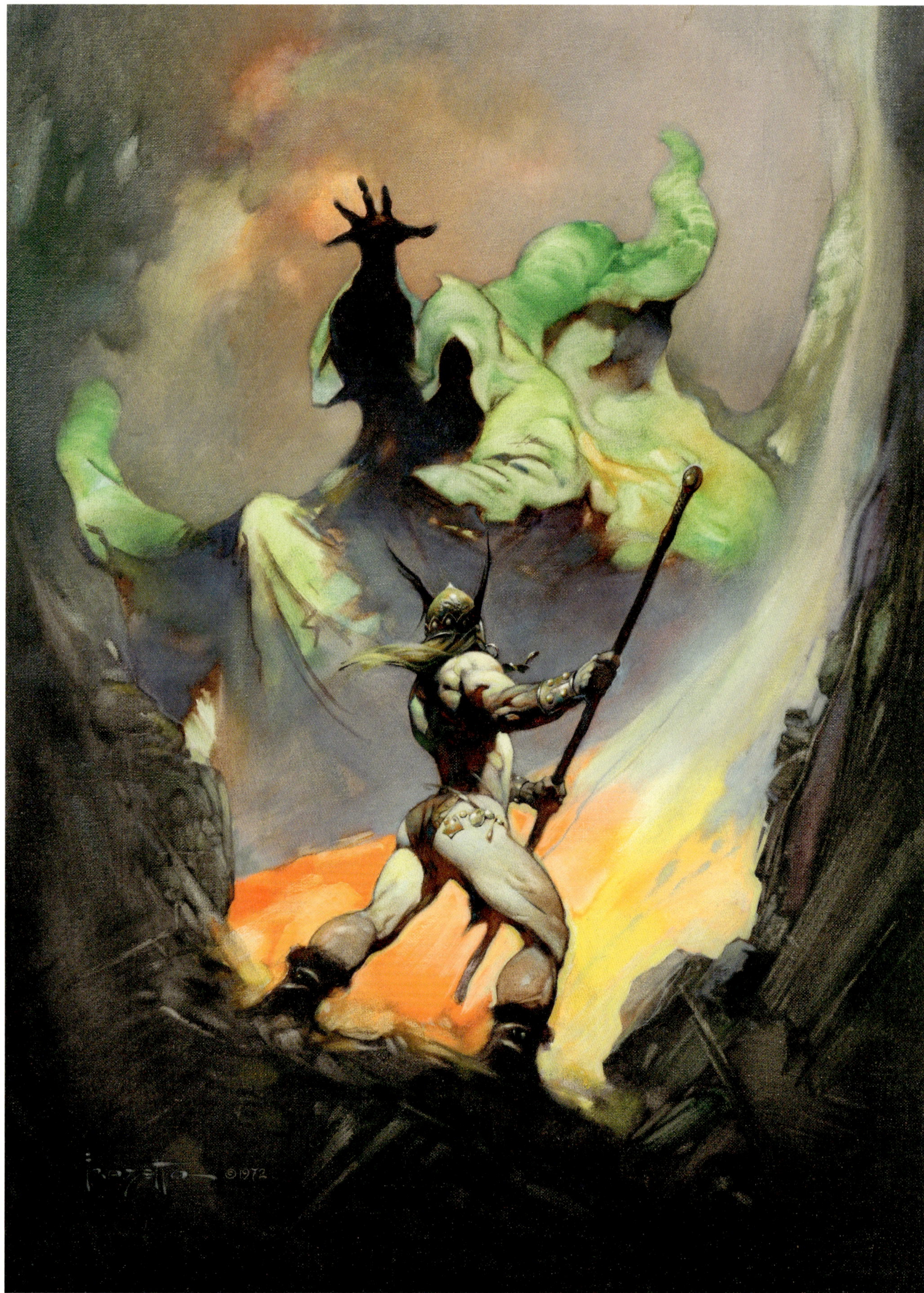

Esquire and Death Dealer
1970–1979

Frazetta was now in demand, doing covers for a variety of publishers; even *National Lampoon* came calling in 1971. He was a strange fit for the counterculture—he liked Sinatra and classical music and his politics mirrored his notions about painting: success would, should, and in his case had come as a result of hard work with no free handouts. That's what had worked for him, and any alternate ideas of social order were above his pay grade. Frank was laconic about *Lampoon*: "They loved my art and they paid well. I didn't tell them to grow up and they didn't lecture me about Nixon."

The Frazetta family now included Frank Jr.'s siblings Billy, Holly, and Heidi—arriving in 1959, '63, and '68 respectively. With money in the bank, Frank began looking for a bigger house, preferably one with a lot of land. There were no longer farms in Sheepshead Bay, so he cast his net wider, finally finding a derelict house on 67 acres in the Pocono Mountains of Pennsylvania. In 1971, the family left Brooklyn for the sticks, eventually building a house based on Frank's own architectural drawings to contain his collection of guns and a tiger-striped couch, while the barn held a menagerie of farm animals straight out of his early cartoons: pigs, ducks, chickens, sheep, and goats.

As the '70s progressed, the Frazetta legend established itself in earnest: there were Awards of Excellence from the Society of Illustrators in '72 and '74; the World Fantasy Award for Best Artist in 1976, and the cover of the (usually quite sedate) *American Artist*, also in '76. In 1977, he not only appeared in *Esquire* and *Newsweek* but reached a crowning pinnacle of any artistic career: turning down work, in Hollywood no less. He refused the poster commission for Dino De Laurentiis's *King Kong*, and the next year turned down a *Star Wars* book, though he did agree to do the letterhead for Bo Derek's production company, formed with her husband John.

The commissions Frank didn't want offer a better window into what drove him than the ones he did. His poster for Clint Eastwood's *The Gauntlet*—commissioned for $20,000 by the actor himself, after convincing Frazetta his call wasn't a prank—was based on Frank's least favorite of five sketches he offered Eastwood. Not only does the *Gauntlet* poster feature Eastwood and his co-star responding to something out of frame, it includes

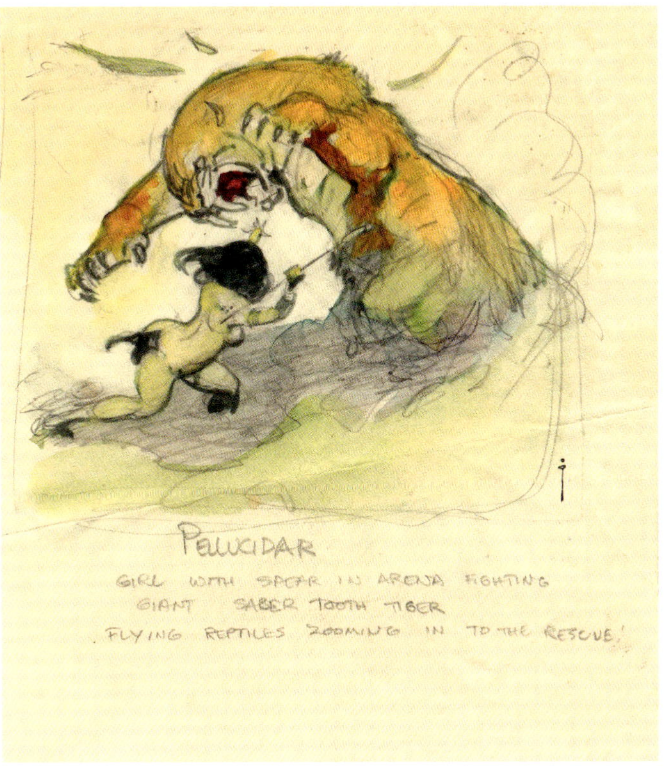

First color preliminary for the cover of Ace Books' *Pellucidar*. Graphite and watercolor on paper, 1971, 20.3 x 17.7 cm (8 x 7 inches). *Courtesy of Heritage Auctions and Edgar Rice Burroughs Inc.*

The Norseman, used on the cover of *Flashing Swords* No. 1, a short story collection edited by Lin Carter, proves power and drama can communicate without eye contact, or even faces. Oil on canvas board, 1972, 59.6 x 44.4 cm (23.5 x 17.5 inches). *Courtesy of Heritage Auctions.*

The original *Moon Maid* oil was created in 1972 for the cover of Ace Books' Burroughs novel, *The Moon Maid*. As was so often the case with Frazetta, he liked it enough to be dissatisfied with his original, and painted this second, darker, more dynamic version, for his own satisfaction. Oil on board, 1974, 50.8 x 40.6 cm (20 x 16 inches). *Courtesy of Edgar Rice Burroughs Inc.*

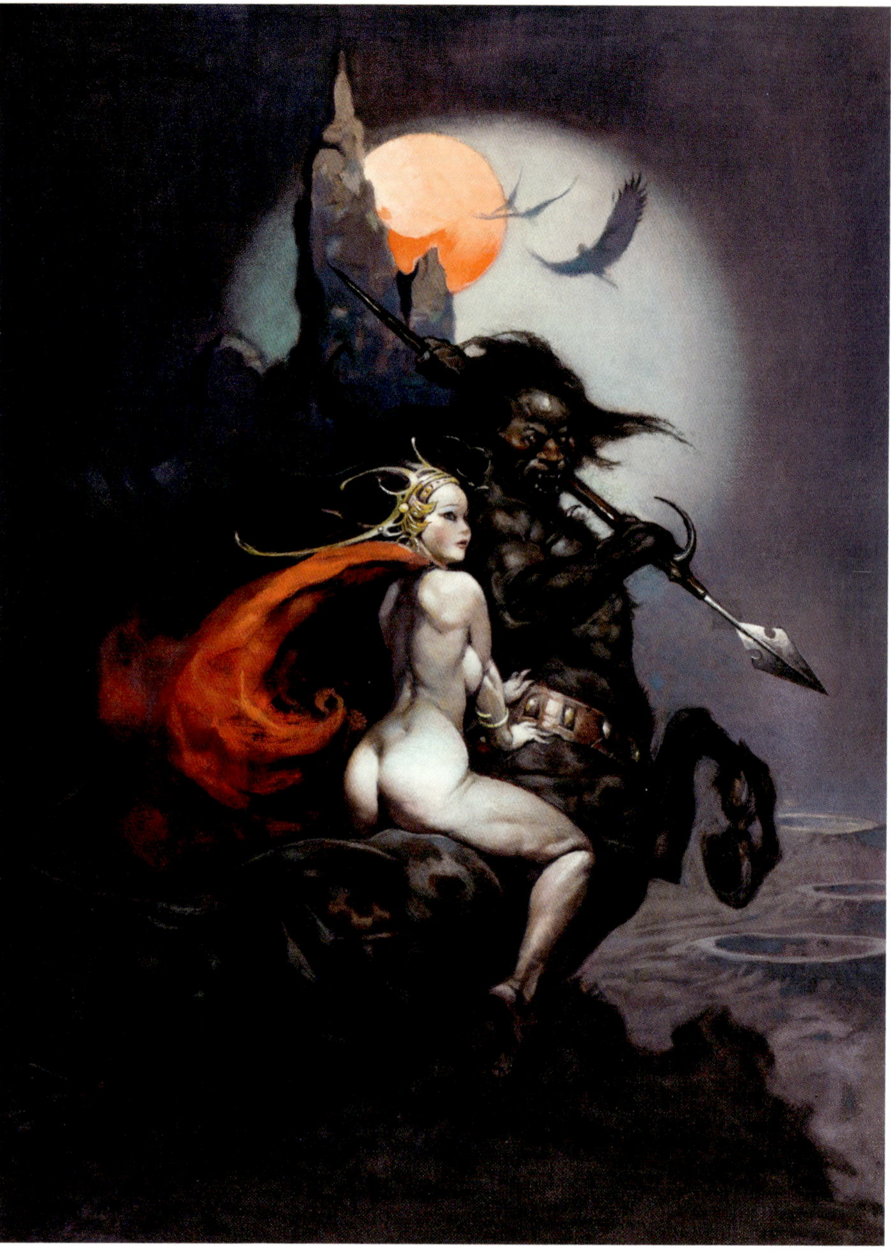

Death Dealer is Frazetta's most enduring and celebrated work, so immediately popular it inspired five more paintings. Originally conceived as a physical representation of death, the figure came to represent indomitable power, leading two U.S. military units to adopt it as a mascot, commissioning life-sized statues for their bases. *Death Dealer* appeared on the cover of Molly Hatchet's debut album in 1978; inspired a novel franchise by Jim Silke and a comic book series from Glenn Danzig's Verotik; and appeared on the cover of the French role-playing game *Bloodlust* in 1991. Oil on board, 1973, 60.9 x 40.6 cm (24 x 16 inches).

a wrecked bus, a rare example of Frazetta painting any vehicle but an organically streamlined Flash Gordon starship. Similarly, when Sylvester Stallone came to the Frazetta farm seeking a poster for his upcoming *Paradise Alley*, he asked for a boxing scene with a variety of details alien to Frazetta's atmospheric burst-of-action style, including both boxers punching simultaneously, a pose most artists avoid unless mocking the combatants, and a crowd full of very specific spectators (Frank Frazetta didn't paint civilians). Frank quoted an insane price, Stallone met it, leaving Frazetta with no recourse but to politely beg off the project.

The late '70s also saw Frazetta become a phenomenon within the burgeoning teen fantasy fandom. Early record album covers for Herman's Hermits, Roger Miller, and Roy Orbison gave way to Dust's *Hard Attack* with *Snow Giants* cover; Nazareth's *Expect No Mercy* with *The Brain* cover; and most famously, Molly Hatchet's self-titled first effort featuring *Death Dealer*. The good fortune spread to other family members: Kiss's classic *Destroyer* cover was done by Ken Kelly—Ellie's nephew, mentored by Frank—after

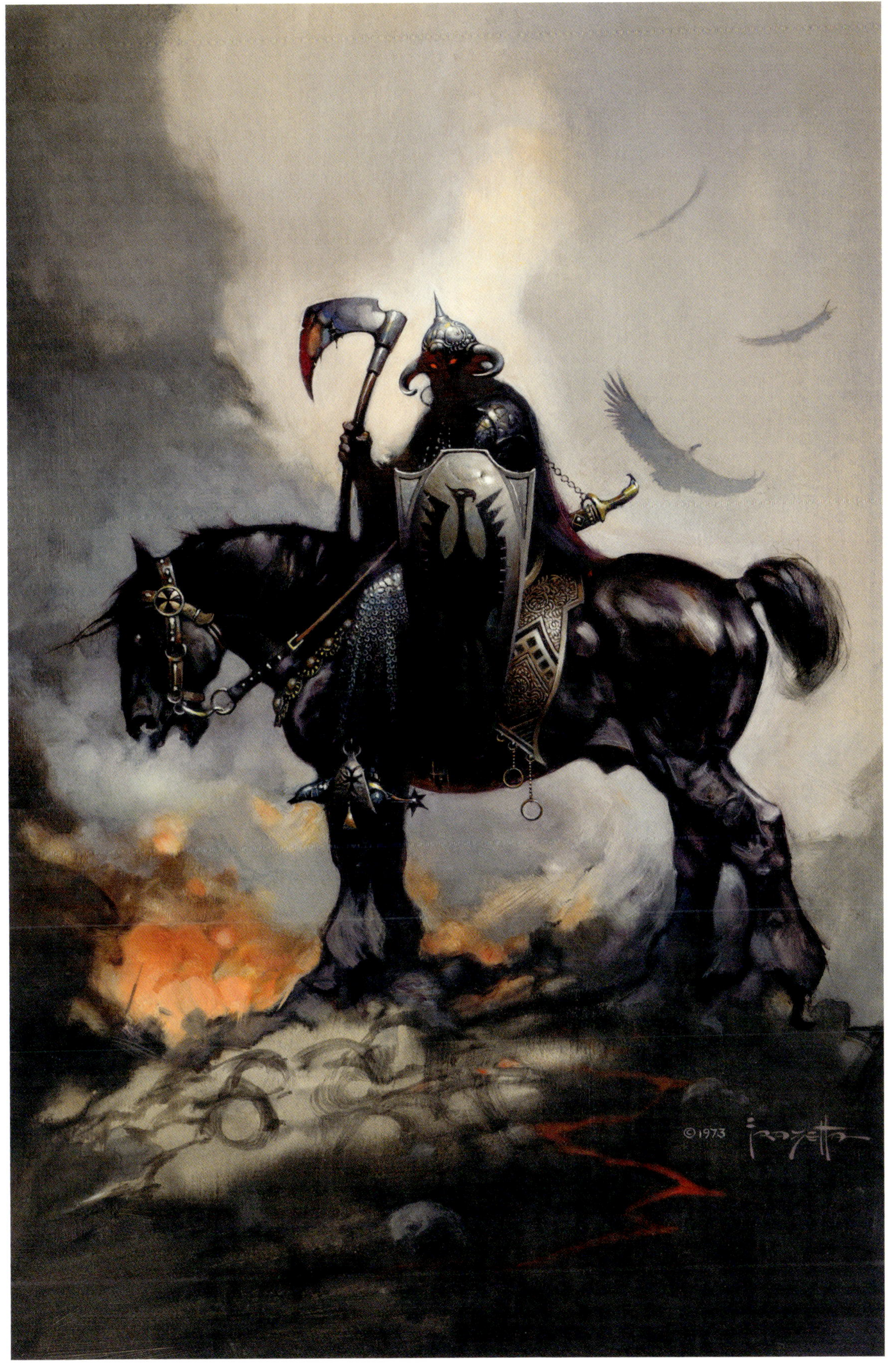

©1973 Frazetta

Color preliminary for *Warrior with Ball and Chain*. Watercolor on paper, 1973. *Courtesy of Daren Bader.*

Warrior with Ball and Chain, for the anthology *Flashing Swords!* No. 1, from Dell Books. It subsequently appeared on the cover of *Wilderlands of High Fantasy*, a *Dungeons & Dragons* campaign book by White Wolf Publishing, 2005. Oil on board, 1973, 58.4 x 48.2 cm (23 x 19 inches). *Courtesy of Heritage Auctions.*

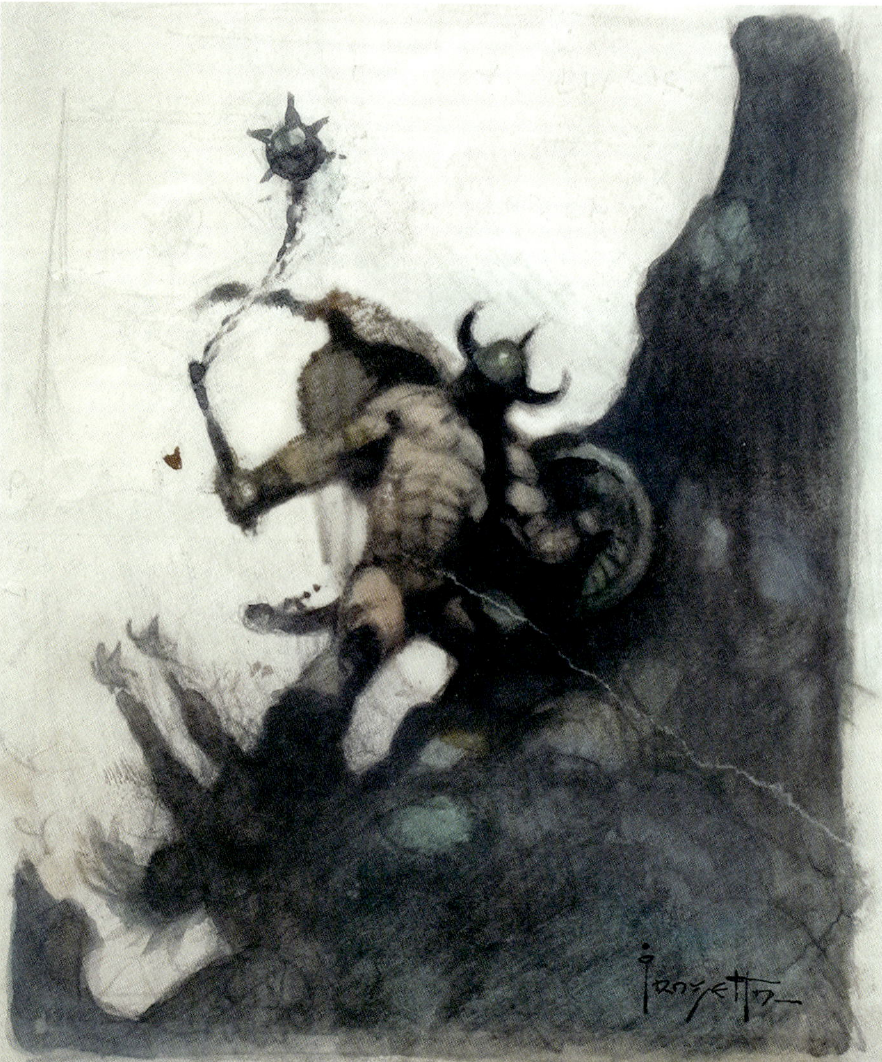

Frazetta's fee proved too high. Ellie was quick to see the opportunities in the growing teen market, running through the door kicked open by the psychedelic album art craze to sell Frazetta posters straight to fans, helping jump start the modern fantasy art print industry. The name "Frazetta" joined Burroughs, Howard, and Tolkien in the pantheon of pop fantasy, and where once subject had reigned supreme, now that he was a "real" artist, people argued the Frazetta technique.

THE FRAZETTA TECHNIQUE

Frank Frazetta was famously tight-lipped about technique, and while for the most part friends, fans, and learned authors of introductions and forewords have been happy to see his paintings as pure and inscrutable emanations of genius, at his peak he developed a very specific oil painting method, custom-built to generate the kinds of images he liked best.

Though capable of tremendous subtlety, Frank was a pulp cover artist at heart and subtlety was never the point: the point was conflict. The classic Frazetta composition spiders out from a central core like a bullet hole in colored glass—broad and simple shapes at the edges, tight linear detail around a few central figures either in action (*Snow Giants*), anticipating action (*Escape On Venus*), or in the aftermath of action (*Death Dealer*)—so most of his preparation for any given painting was deciding how to draw the figure or

60

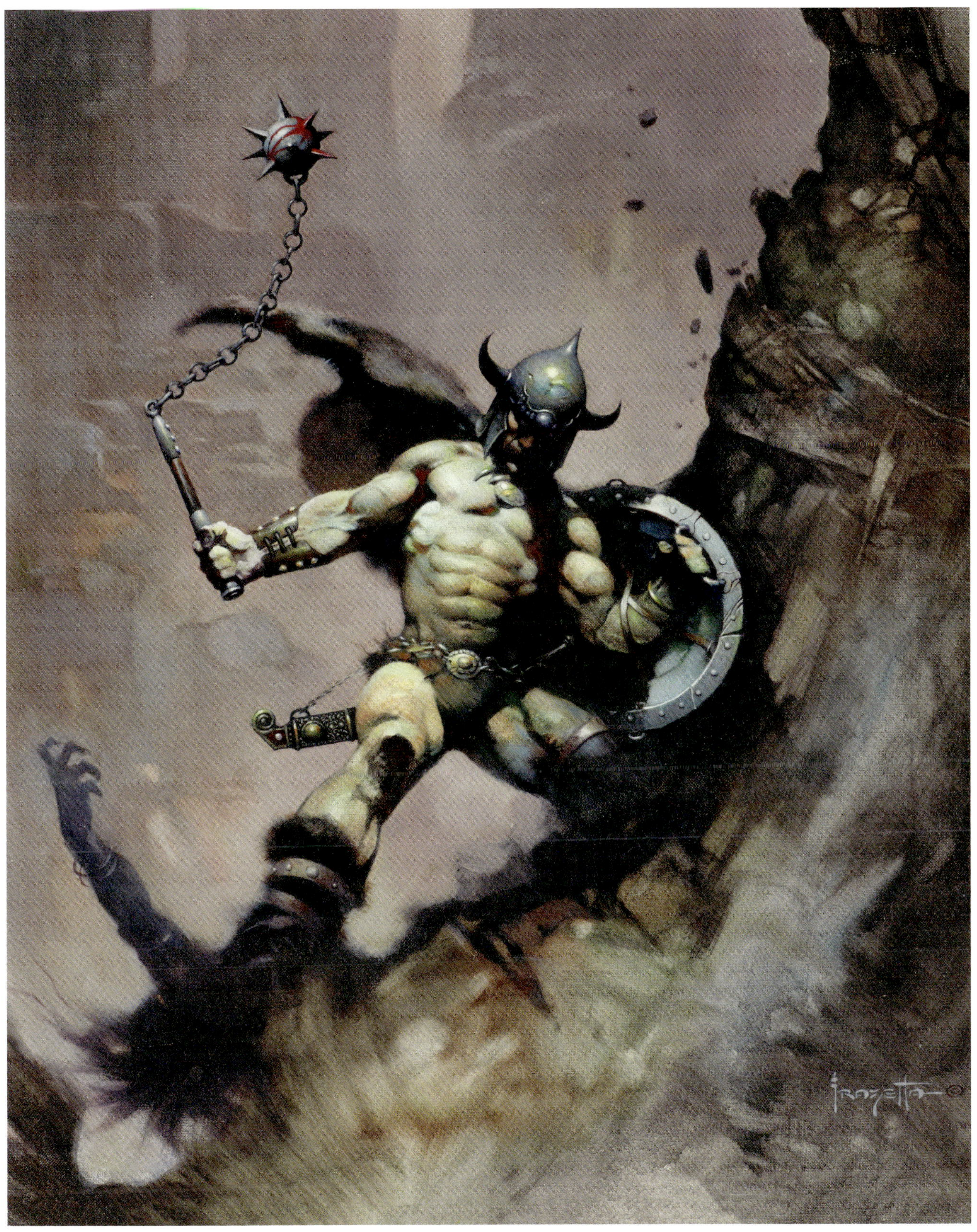

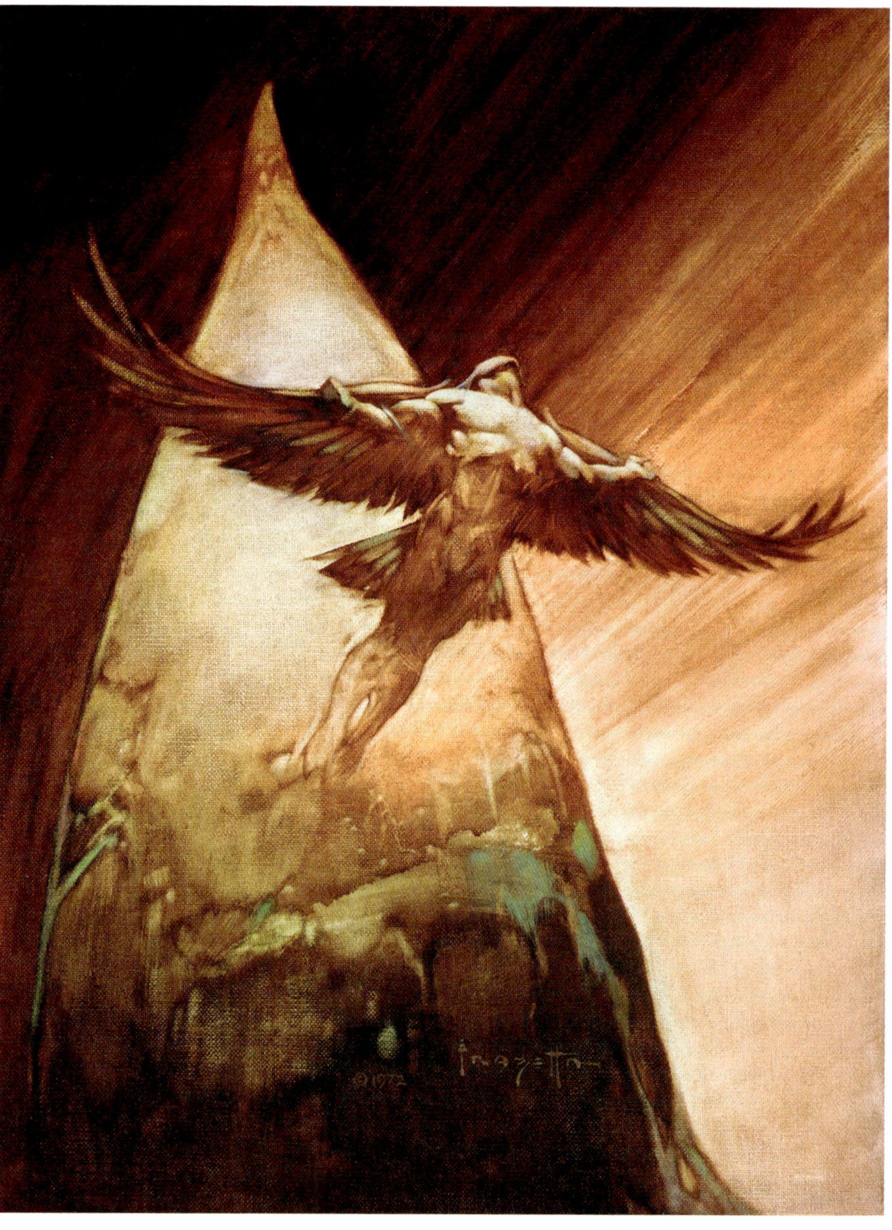

figures. This was equally true for the rarer paintings where the central event was just a Frazetta girl looking curvy.

Frazetta could spend a week or more with a sketch pad (often while watching a ball game, at the zoo, or otherwise out in the world) trying to get figures that worked. Once the figures were found, these were developed and assembled, with the help of a Mickey Mouse–brand watercolor set, into a full-color preliminary painting. The preliminary paintings show a clear distinction in focus between things that have to be gotten "right" (people, animals, anything big requiring right angles and therefore perspective) and things that can be worked out later (plants, invented monsters, skies). In the final picture, these latter elements are often freely distorted to help balance the composition or make the figures "sit" right in the space—Frazetta loved to use twisting tree branches to help poses look natural.

He then moved to the final surface—canvas, Masonite, or board—usually small enough that the major figures would be about the size of his outspread hand, so a muscle could be defined with a single turn of the wrist. Frazetta started with a thin oil

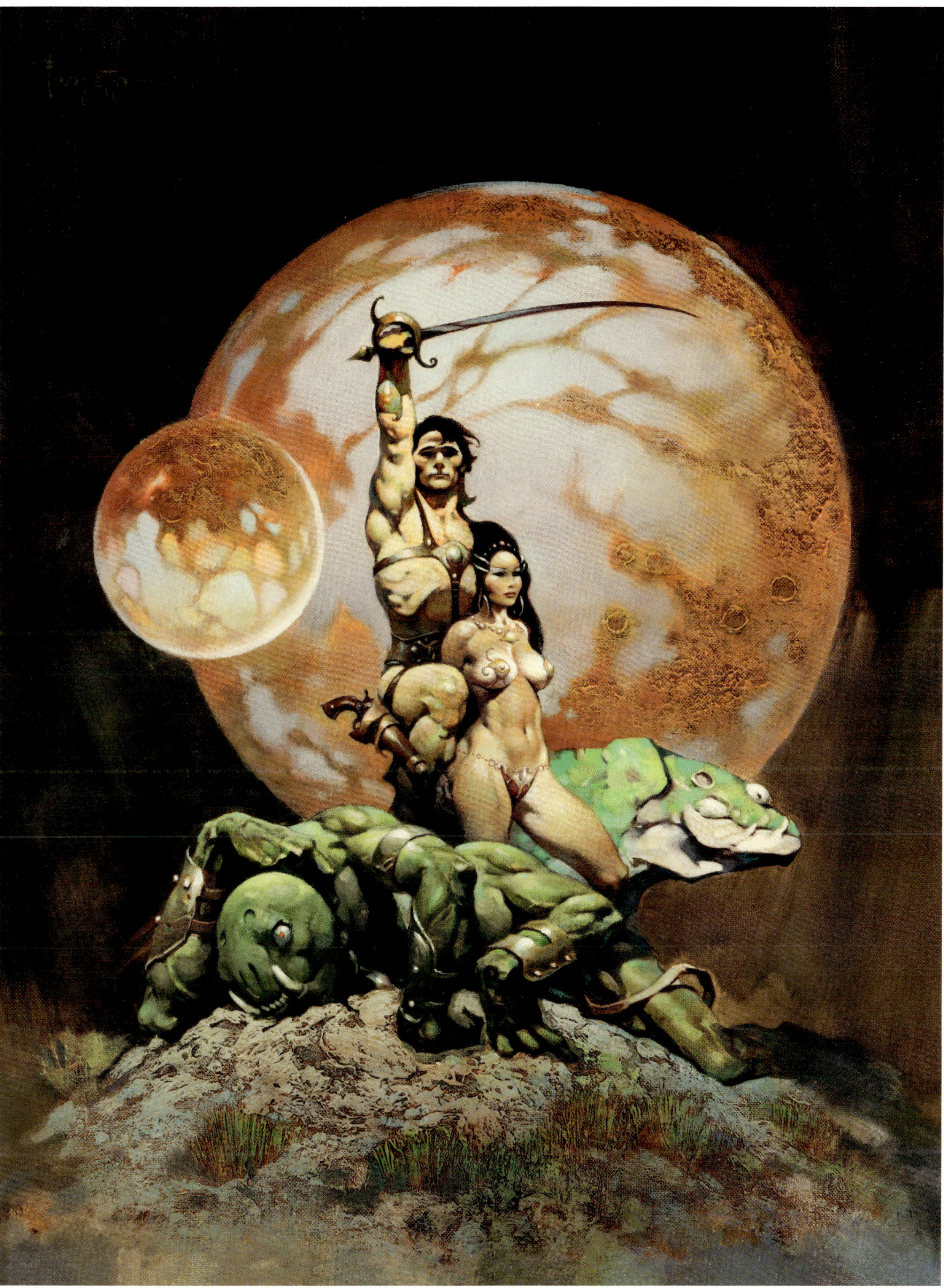

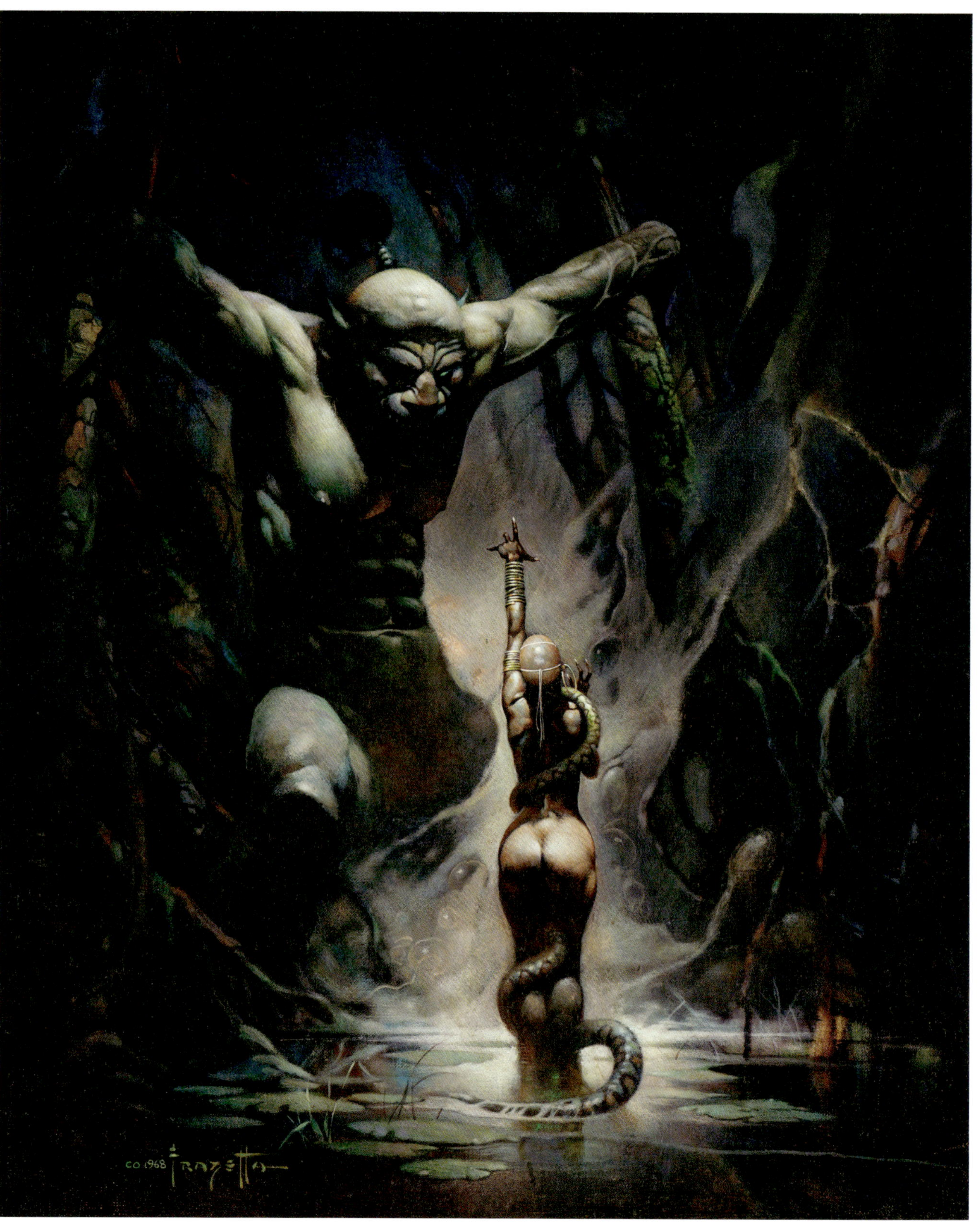

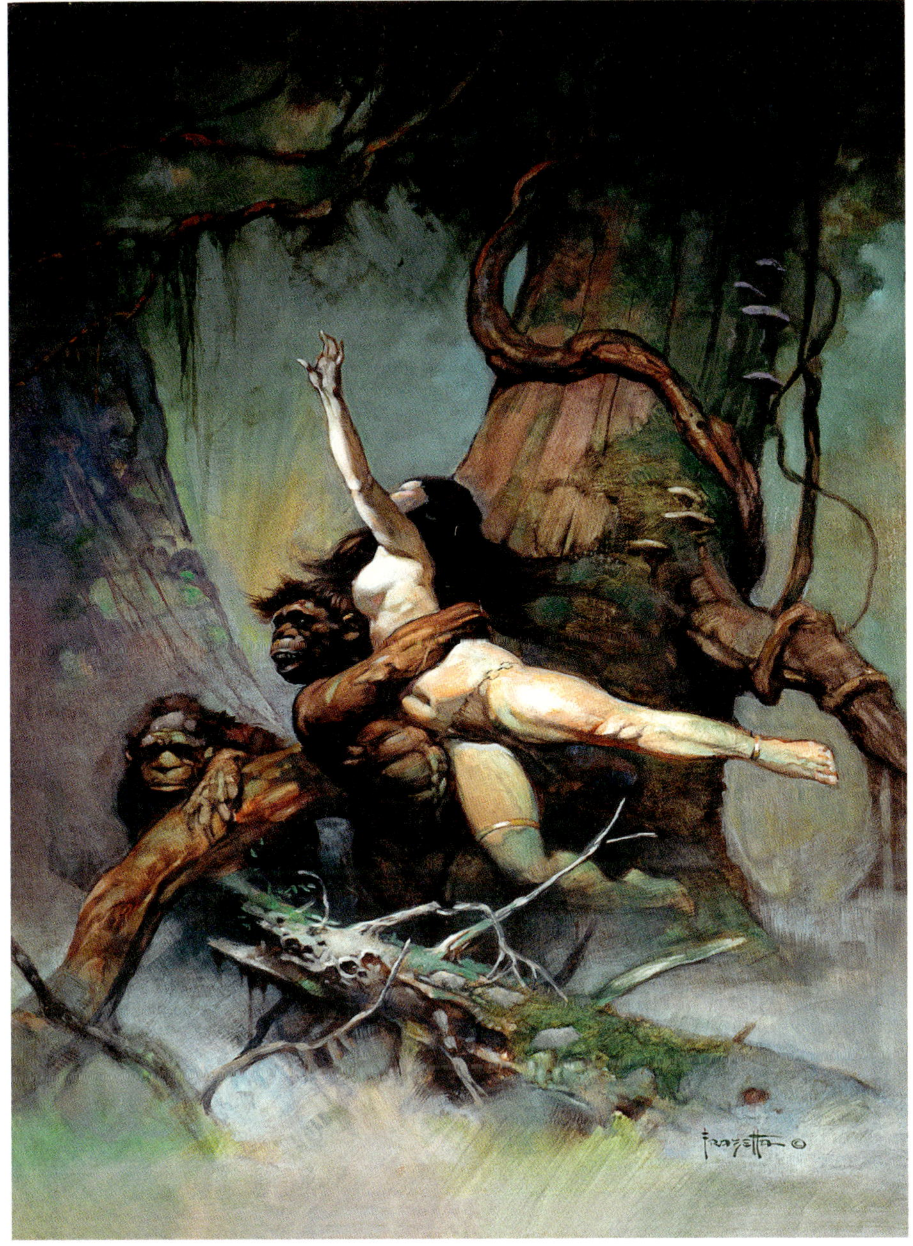

Captive Princess, for the cover of Burroughs's *The People That Time Forgot*, from Ace Books. Oil on Masonite, 1973, 50.8 x 40.6 cm (20 x 16 inches). *Courtesy of Edgar Rice Burroughs Inc.*

underpainting that sunk into the surface quickly and through which much of the texture of the surface (the weave of the canvas or the irregularities of the Masonite) could be seen, usually with a gray or brown in the center that would act as the darkest, or second-darkest, shadow color in the figures' flesh, surrounded by a blocky, more brightly colored mapping out of the remaining painting. The figures often got bigger in the transition from watercolor to oil.

Ironically, all this preparation gave Frazetta's oils the spontaneity of paint handling that is their most distinctive feature. Although he would then go on to apply the thicker, final layers of paint quickly, these strokes sat on top of a painting he already knew worked, and whose basics he'd practiced several times.

It also allowed for Frazetta's distinctive color variations: making sure up front that the figures were going to look like figures gave him room to experiment with colors outside the expected palette in the last layer, with flashes of blue, green, or purple animating otherwise naturalistic surfaces.

The Swamp Demon appeared on John Jakes's *Witch of the Dark Gate*, 1972, and was repurposed by Joshua Ortega, Josh Medors, and Jay Fotos in 2008 for *Swamp Demon*, a one-shot comic book. Oil on board, 1968, 45.7 x 40.6 cm (18 x 16 inches).

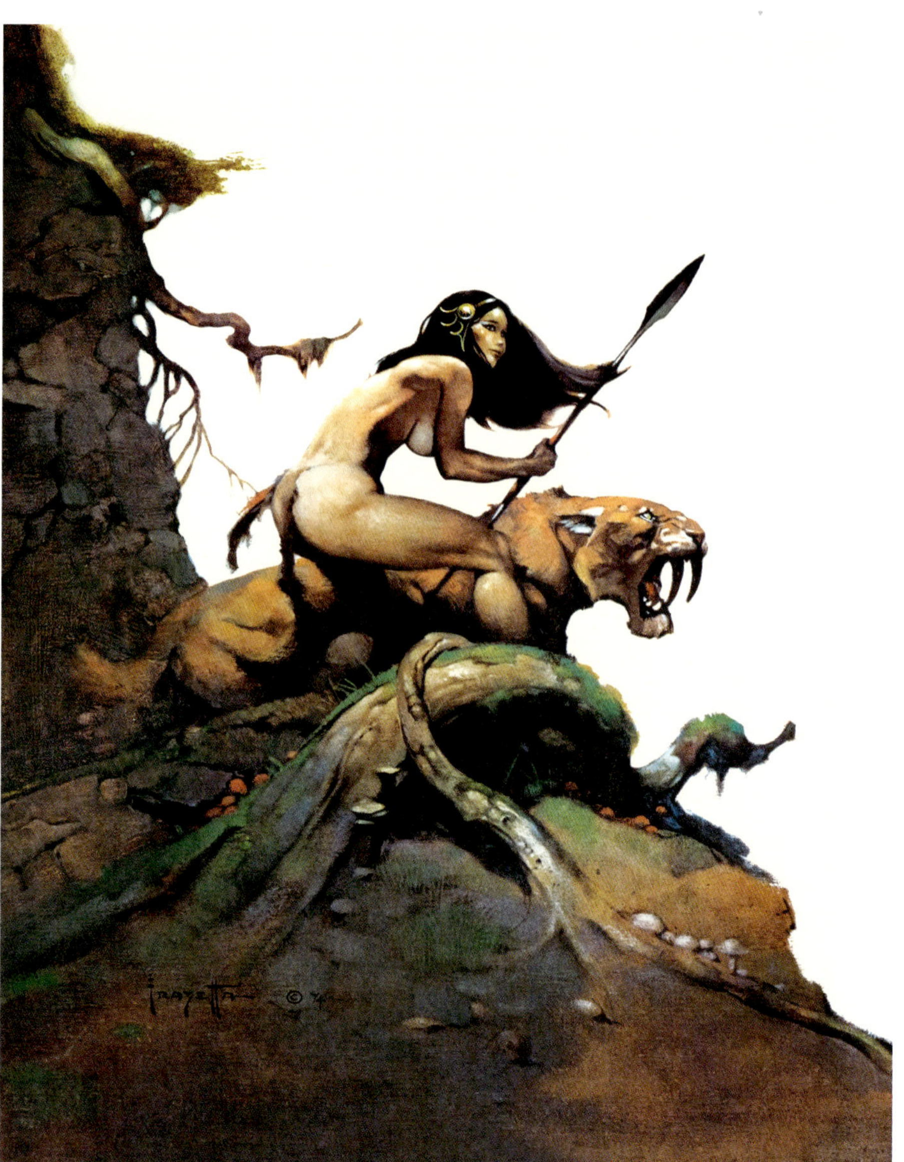

Luana repurposed as Dian for the cover of Ace Books' *Savage Pellucidar*. Oil on board, circa 1970, though dated 1974. *Courtesy of Edgar Rice Burroughs Inc.*

The general pattern of a Frazetta painting, therefore, is misty, dark, and translucent on the bottom; light, sharp, and opaque on top—giving the impression of definition or action emerging crisply into reality from a more generalized dream haze. That top layer of paint acts like the focus of a camera's lens—for example, a mostly underpainted red-brown haze gives way to a sharply rendered thick gold-over-orange in the sabertooth's fur in *Flying Reptiles* (cover for *Pellucidar*, 1972), and the red-brown of the beast's shadow is also the first and darkest layer laid down to define Dian the Beautiful in the foreground, the pterosaur in the middle distance, and the mountains behind.

Flying Reptiles, for the cover of Ace Books' *Pellucidar*, a sequel to Burroughs's *At the Earth's Core*. Here, Dian the Beautiful battles a sabertooth. Oil on board, 1971, 58.4 x 38.1 cm (23 x 15 inches). *Courtesy of Edgar Rice Burroughs Inc.*

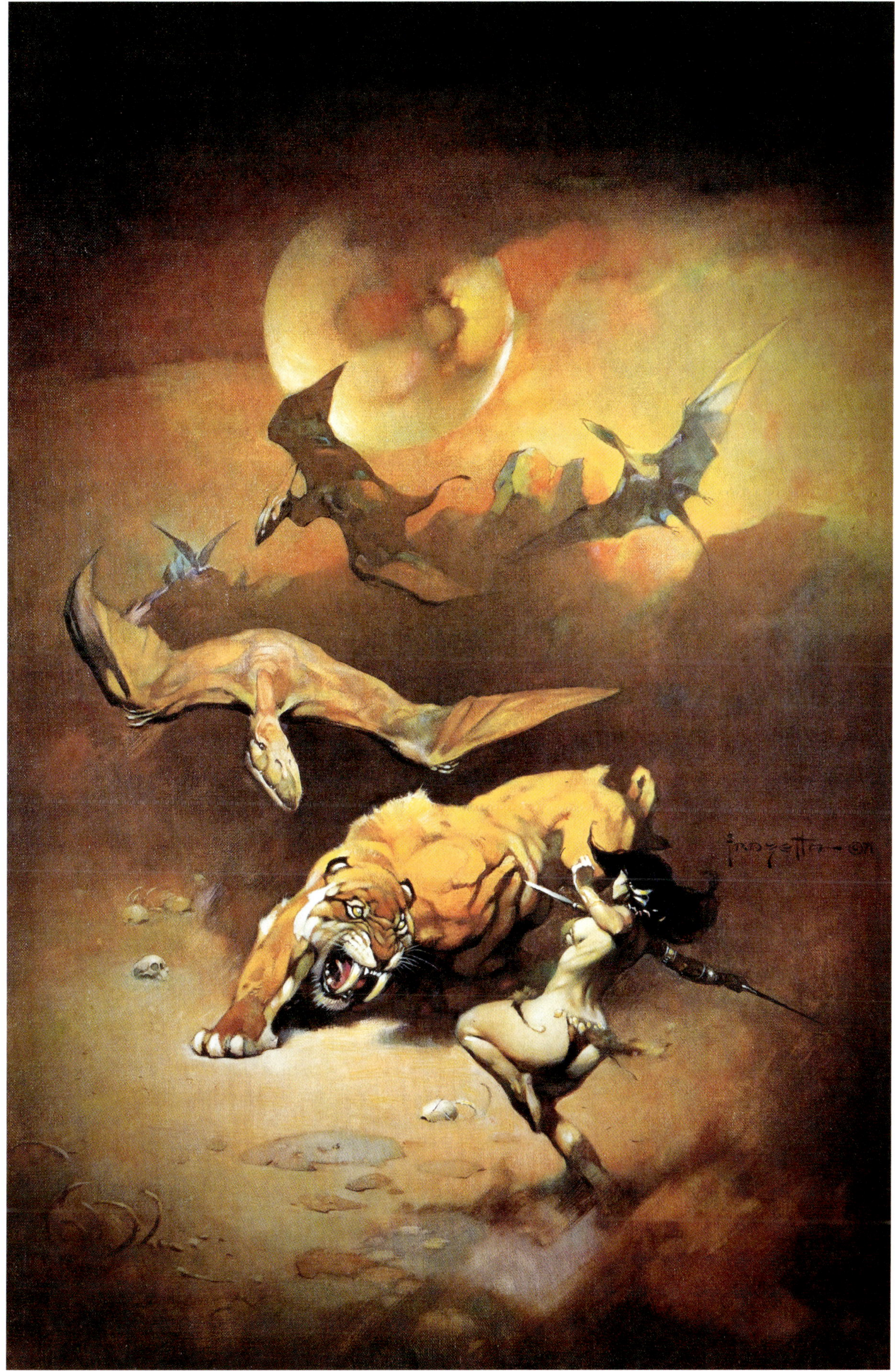

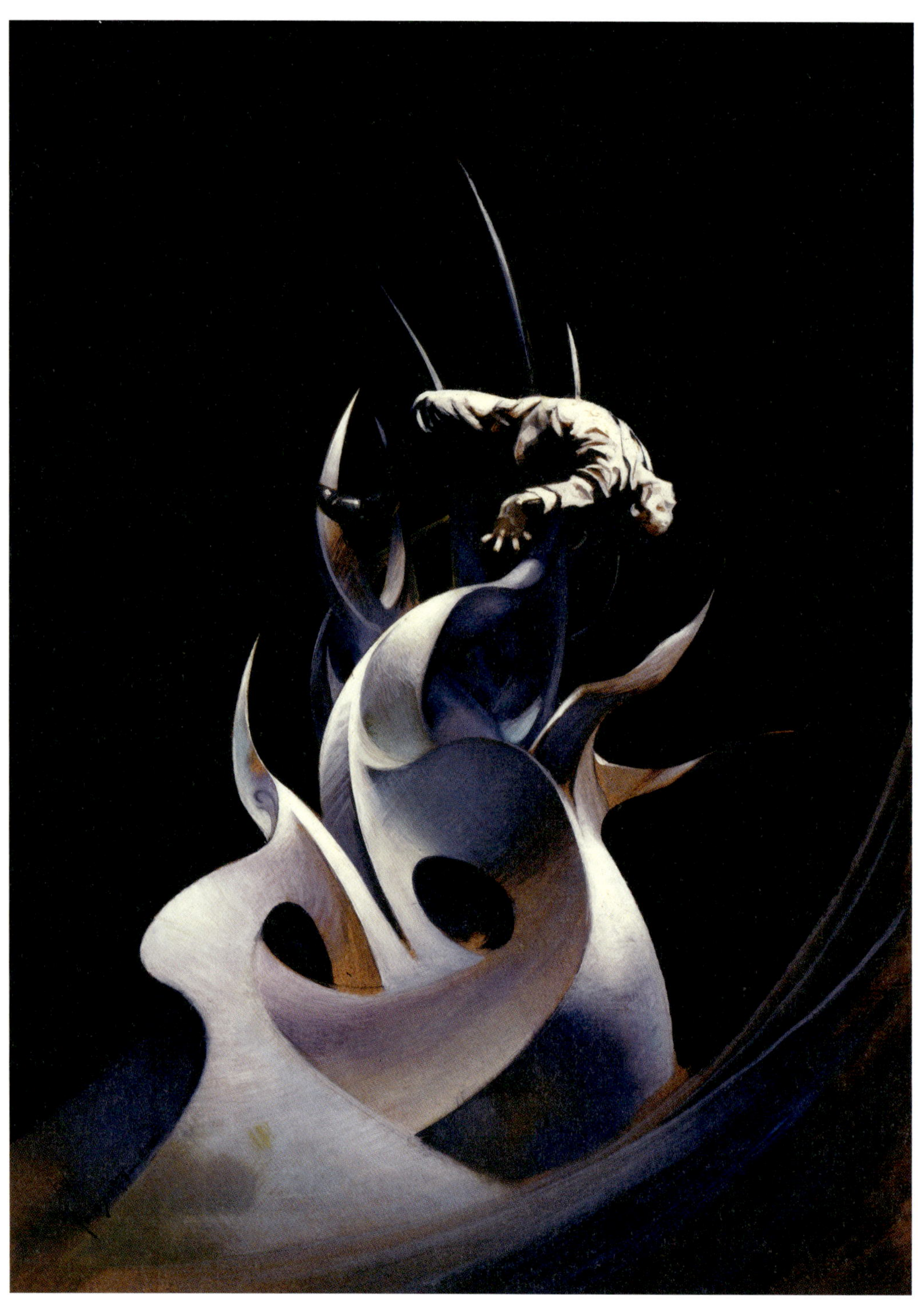

ABOVE
Torment, a promotional piece for the
Nelson Doubleday Mystery Guild Book
Club. Oil on board, 1975.

OPPOSITE
The Godmakers, art for Pinnacle Books.
Oil on Masonite, 1970, 60.9 x 40.6 cm
(24 x 16 inches).

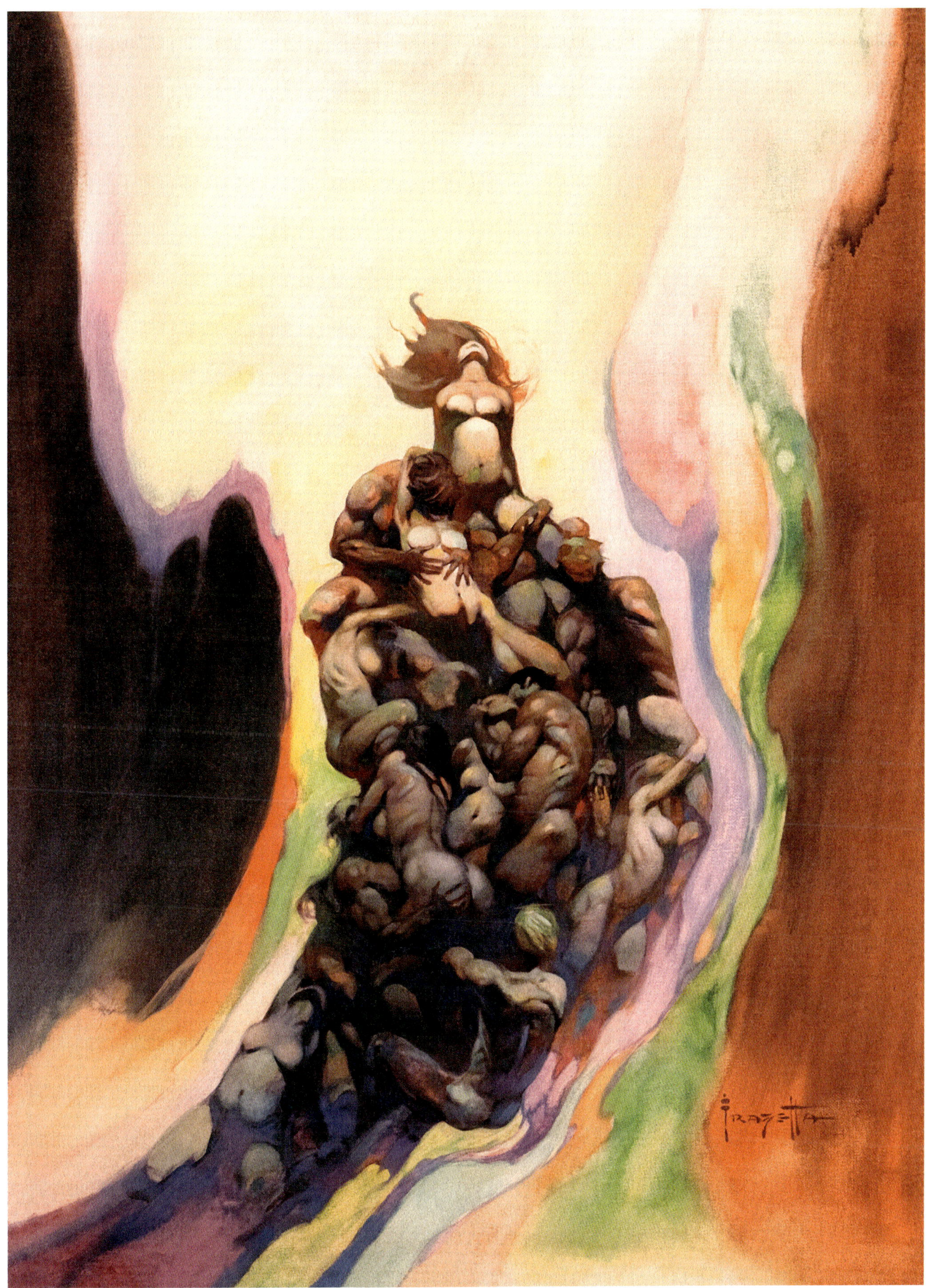
Frazetta

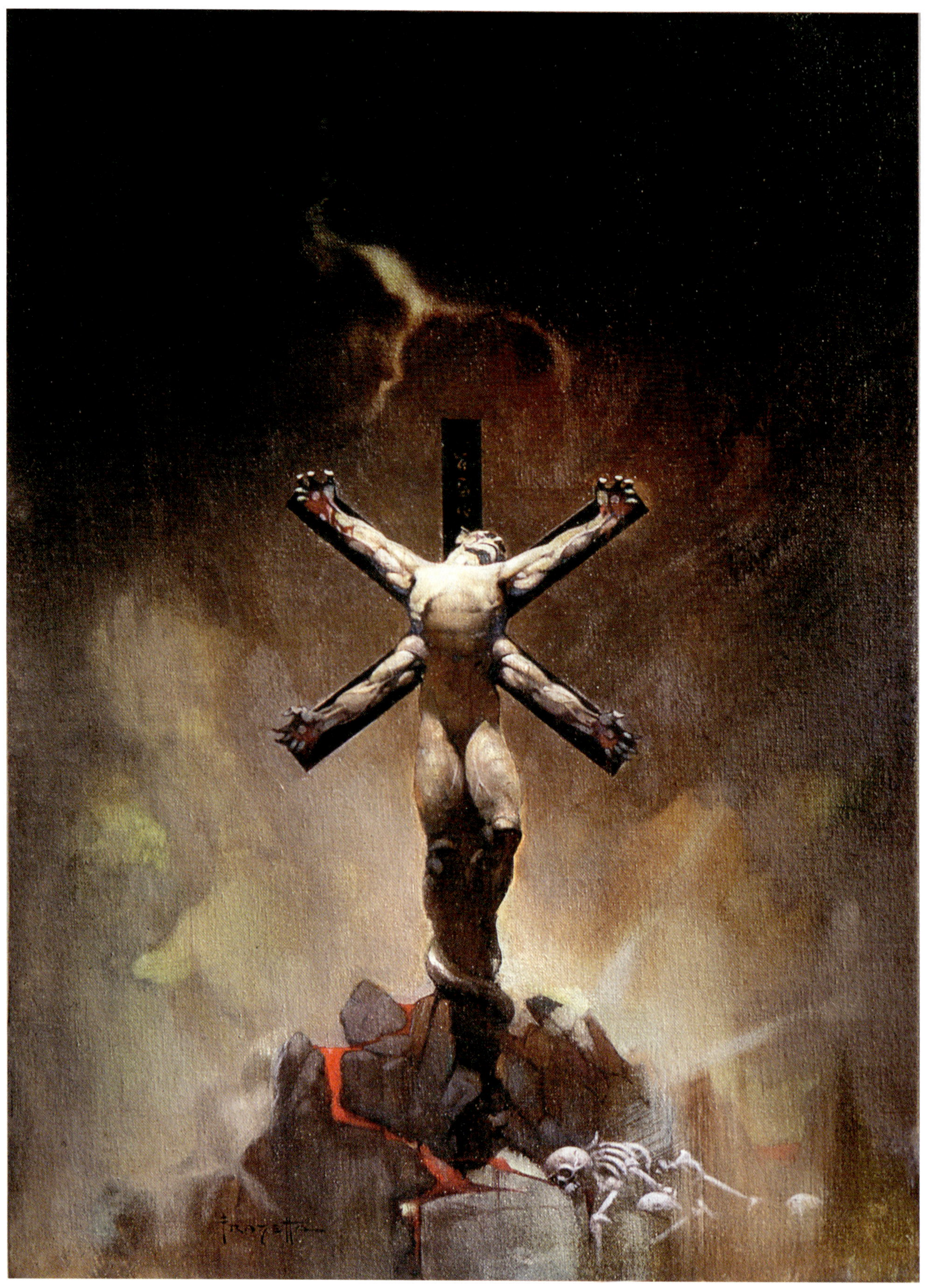

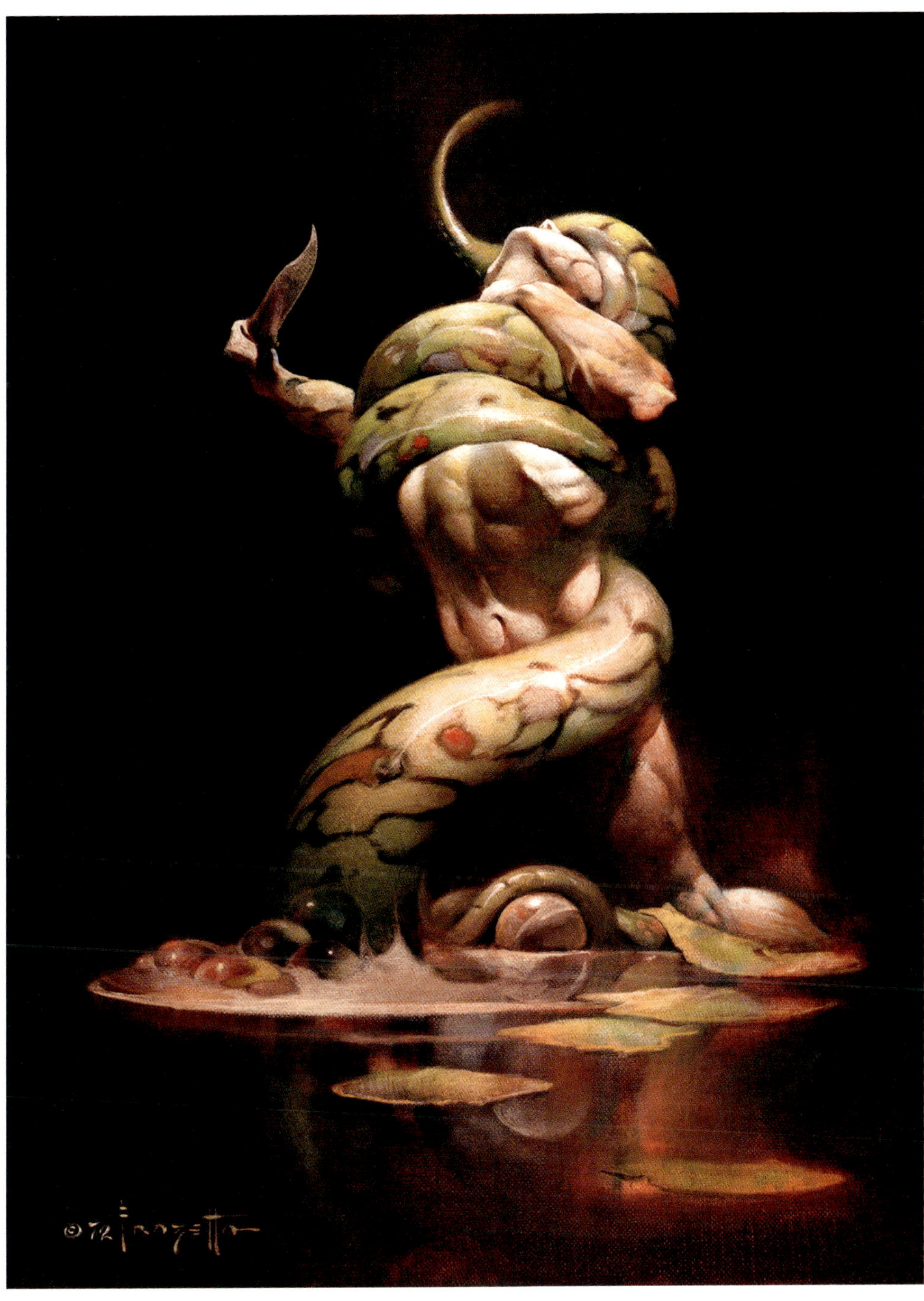

A variant of *Alien Crucifixion*, for the June 1972 cover of *National Lampoon*. Frazetta often rethought paintings after they were returned from publishers, and altered them to his satisfaction. In the original *Lampoon* image the alien has a snakelike lower body that twines around the upright. Frank added legs and the suggestion that it's a tail encircling the post. Oil on board, 1972.

The Serpent, for the cover of Andrew Offutt's novel *Ardor on Aros*, for Dell Books. Oil on board, 1972.

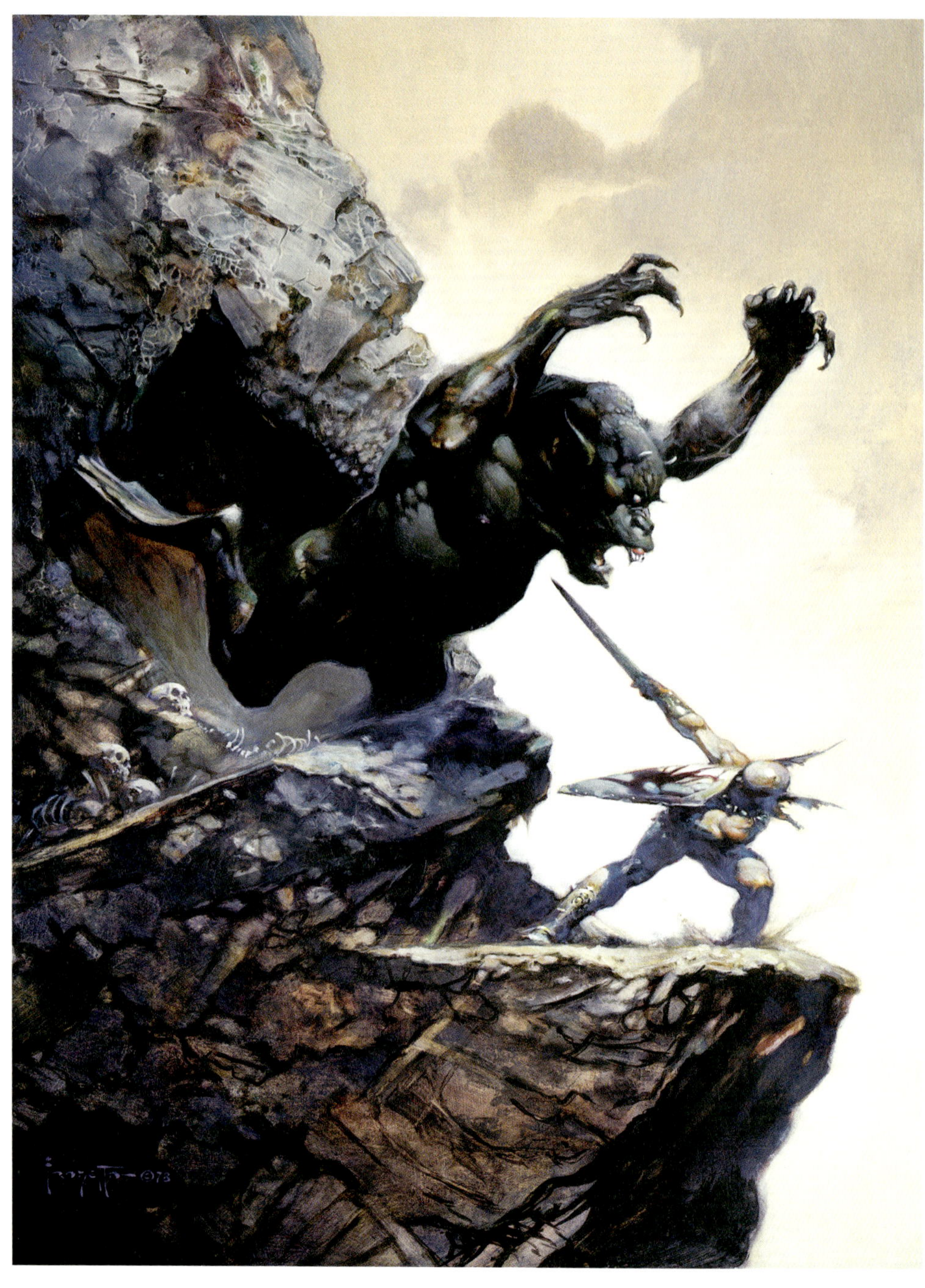

The Cave Demon, for the cover of *Death Angel's Shadow*, part of Karl Edward Wagner's Kane series. Oil on board, 1978, 53.3 x 40.6 cm (21 x 16 inches).

OPPOSITE
Dark Kingdom, for the cover of Karl Edward Wagner's *Kane in Dark Crusade*, sold for an astounding $6 million in 2023, setting records for the highest price ever paid for fantasy or comic art, let alone a Frazetta. The painting is best known as the album cover for Molly Hatchet's *Flirtin' with Disaster*, released in 1979. Oil on board, 1976, 50.8 x 40.6 cm (20 x 16 inches).

72

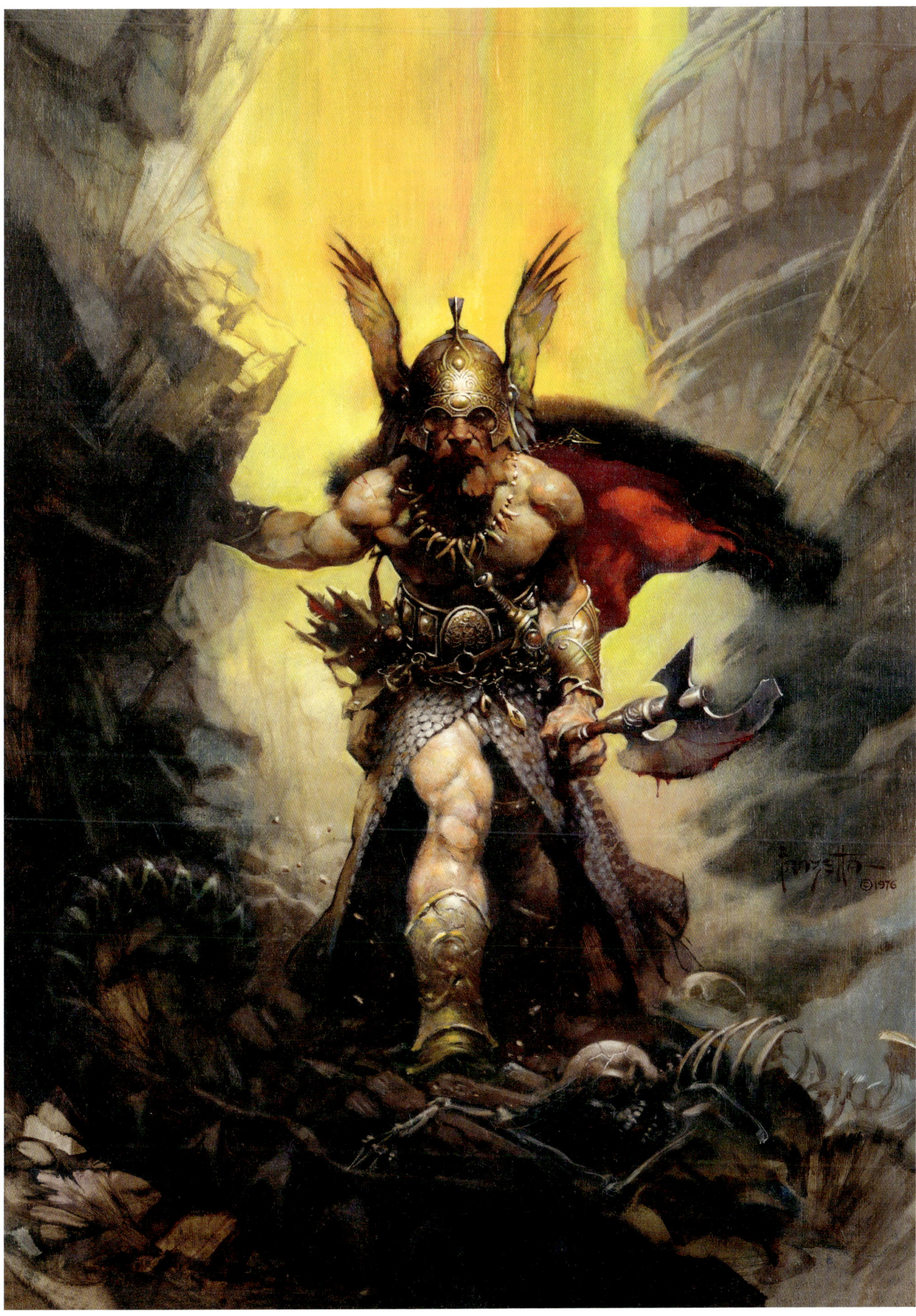

FRAZETTA ©1976

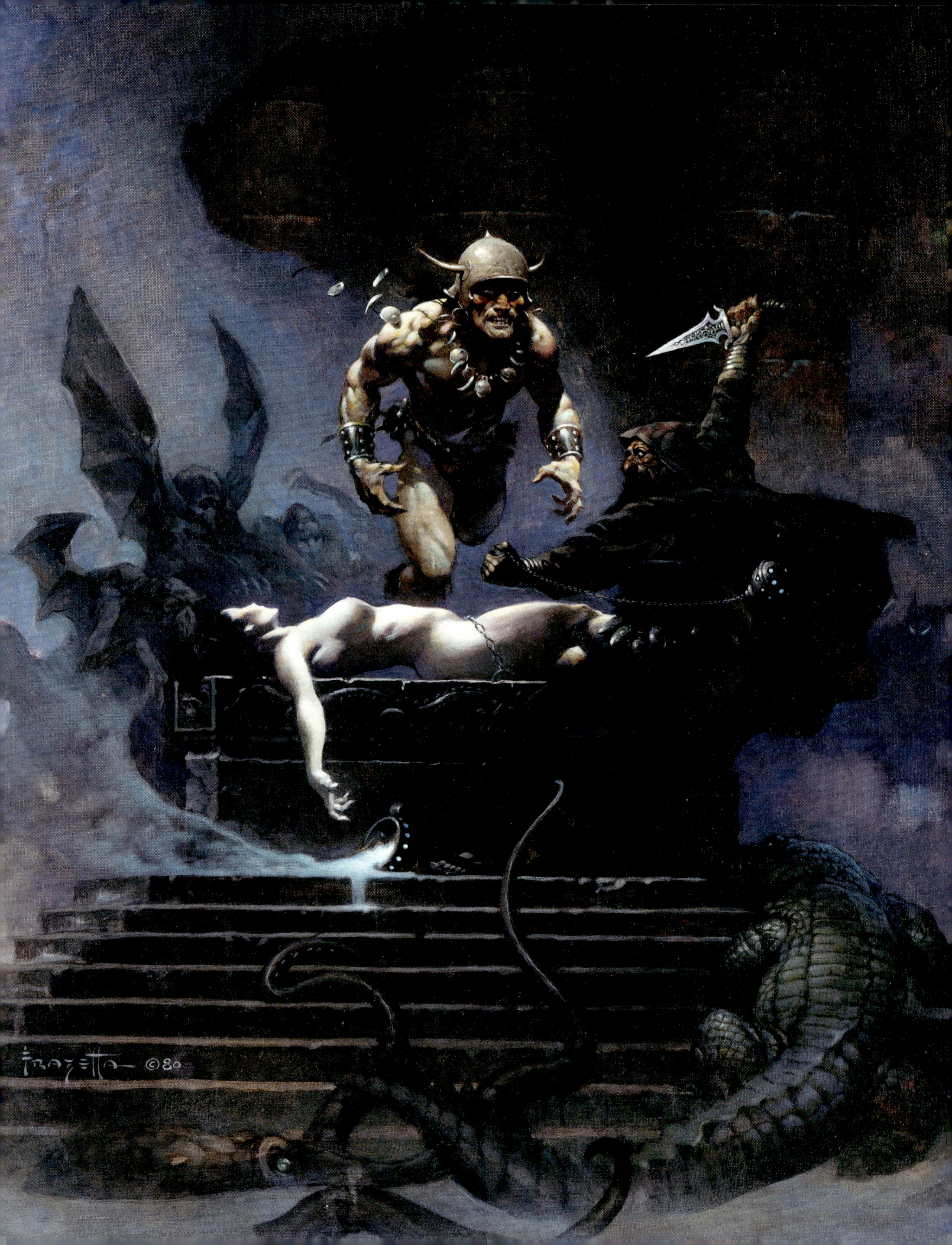

Fire and Ice and *Dusk Till Dawn*
1980–2010

In 1981, Frazetta began working with film director Ralph Bakshi on *Fire and Ice*, doing concept art, supervising the creative team (including a young Thomas Kinkade and future *Dinotopia* creator James Gurney), and making head sculpts of key characters to keep the animators on-model. Bakshi's rotoscope process—whereby animators trace over live-action footage—allowed Frank to work with actors as well. Frazetta spent a year on the film, and a handwritten note from the time records not only the depth of his participation, but also his dedication to craft:

Fire & Ice: *The making of a "Frazetta" film*

Conceived of the original concept
Created the characters of Larn, Teegra, Darkwolf, Nekron, subhumans.
Directed most of the action scenes, particularly the Larn and Darkwolf
*   fight scenes, Darkwolf vs Nekron, giant lizard scene, wolves scene*
In short, I was responsible for the action scenes, attitudes, backgrounds,
*   atmosphere, color, casting, costumes etc.*
I drew as many key drawings as possible. Drew the wolves & lizard
*   & panther almost in [their] entirety.*
Worked with actors and stunt men on all live-action shots. Demonstrated
*   actions personally. How to run, leap, kill Frazetta style.*
Conceived of rolling up newspapers in lieu of phony weapons, for a more
*   convincing follow through in fight scenes. No choreography here!*
*   Just natural actions and reactions.*
I was the iron hand in maintaining that the film be kept clean and inoffensive.
I insisted on a classical score for the background music; I introduced Bakshi
*   to the likes of Stravinsky, Mussorgsky, Prokofiev. Sources of inspiration*
*   for me for many years.*
I found myself very much alone concerning the Darkwolf character. I insisted that
*   he remain a mystery, an enigma, throughout the film. I didn't feel as they did,*
*   that we owed the audiences an explanation for his being. To me this was*
*   the most critical point of the entire film. I stuck to my original concept right*
*   thru the film.*
Of course, there were countless art lessons & private exhibits of my art.

All of this to help inspire them and keep them up for the long haul.

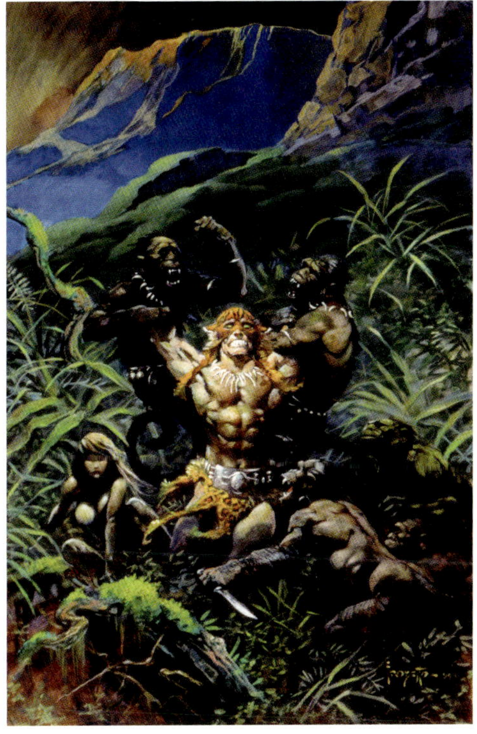

Jaguar God, for the cover of
Jaguar God No. 1, a comic series
from Glenn Danzig's Verotik.
Oil on board, 1995.

Sacrifice, a revised version of the cover
painting for *Conan the Avenger* by Björn
Nyberg from Lancer Books, 1968. Frazetta
made Conan more muscular, more
menacing, and gave him a simpler helmet,
while stripping the costume completely
from the sacrifice. Oil on board, 1980,
55.8 x 40.6 cm (22 x 16 inches).

Artwork for *Fire and Ice* film poster.
When director Ralph Bakshi approached
Frazetta to turn his characters and their
worlds into a feature-length animated film
Frank was thrilled, but the rotoscope ani-
mation didn't live up to expectations and
Bakshi couldn't get the film into theaters.
But, what a great poster. Oil on board,
1983, 66 x 50.8 cm (26 x 20 inches).

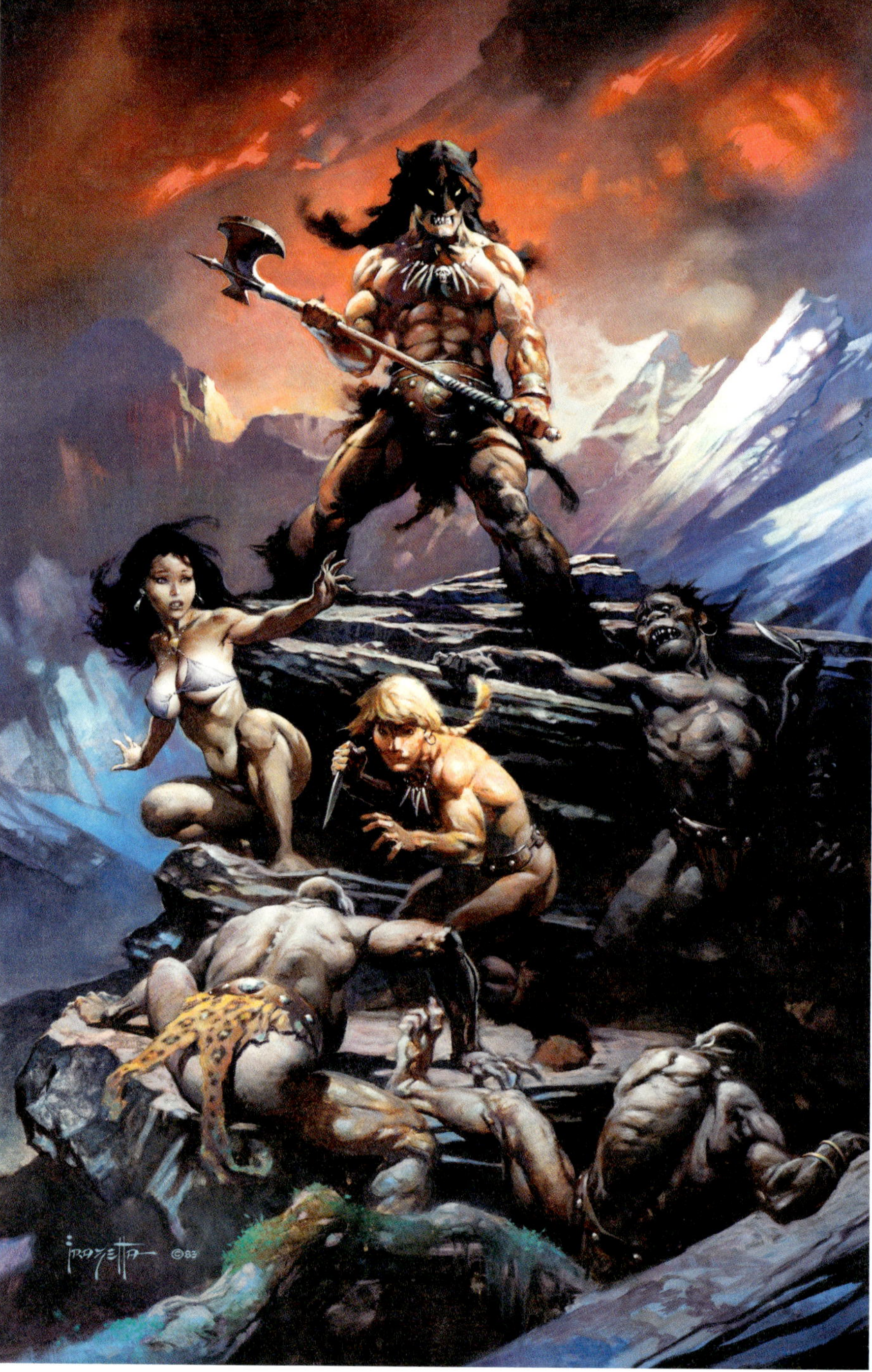

Days of Wrath, also known as *Darkwolf*,
started as a study for the mysterious character in *Fire and Ice*. Frank later altered
it yet again, but this remains the most
detailed and wrathful. Oil on Masonite,
1982, 58.4 x 40.6 cm (23 x 16 inches).

Unfortunately, while the "action scenes, attitudes, backgrounds, atmosphere, color,
casting, costumes, etc." were indeed impressive, the less visual elements of the film didn't
land with audiences, for many of the same reasons fans threw their Conan paperbacks
away after ripping off the covers and pinning them to the wall. Frazetta's ability to capture
the heart of an exotic, heroic narrative in a single image often left nothing else to say,
and in the coming decades artists inspired by Frazetta would learn they had to bring just
as much to the table to counterbalance or compete with the master's shadow.

The year before *Fire and Ice* came out the first film version of Conan appeared, clearly
influenced by Frazetta's creation—the preview poster featured Frazetta's *Conan the*

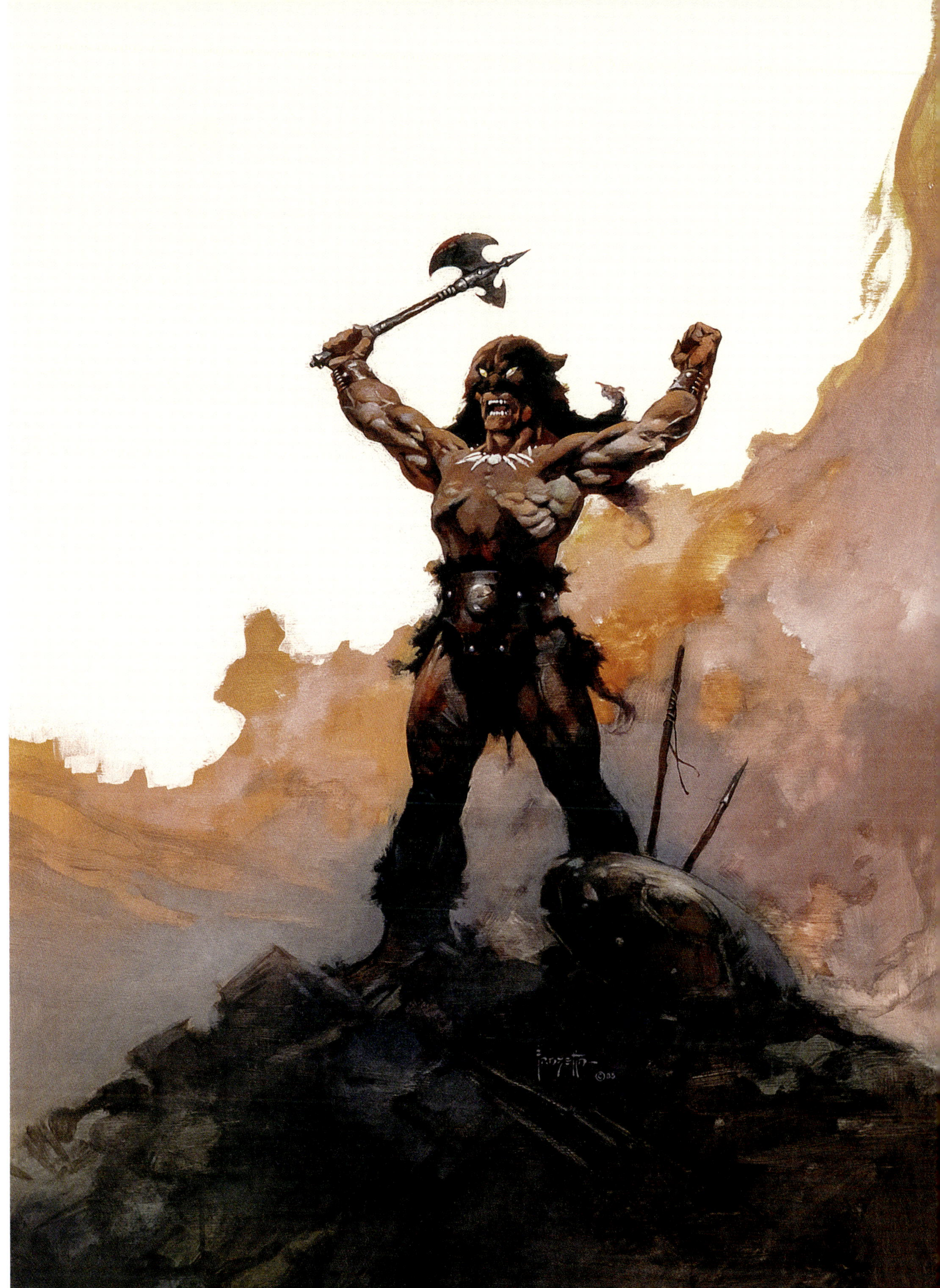

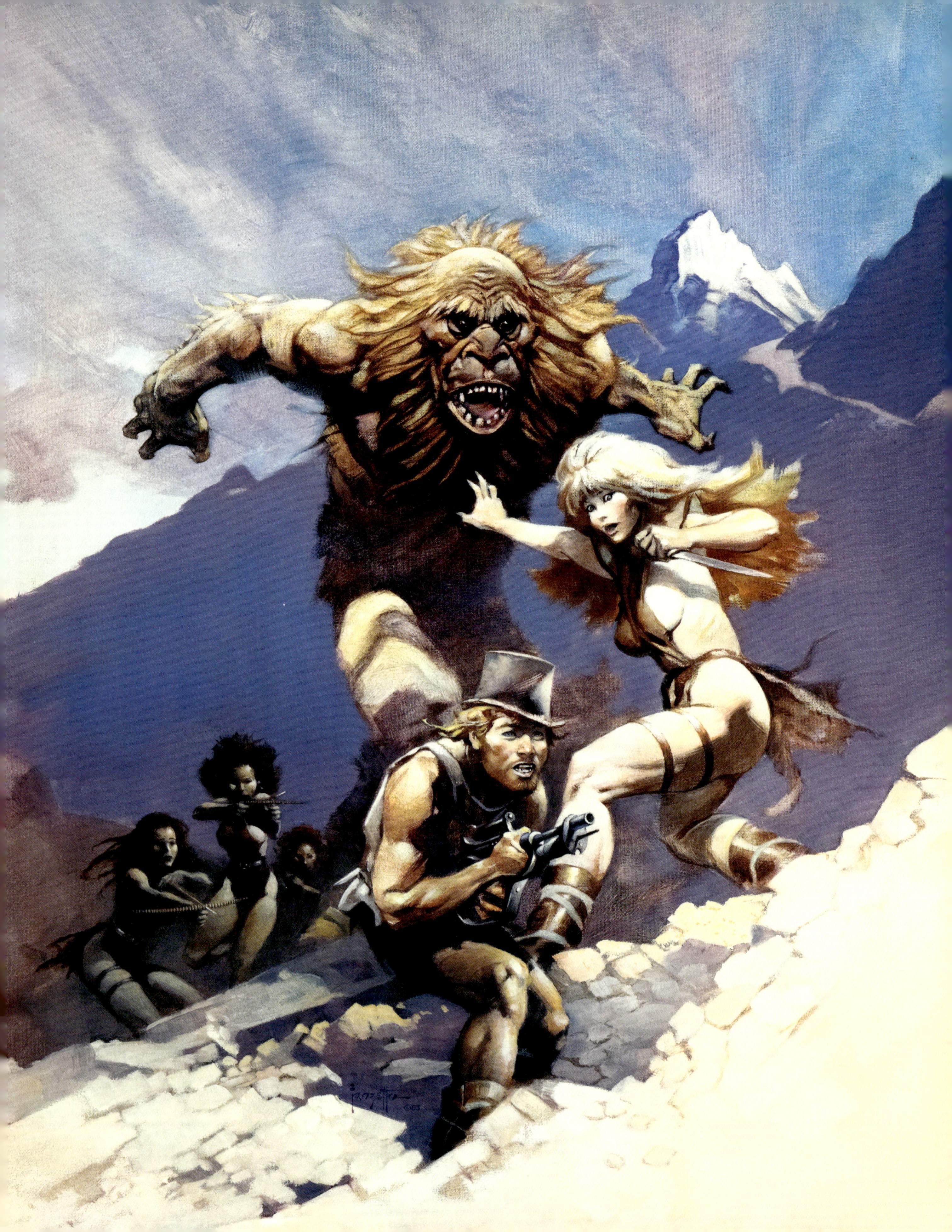

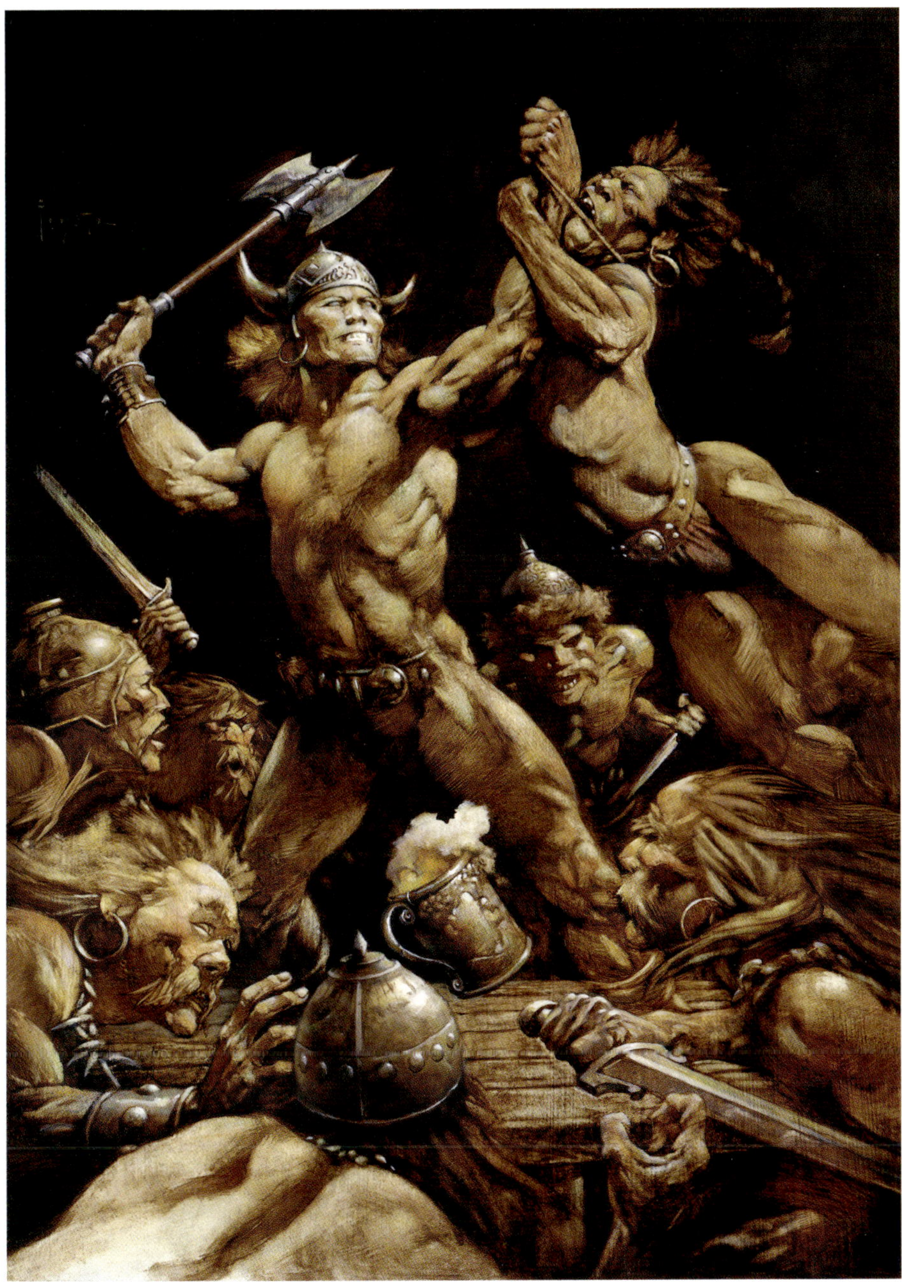

Adventurer from the 1966 Lancer Books paperback. Director John Milius, the screenwriter behind *Apocalypse Now*, said, "Not that I could ever redo Frazetta on film. He created a world and a mood that are impossible to simulate—but my goal in *Conan the Barbarian* was to tell a story that was shaped by Frazetta and Wagner." (And Arnold Schwarzenegger.)

Along with the continuing success of other Frazetta-inspired franchises like *Star Wars*—Leia's *Princess of Mars* style bikini in 1983's *Return of the Jedi* is the most obvious tribute to Frazetta in the original trilogy—young painters and comic artists were emerging who managed to learn from Frazetta without stealing outright. Frazetta's influence was clear in Boris Vallejo's operatic realism, Simon Bisley's bodies in violent motion over boldly colored underpainting, and Mike Mignola's faceted animal anatomy and use of shadow to convey movement and mood in *Hellboy*. A generation that had grown up on

Poster painting for the low budget 1986 film *America 3000*, about a post-apocalyptic world where women rise (in skimpy outfits) and hold men in slavery. Can B-movie star Chuck Wagner (seen in the foreground) free his brothers? For reasons unknown a far inferior photomontage was used instead of Frank's great painting for the poster. Oil on Masonite, 1985, 76.2 x 60.9 cm (30 x 24 inches).

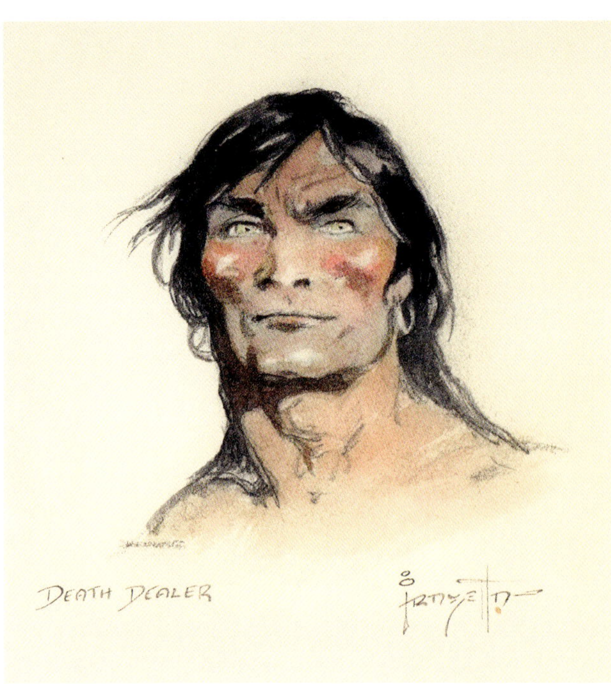

Death Dealer with his helmet removed, a preliminary test for a planned, and abandoned, oil portrait of the barbarian. In the end Frazetta realized anonymity is key to the character's popularity. Graphite, ink and watercolor on paper, 1986, 10.1 x 10.1 cm (4 x 4 inches). *Courtesy of Heritage Auctions.*

Death Dealer No. 4, for the cover of Jim Silke's *Death Dealer Book 3: Tooth and Claw*. Oil on board, 1987, 60.9 x 40.6 cm (24 x 16 inches).

Frazetta was emerging, his stature growing as they sung his praises, and the price of his originals went through the roof.

By the mid-1980s Frazetta was only taking rare commissions, enjoying life with his family and a variety of hobbies. In addition to baseball, Frank liked golf, target shooting and gun collecting, bowling, model planes, martial arts, and—especially as he got older—photography. Although never a slave to the photograph, Frazetta did take pictures to reference pose and shadows, and his art shows an attention to how tonality can change dot-by-dot that sets it apart from Old Master paintings. His interest in photos went far beyond what turned up on board, however. He had a collection of over 100 cameras and a home darkroom, and when digital photography emerged he eagerly took to the new technology. "He'd trade originals for cameras," his granddaughter Sara later remarked, "and my grandma had to kick people (looking for trades) out of the house because she was the fierce one … my grandfather, he just wanted to make people happy."

Ellie busied herself managing the licenses and legacy: in addition to the print company, a Frazetta Museum was established adjacent to their home in East Stroudsburg (it would eventually move to Florida and then back to Pennsylvania) where fans could meet the ever-sociable artist. In 1988, James Silke wrote the first licensed *Death Dealer* novel, with three more to follow. Frazetta's finances had never been better, but health problems in the form of an undiagnosed and debilitating case of Graves' disease—an overactive thyroid—began plaguing Frank in 1986 and would continue for eight years until a local doctor noticed his bulging eyes—characteristic of the condition—and prescribed medication. After relapse and medication adjustment he appeared to recover, but damage had been done.

Meanwhile, the maturing and increasingly creator-conscious fandom of the '90s brought more awards (from Spectrum, the Society of Illustrators, the Kirby and Eisner Halls of Fame, and the Association of Science Fiction and Fantasy Artists) and more usage licenses: Frazetta's work appeared as sculpture, including a larger-than-life fiberglass statue of Death Dealer created for the U.S. Army's III Corps at Fort Hood, Texas; on the covers of new comics from Glenn Danzig's Verotik; on trading cards; T-shirts; Zippo lighters; Halloween masks; pillowcases; skateboard decks; motorcycle gas tanks; ceramic tiles; pinball machines; and even on Scientology founder L. Ron Hubbard's 1994 hologram phone cards. Work like 1994's *Tooth and Claw* proves he was painting as well as ever, if a little slower.

In 1996, film director Robert Rodriguez commissioned him to do a poster for his horror/action film *From Dusk Till Dawn*. Rodriguez, a major fan, based Salma Hayek's look in the film on the girl in Frazetta's *At the Earth's Core* and said in a 2015 interview with *Ain't It Cool News*:

"That's why when Frank Frazetta saw the movie originally (sent to him for the poster commission) he called me and said 'Where did you find this gal? I wish I was painting her when I was painting these things!' I said, 'She's based on your paintings, that's why she looks like your paintings!' He said, 'Oh, OK.' The whole costume design and headdress was all based on that painting.... His whole comment on the poster is, 'That's all you need on the poster. You don't need anybody else but her and that snake.' I said, 'Well, we kind of have to put in the other actors, too, because it's George Clooney and Harvey Keitel …' He said, 'Alright, alright.' But if you look at the painting it's 90 percent Salma and at the very bottom is George Clooney. He didn't even bother to put Harvey Keitel on the poster! It's just George Clooney, Richie and he didn't even draw in the vampires, he just [put in] the monkey guys he usually does. (Scriptwriter) Quentin

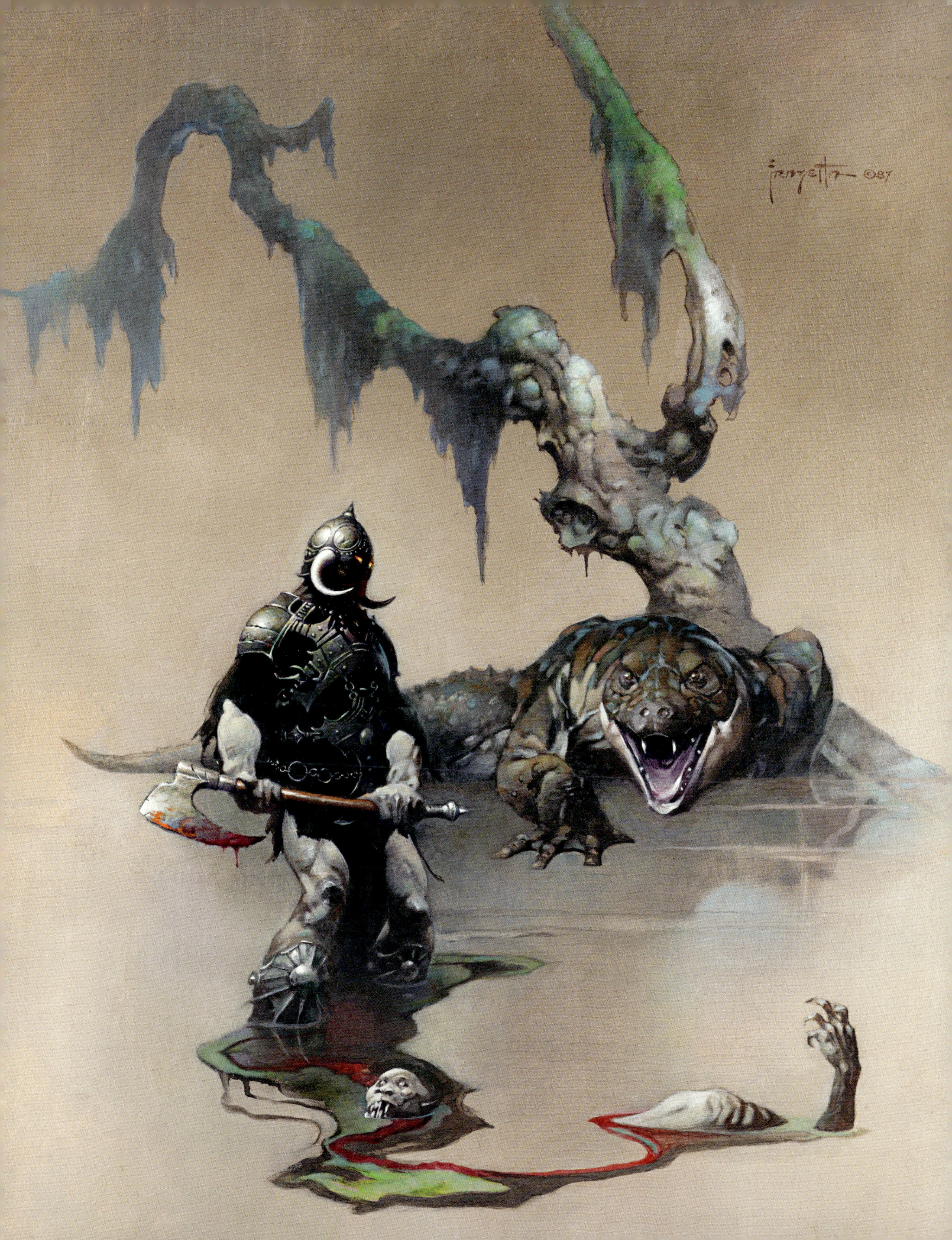

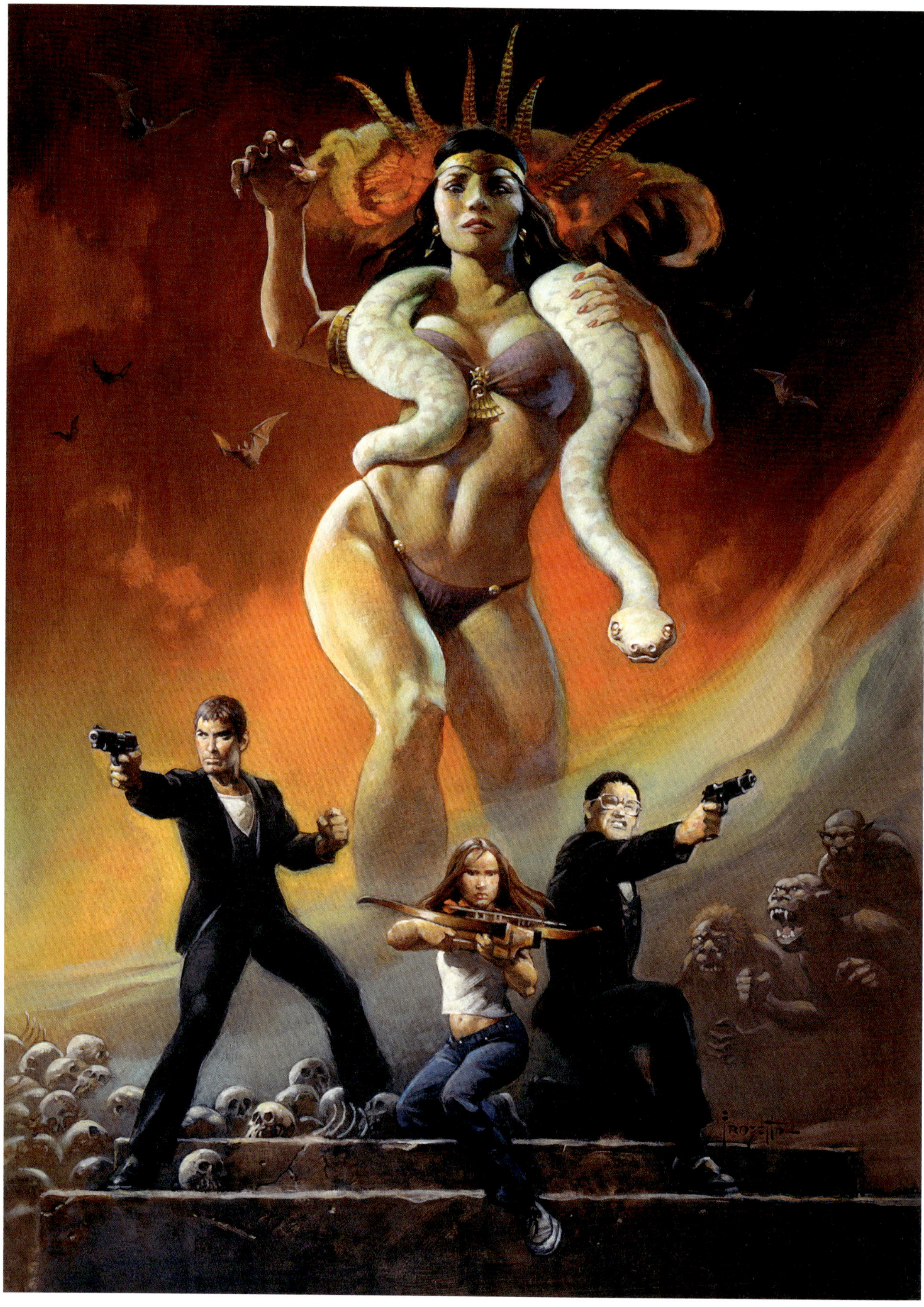

Sadly, shortly after accepting the commission Frank suffered
a stroke: the years of hyperthyroidism had damaged his vascular
system. He soldiered on in his stoic way, but the painting had to be
done left-handed and arrived two months too late to be the official
poster. The image—dominated by the voluptuous Hayek and her
white snake in a way the film (oddly) was not—was still a classic
Frazetta, perhaps the last.

The stroke in '96 was the first of eight. As his health and painting
ability declined, the family watched Frazetta become first resigned,
and then eager, for his end: "'I'm done, just get me outta here,'—he'd
always say that," Sara Frazetta reported in a 2019 interview. "'Frank
Sinatra's gone, all the greats are gone, they're all dying, my friends
are gone, I want outta here.'"

When Ellie died from lung cancer in 2009, Frank moved to
Florida, leaving the house they'd shared for 38 years, and never
returned. A final stroke took him a year later, on May 10, 2010.

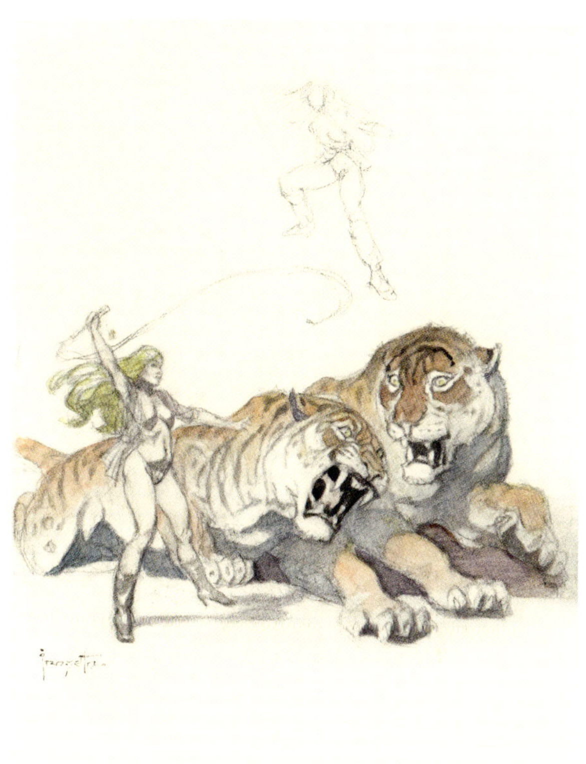

Color preliminary for *The Countess*,
one of three paintings inspired by
L. Ron Hubbard's sci-fi writing. Watercolor over graphite on paper, circa 1988,
30.4 x 20.3 cm (12 x 8 inches). *Courtesy
of Heritage Auctions.*

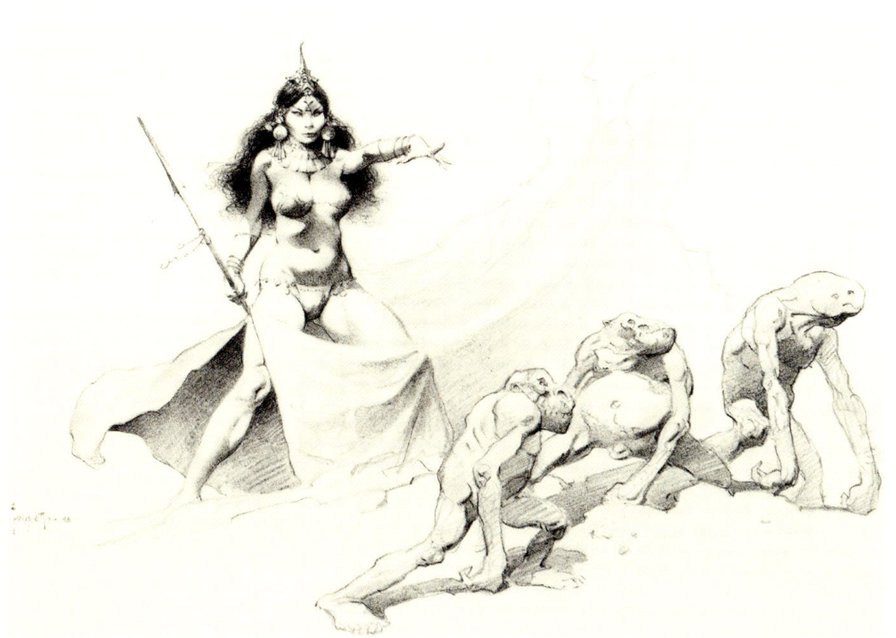

LEFT
Interior drawing for Verotik Publications'
Frazetta: Illustrations Arcanum, 1994.
Graphite on board, 1993, 35.5 x 50.8 cm
(14 x 20 inches). *Courtesy of Heritage
Auctions.*

OPPOSITE
Film director Robert Rodriguez is a huge
Frazetta fan, so much so he opened a tem-
porary Frazetta museum in Austin, Texas,
in 2015, and pursued Frank to paint the
poster for his 1996 film *From Dusk Till
Dawn*. Sadly, the commission came in the
middle of Frazetta's hyperthyroid health
crises and shortly after his first stroke, so
he was unable to complete the painting in
time for it to be used as the official poster.
Still great for a sick old man. Oil on
Masonite, 1996.

RIGHT
Leaping Lizards, for the wraparound
cover of *L. Ron Hubbard Presents
Writers of the Future, Volume VI*, 1990.
Oil on board, 1989.

PAGE 86
Death Dealer No. 5, for the cover of Jim
Silke's *Death Dealer Book 4: Plague of
Knives*, and reused on Yngwie Malmsteen's
2001 record album *War to End All Wars*.
Oil on board, 1989, 50.8 x 40.6 cm
(20 x 16 inches).

PAGE 87
Death Dealer No. 2, for the cover of
Jim Silke's first novel for TOR Books,
*Death Dealer Book 1: Prisoner of the
Horned Helmet*. Oil on board, 1986,
50.8 x 40.6 cm (20 x 16 inches).

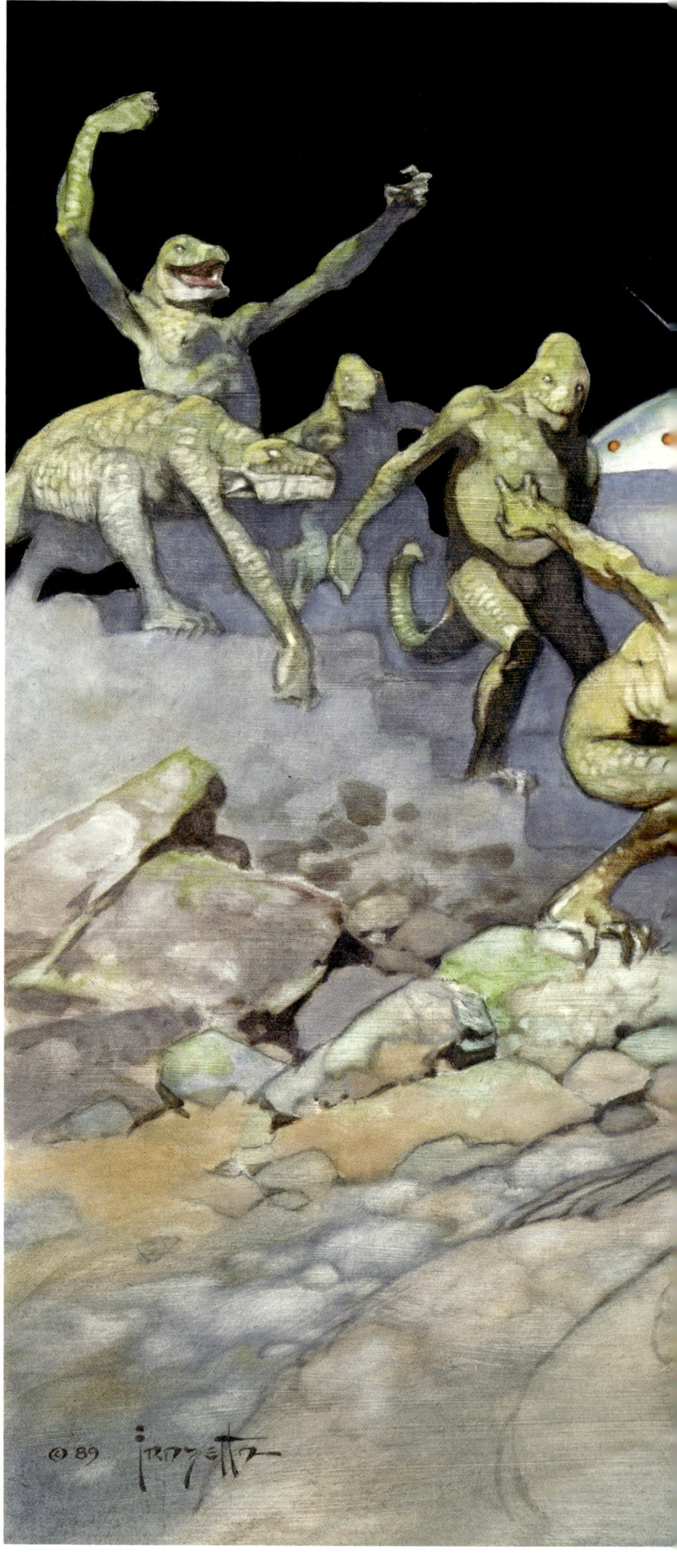

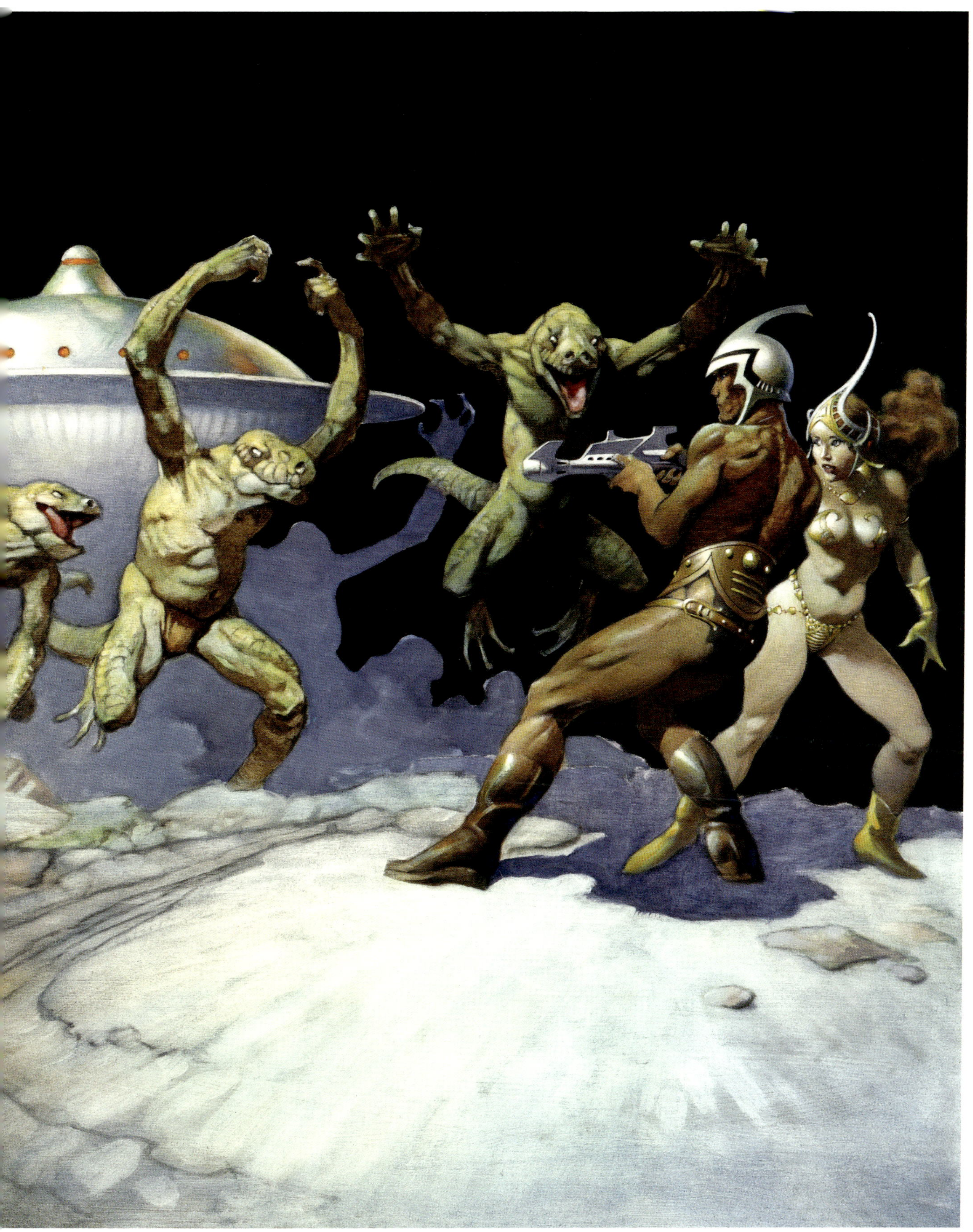

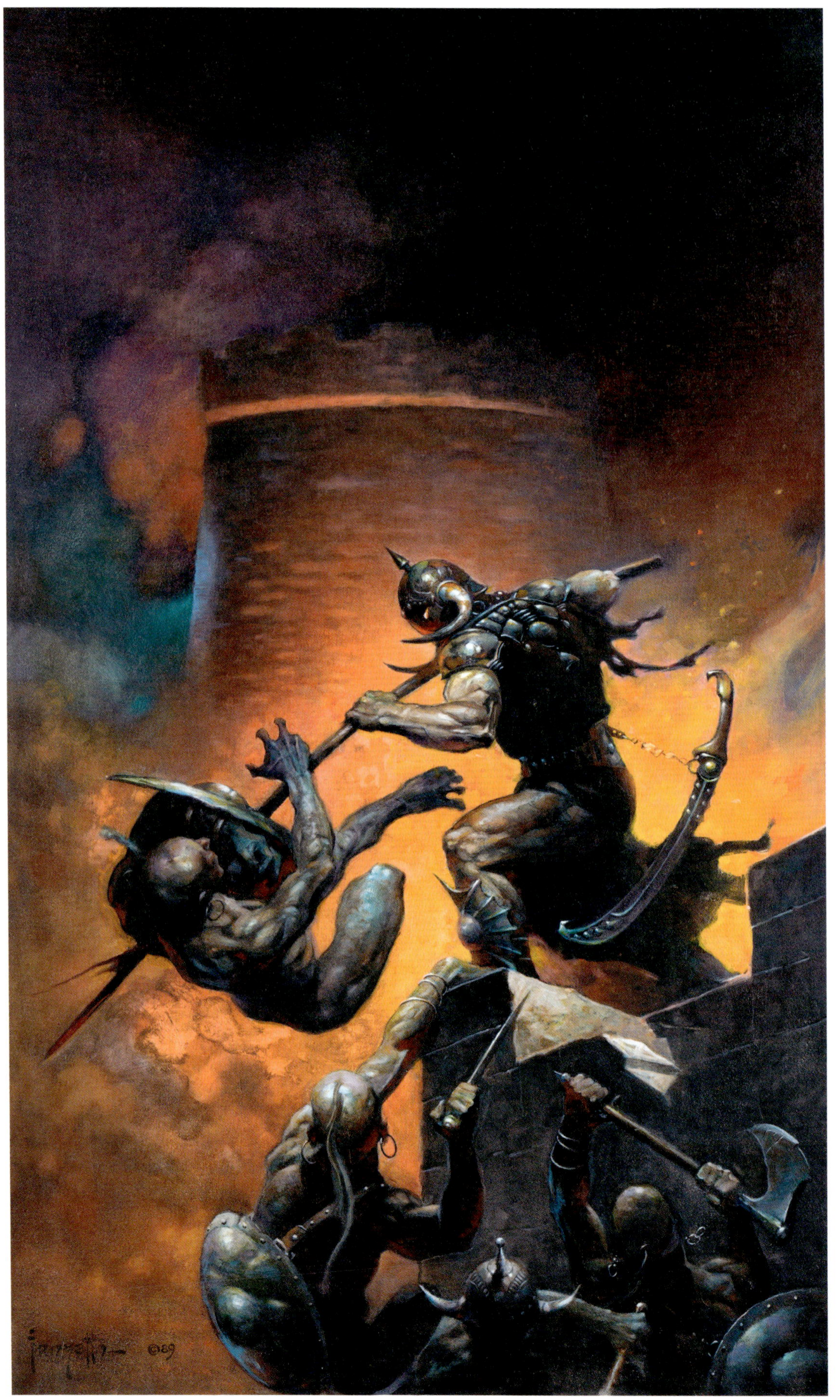

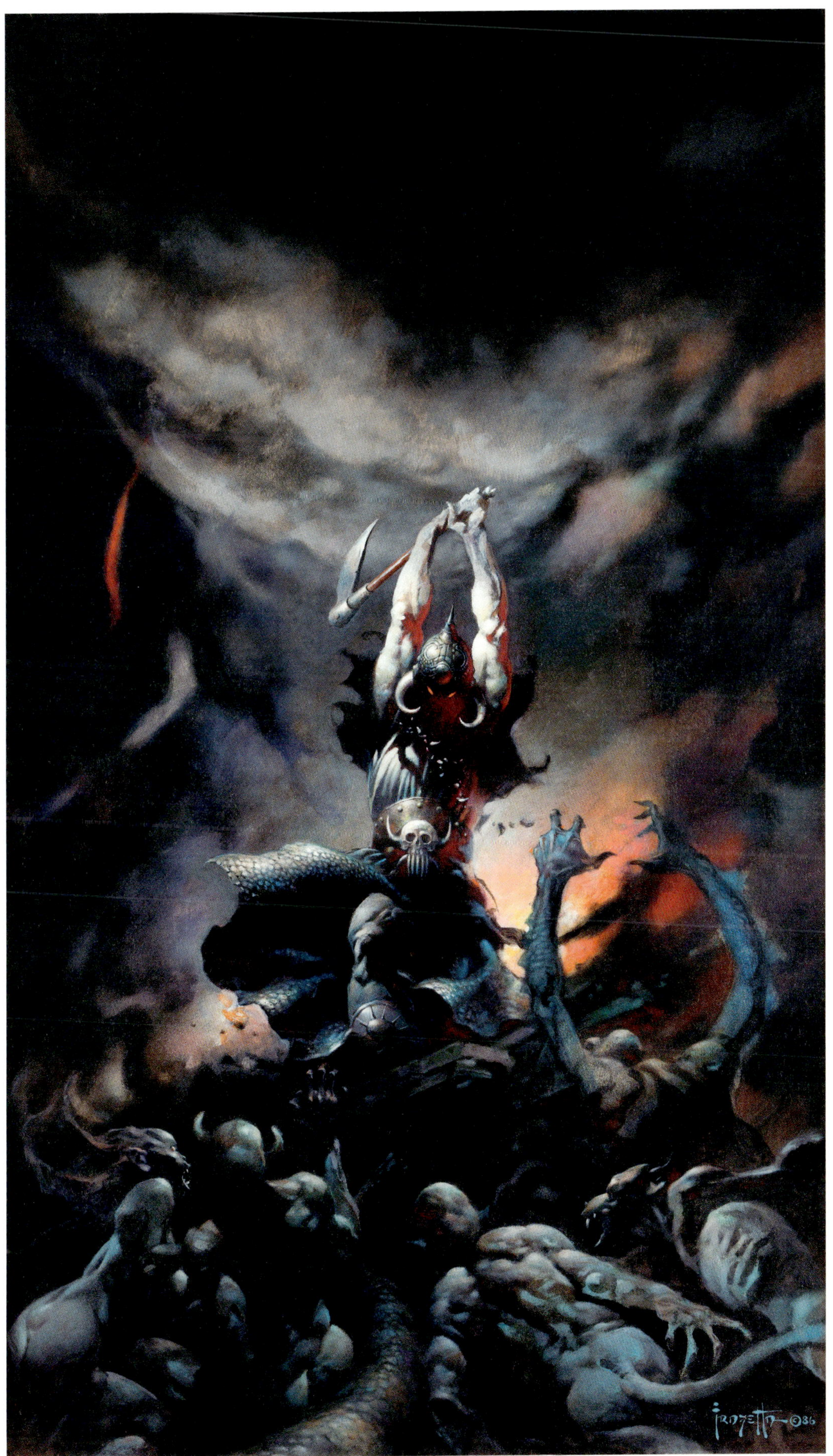

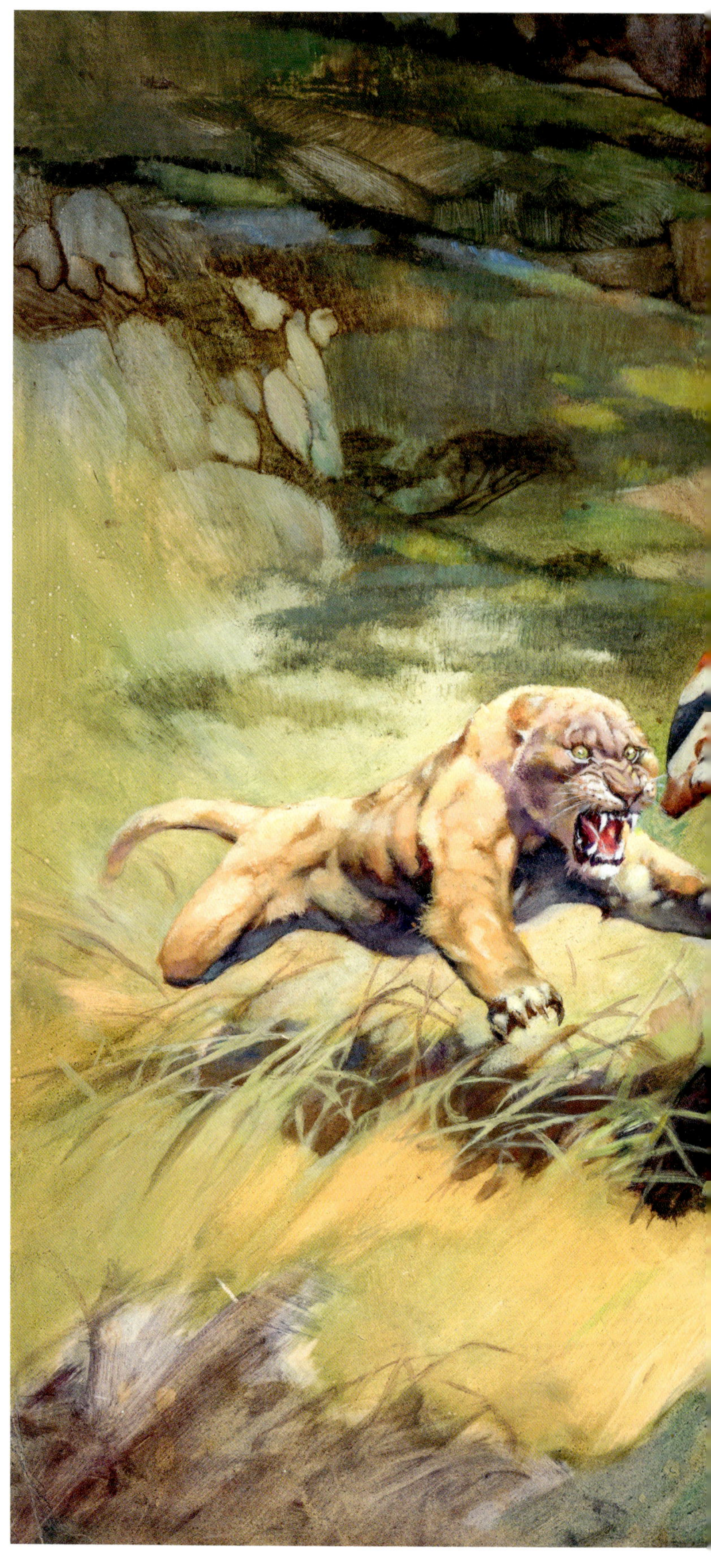

Predators, another personal painting, was one in a series of works exploring Frazetta's fascination with African warriors, begun around 1960. Though Frank was not much for reading or research, these works all show accurate detail in clothing, hair, and weaponry. Oil on Masonite, circa 1987, 40.6 x 50.8 cm (16 x 20 inches).

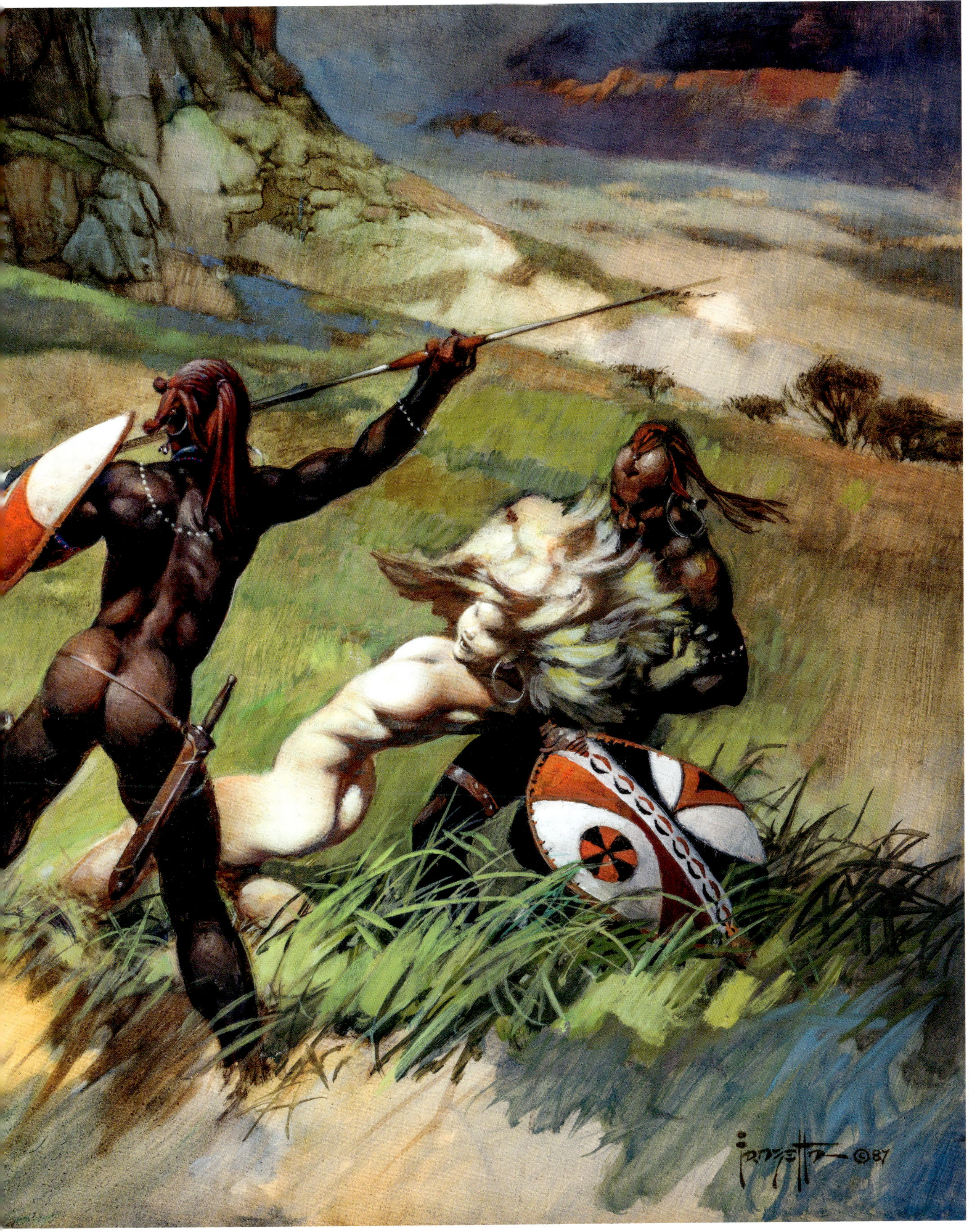

Frazetta ©87

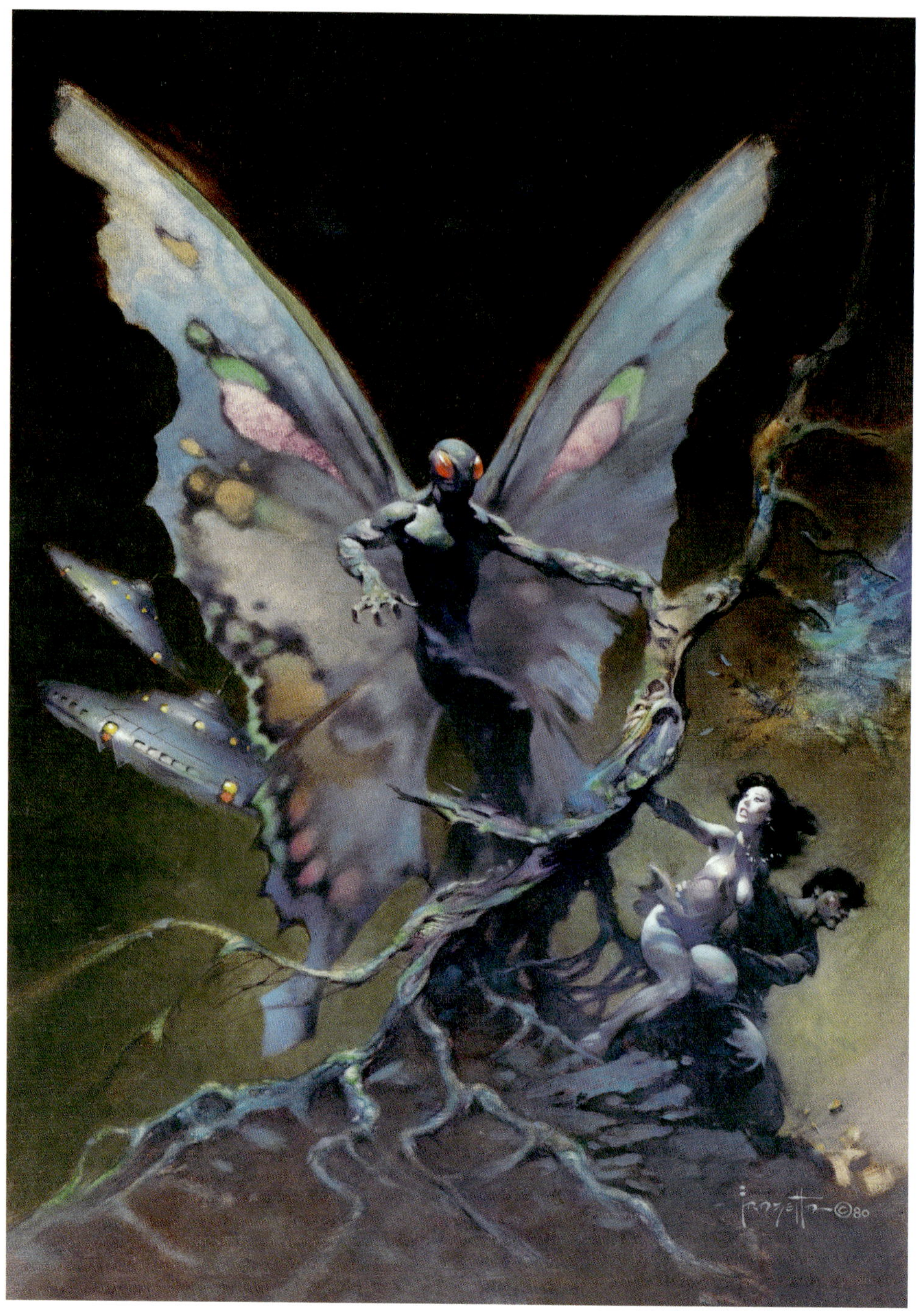

ABOVE

The Mothman, for the May 1980 cover of
High Times magazine, to illustrate a story
titled "Beware of the Mothman." It later
appeared on the cover of John Keel's *The
Mothman Prophesies*, 1991. Oil on board,
1980, 50.8 x 40.6 cm (20 x 16 inches). *Courtesy of the Lucas Museum of Narrative Art.*

OPPOSITE

The Encounter, wherein a sexy space
fairy meets a space explorer on a seemingly airless alien world, for the cover
of *L. Ron Hubbard Presents Writers of
the Future, Volume V*. Oil on board, 1988,
60.9 x 45.7 cm (24 x 18 inches).

PAGES 92/93

Dawn Attack, for the wraparound cover
of *L. Ron Hubbard Presents Writers
of the Future, Volume VII*, a short story
compilation by winners of the annual
Writers of the Future competition established by Hubbard in 1985. Oil on board,
1991, 40.6 x 60.9 cm (16 x 24 inches).

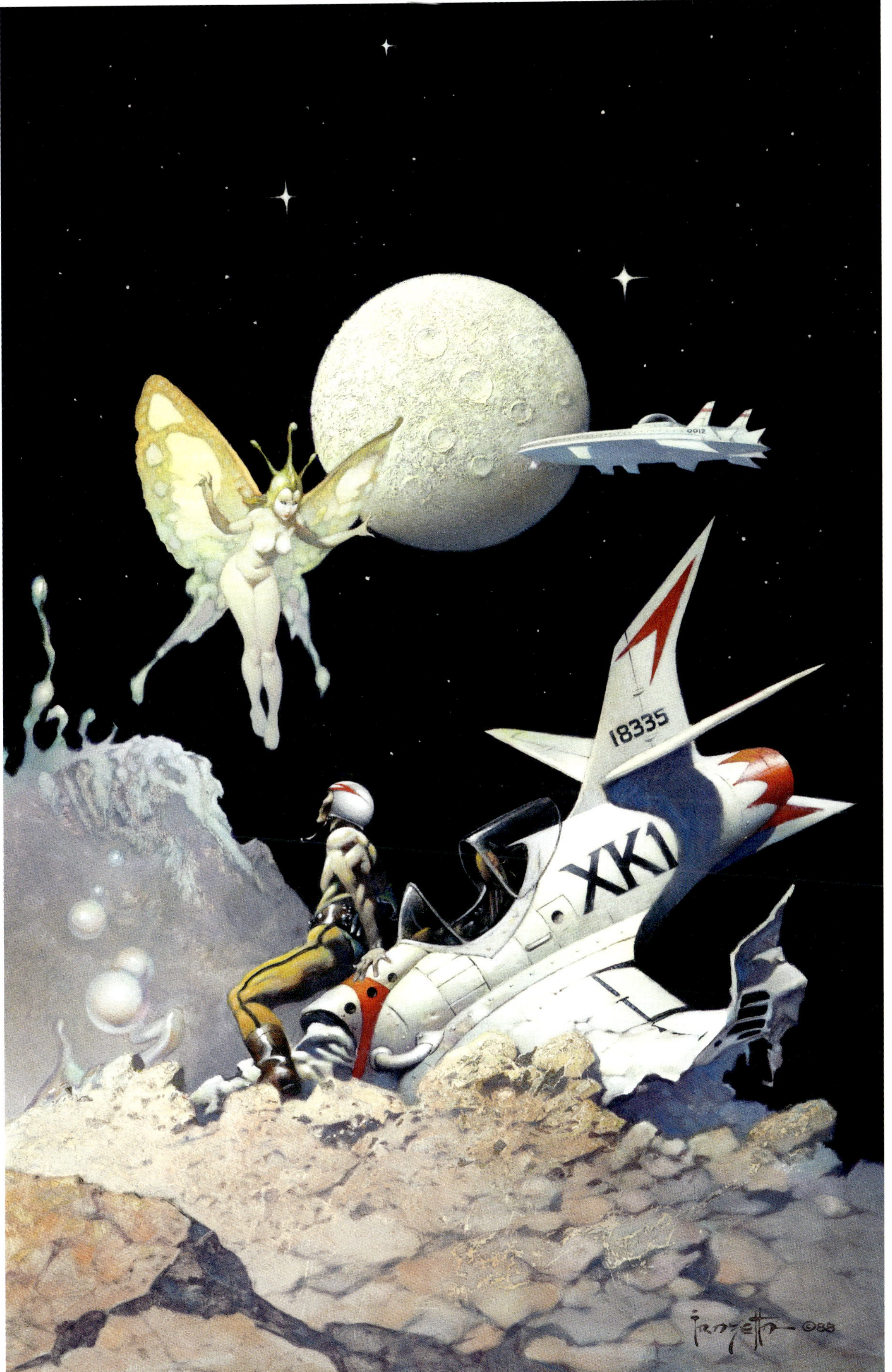

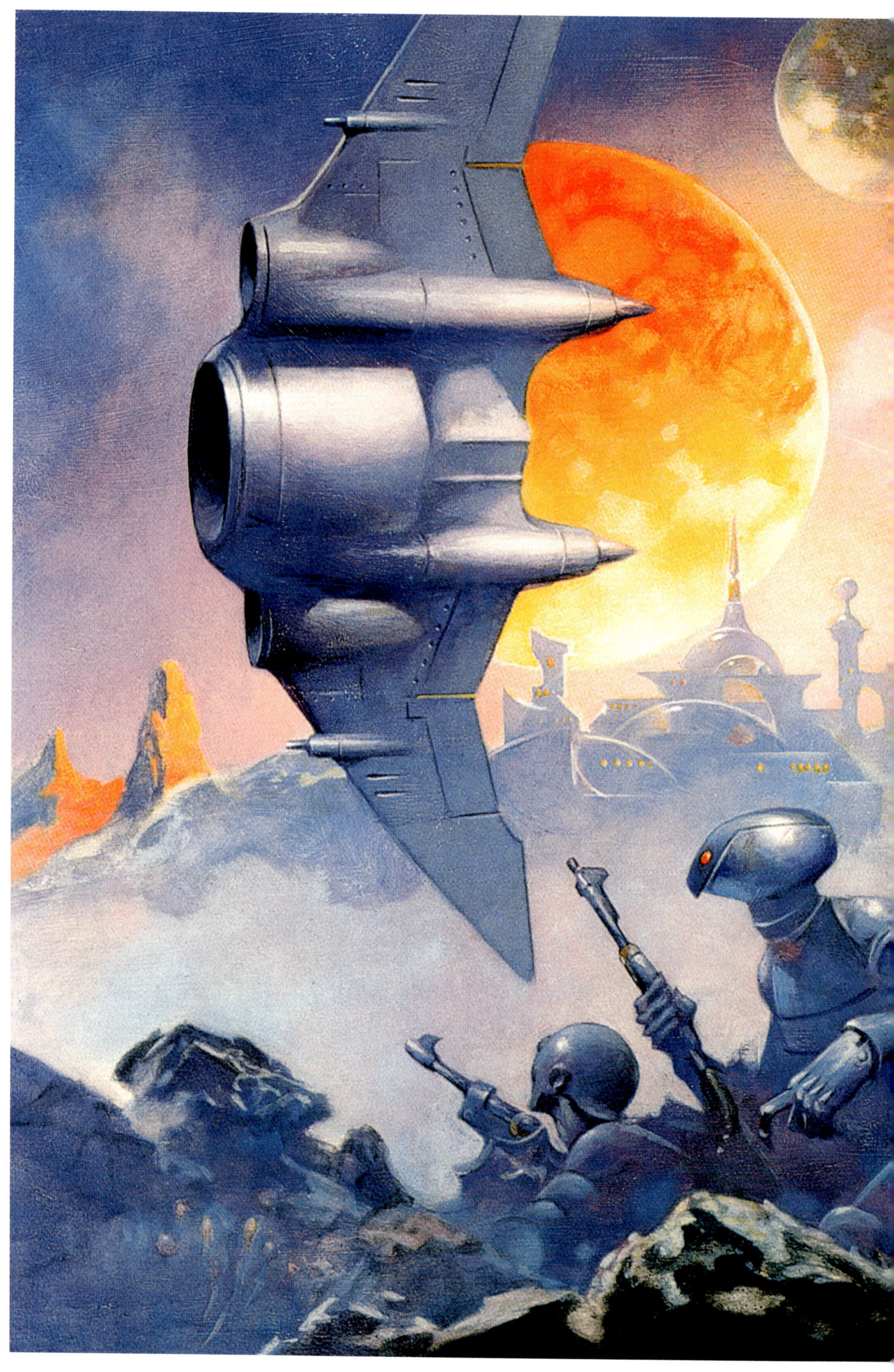

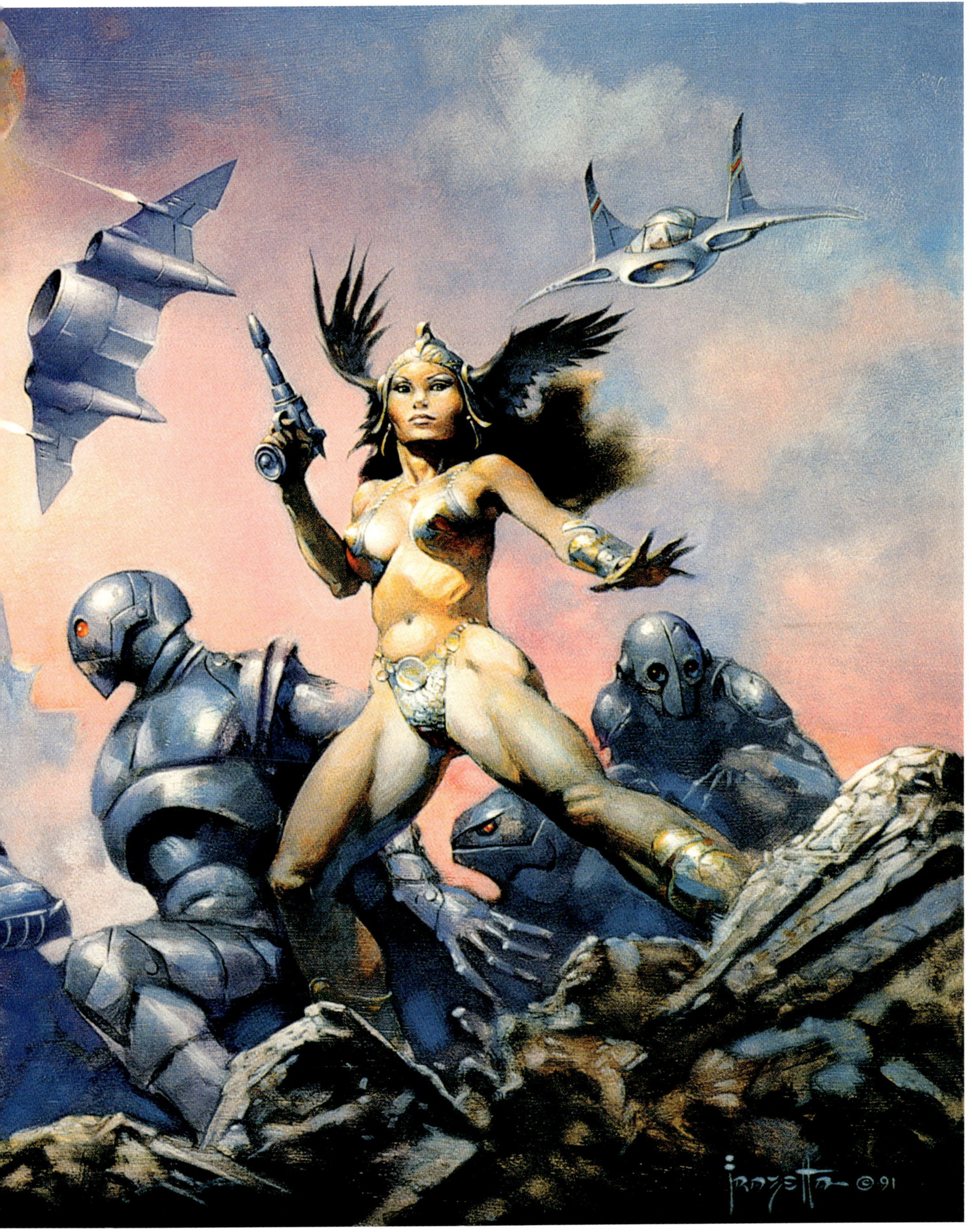
Frazetta ©91

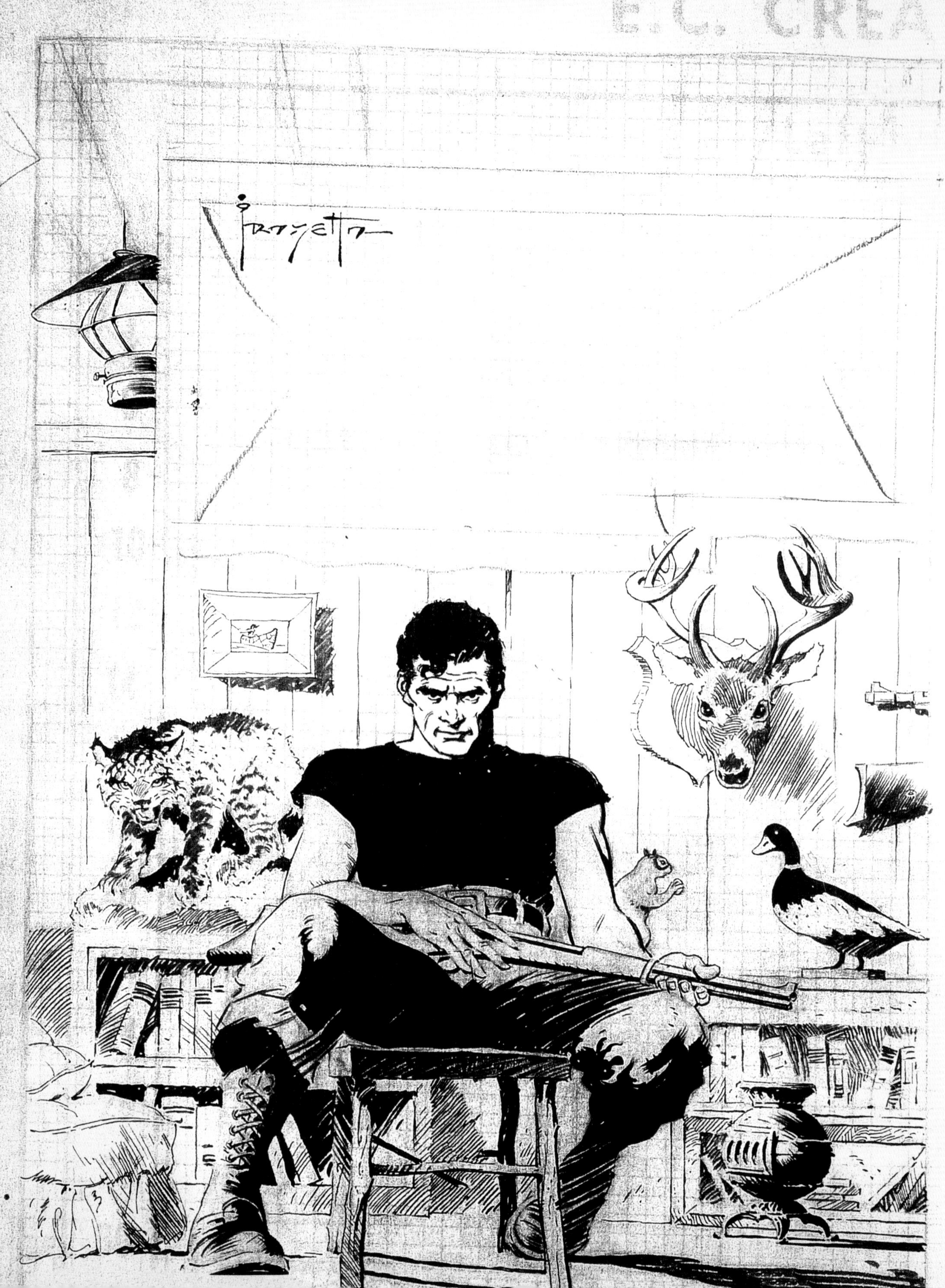

Frank Frazetta
1928–2010
Life and Work

1928 Frank Alfonso Frazzetta is born into a Sicilian family in Sheepshead Bay, Brooklyn, New York.

1936 Frank, aged eight, enrolls in Michele Falanga's Brooklyn Academy of Fine Arts, a humble neighborhood school with one teacher, despite the elegant name. Falanga declares him a genius on his first day.

1942 Teacher Falanga dies, leaving the students to carry on without him, teaching each other. Frank has no further higher education.

1944 At age 16, Frazetta drops one "z" from his name and begins work in comic artist Bernard Baily's studio. He inks his first 8-page story "Snowman," which is published in *Tally-Ho Comics* that December.

1952 After six years drawing spot features for comic books, Frazetta produces the daily newspaper strip *Johnny Comet*.

1954–1961 Frazetta takes over the popular newspaper comic strip *L'il Abner*, while creator Al Capp maintains his byline.

1956 Eleanor Kelly becomes Mrs. Frazetta. She is his artistic muse, business partner, and constant domestic combatant.

1961 After falling out with Capp over money, Frank is unable to find comic work and produces illustrations for men's magazines and a series of seedy sex novels.

1962 Roy Krenkel invites Frank to help paint covers for Ace Books' line of Edgar Rice Burroughs paperbacks, launching his successful book cover career.

1964 A painting of Ringo Starr for *MAD* magazine gains the attention of United Artists Studios. Frazetta paints the poster art for *What's New Pussycat?* (1965), the first of many film posters.

1971 The Frazetta family, now including four children, moves to East Stroudsburg, Pennsylvania, where Frank builds his dream house.

1976 The World Fantasy Awards declares Frazetta Best Artist. *American Artist* magazine profiles Frazetta and gives him the cover, a fantasy art first.

1981 Frazetta teams with filmmaker Ralph Bakshi to make *Fire and Ice*, an animated film of his art.

1986 Frazetta develops Graves' disease, leading to eight years of undiagnosed illness.

1996 The years of untreated hyperthyroidism lead to the first in a series of strokes, paralyzing Frazetta's right hand. Frazetta paints the poster art for Robert Rodriguez's film *From Dusk Till Dawn* left-handed. Though he finishes too late for the artwork to be used, learning to paint left-handed allows him to keep working.

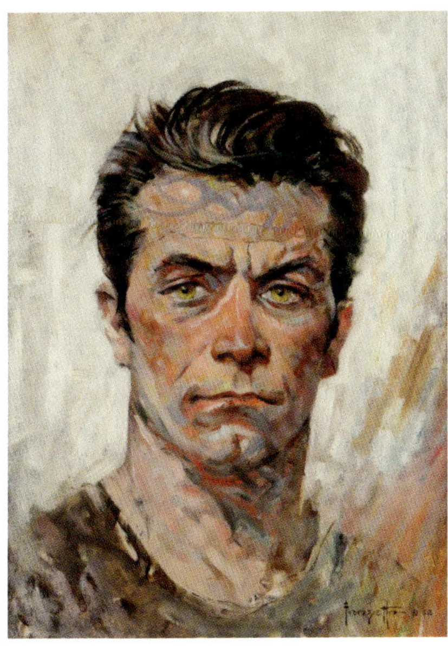

1999 Frazetta is inducted into the Jack Kirby Hall of Fame.

2010 Frazetta dies on May 10, 2010, leaving two sons, two daughters, and 11 grandchildren.

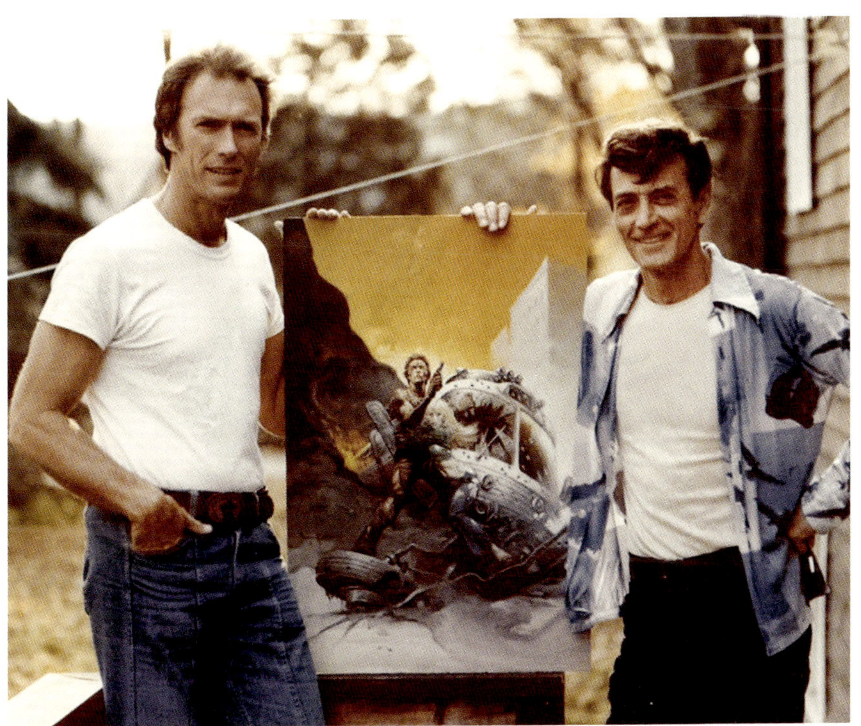

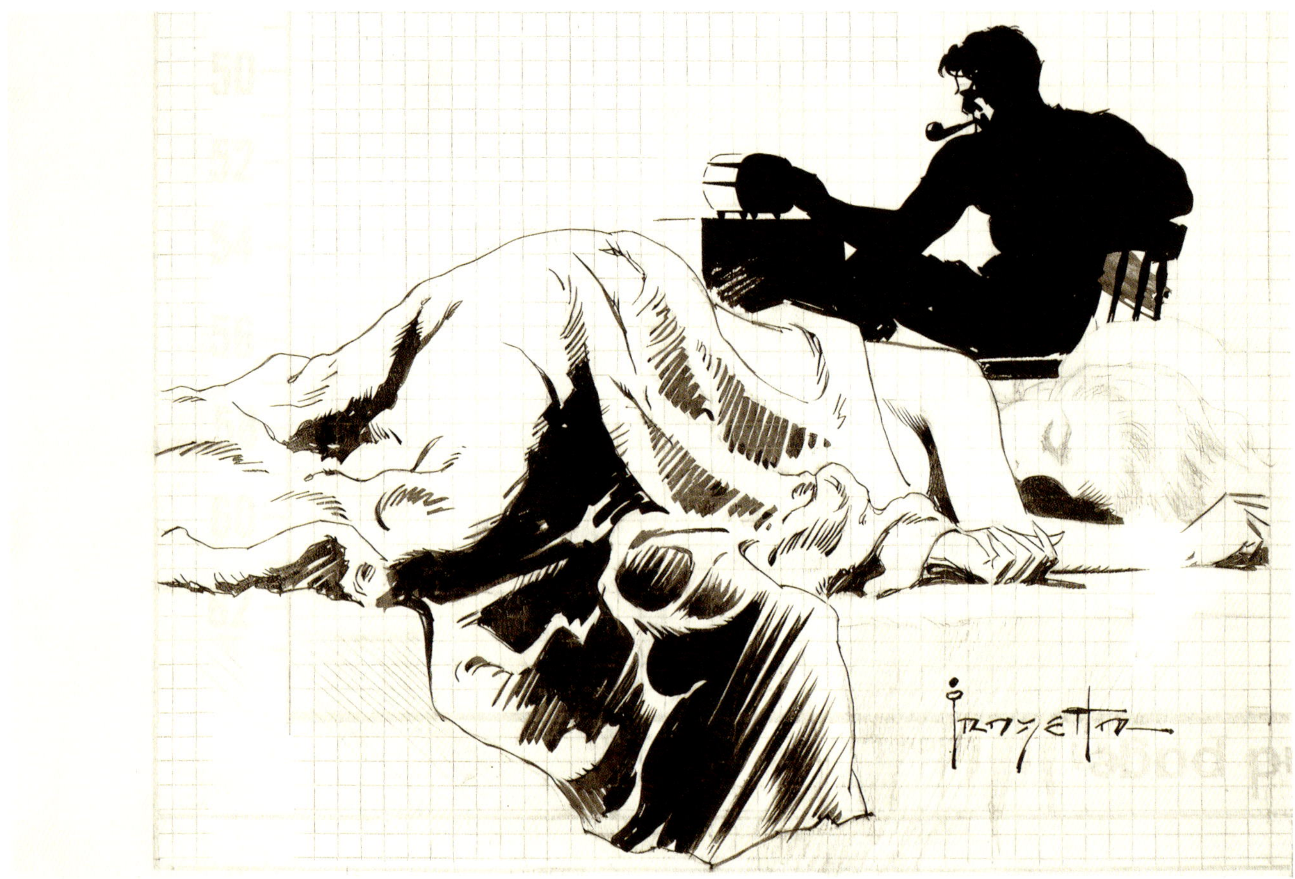

Credits

All images in the book are copyright
© Frazetta Girls Inc. unless otherwise stated
and may not be reproduced in any form without
written permission from the rights holders.
Visit them at *frazettagirls.com*.

Cover art for *Beyond the Farthest Star* (1964)
© 1964 Edgar Rice Burroughs, Inc. All rights
reserved.

Tarzan®, John Carter®, and other characters,
names, and titles created by Edgar Rice
Burroughs are trademarks or registered trademarks of Edgar Rice Burroughs, Inc.

Conan the Barbarian® and © 2022 Conan
Properties International LLC.

The Editor

Dian Hanson is a senior editor and writer for
TASCHEN, with over 50 books to her credit. In
addition to *ARNOLD*, her recent works include
The Art of Pin-up, *Masterpieces of Fantasy Art*,
and *The Fantastic Worlds of Frank Frazetta*.

Imprint

**EACH AND EVERY TASCHEN BOOK
PLANTS A SEED!**
Each year, we offset our annual carbon emis-
sions with carbon credits at the Instituto Terra,
a reforestation program in Minas Gerais, Brazil,
founded by Lélia and Sebastião Salgado. To find
out more about this ecological partnership,
please check: *www.taschen.com/institutoterra*.
Inspiration: unlimited.
Carbon footprint: (almost) zero.

Want to see more? Visit *taschen.com* to view
our current publications, browse our latest
magazine, and subscribe to our newsletter.

© 2026 TASCHEN GmbH
Hohenzollernring 53, 50672 Köln, Germany
www.taschen.com

Original edition:
© 2022 TASCHEN GmbH

Printed in Bosnia-Herzegovina
ISBN 978–3–7544–0044–9